Maritime Security for India

New Challenges and Responses

Maritime Security for India

New Challenges and Responses

K.R. SINGH

New Century Publications
New Delhi, India

NEW CENTURY PUBLICATIONS
4800/24, Bharat Ram Road,
Ansari Road, Daryaganj,
New Delhi-110 002

Tel.: 23247798, 65396605
Telefax: 011-41017798
E-mail: indiatax@vsnl.com
www.newcenturypublications.com

Editorial office:
34, Gujranwala Town, Part-2,
Delhi - 110 009
Tel.: 27247805, 27464774

First Published - 2008

ISBN 13: 978-81-7708-156-5
ISBN 10: 81-7708-156-x

Published by New Century Publications and printed at Singhal Print Media, New Delhi -110 005

PRINTED IN INDIA

CONTENTS

Admiral Arun Prakash, IN (Retd.)
Tele: 0135-2645102
E-mail: arunp2810@yahoo.com

"Anchorage"
219, Turner Road,
Clement Town
Dehradun - 248002

FOREWORD

Writing of naval history, must arguably, be counted as one of the more difficult and demanding human pursuits, because it requires knowledge, not just of political, social, and economic conditions prevailing in different eras, but also the tactical, administrative, logistic and technological aspects that underpin the operation of ships and naval forces extant in that era. The transition from sail to steam, which took place in the mid-19th century, was just the beginning of an interminable progression of technological advances which are now being collectively termed as the Revolution in Maritime affairs, and which have added to the historians' difficulties.

It was perhaps for this reason that a learned speaker at a recent seminar on maritime History in Kochi, while cautioning the audience about against "mythologizing" history in order to glorify nations or cultures, went on to disclose the disheartening reality that "…Indian historians have neither the wherewithal to look for marine artefacts, nor sufficient nautical expertise to interpret whatever they do find." The resultant paucity of writings, and consequently of discourse, on the subject of India's maritime history has had many adverse consequences; some direct and others indirect.

For one, the field having been left clear to Western historians, we have had little choice but to accept their version of the past, with all the embellishments about their own history, and blemishes that "literary licence" permitted them to attribute to India's ancient culture, and civilization. While one comes across lengthy accounts about the "birth" of maritime tradition in the Mediterranean basin, there is no mention at all, of the seafaring skills and accomplishments of ancient Indians.

It is the lonely voice of Sardar KM Panikkar which informs his ignorant compatriots about their precious maritime heritage, and the fact that, "... millenniums before Columbus... and Magellan, the Indian Ocean had become thoroughfare of commercial and cultural traffic..." He then goes on to describe India's deep and abiding cultural symbiosis with SE Asia which could only have been created and sustained by intense maritime activity over centuries.

The other deleterious impact of this hiatus in indigenous historiography has been the total indifference of our rulers and countrymen alike, towards maritime threats. This syndrome, which has grown over the years, has come to be known as our "maritime blindness".

It was as a part of the Indian Navy's endeavours to redress this inherited cultural lacuna that the University of Calicut was selected for establishing a Chair of Maritime Studies and Research, with financial assistance obtained, after much persuasion, from the Ministry of Defence. In October 2004, I was privileged to inaugurate this Chair, the first of its kind to be established anywhere in India. In choosing Calicut, the Navy accorded recognition to Kerala's rich maritime heritage nobly symbolized by the epic struggle waged off the Malabar Coast by the Zamorins and the Kunjali Marrakars against the Portuguese invaders in the 16th century.

Professor KR Singh was the second incumbent of the Maritime Chair (2005-06), and this book is tangible proof that the Navy's objective of imparting an impetus to maritime studies, is well on the path of fulfilment. In choosing as his subject, *Maritime Security for India: New Challenges and Responses,* the Professor has brought into focus, many maritime issues which are of great relevance and importance at this particular juncture. What is contemporary today will be history tomorrow, and the author's work will endure as a significant contribution towards redressing the shortcomings that I have just mentioned.

Contrary to expectations, the post-Cold War era brought with it, not just changes, but many conundrums and contradictions, with serious security implications for India. These are examined by Prof KR Singh in the regional maritime context. He also evaluates the strengths and motivation of significant navies which are either resident, or operate in our neighbourhood, and then goes on to gauge the challenges posed to India's interests by them as well as by non-state entities in the maritime domain.

Force planning issues attract his close attention, and for an outsider (by which I mean a non-naval person), many of the Professor's analyses and evaluations of capabilities, situations, weapon systems and warfare areas are surprisingly accurate. Whether they agree with him or not, maritime strategists as well as naval officers would be greatly interested in some of the prognostications and suggestions offered by him.

In consonance with the navy's current thinking, he devotes a full chapter to "Maritime Security Through Co-operation". On this and the other issues that he examines, Professor Singh brings to bear not only his vast teaching experience in International Studies, but also his research background in Indian Ocean and Security Studies. His erudition and scholarship notwithstanding, the Professor is meticulous about footnotes, citations and references, and frequently quotes senior naval officers in support of his assertions; perhaps overlooking the fact that rank rarely brings with it wisdom!

This is a timely and useful assessment of India's current maritime environment, which not only points out the opportunities and challenges, but also hints at the way ahead. I sincerely hope that this book will find the readership that it richly deserves.

(Arun Prakash)
Admiral (Retd)
Dehra Dun
15th July 2007

ABOUT THE BOOK

India, part of a land-locked sub-continent, has no option but to emphasise its maritime perspective if it has to attain its destined role in the emerging regional and global order. Despite its inherited continental mindset, Indian elite has, over the decades, taken slow but steady steps in the field of maritime development. India has also learnt the hard lesson that a nation which neglects its maritime defence can even lose its sovereignty. Post-Cold War environment has offered India multiple options to strengthen its maritime security through regional and international cooperation. This has assumed strategic significance in view of the new threat posed by maritime terrorism.

The book evaluates India's maritime defence capability in the years to come. It also analyses challenges that are likely to be posed as also options that are available to neutralize them.

AUTHOR'S PROFILE

Professor K.R. Singh (b.1932) had been teaching in the School of International Studies, Jawaharlal Nehru University (JNU), New Delhi till 1997. He was Visiting Professor (2005-06), Chair for Maritime Studies, University of Calicut. His field of specialisation includes West Asia, Indian Ocean Region and strategic studies with special reference to maritime affairs. Professor Singh has written several books and articles dealing with contemporary developments in West Asia, Indian Ocean, naval history of South Asia and also legal dimensions of maritime security.

PREFACE

Six decades of India's independence have witnessed major restructuring of regional and global environment as also a transformation in India's own perception as an emerging regional maritime power. That was in stark contrast to the perceived continental mindset that had for several long years confined India within the narrow territorial bounds of the Indian Peninsula thereby fostering a sub-continental perception of itself. This gave primacy to land-based developments as also threats. As decades passed India, while retaining its sub-continental identity, has sought to acquire a new maritime perspective as well. Having found itself hemmed in within the narrow confines of what is now termed as South Asia it has sought to breakout into the only available space—the seas around it.

Beside the geo-strategic compulsions of breaking out of the sub-continental bondage, other factors like promises of exclusive economic rights for exploitation of sea-based resources under the terms of UNCLOS-III gave India's traditional continental mindset a new as also an additional space in the seas around it. India's EEZ constitutes about two-thirds of its total land mass. In case India's claims for the delimitation of its continental-shelf are accepted, that will add an area of ocean bed that will be almost the size of India's land mass. Hence, India will have two types of land masses; one above the sea-level and the other under the sea. The need for development, especially for food and energy, will compel India to look more and more towards its maritime zone.

As India develops and as its economy grows, India will depend upon its foreign trade and associated institutions like ports and harbours, ship building and repair yards, institutions specializing in training in navigation, management of maritime affairs and related aspects of merchant marine etc. This economic growth will also stimulate greater urbanization along the coast. India's energy requirements, based upon its own offshore oil and gas fields as also upon imported fuel, will also make security of India's adjoining waters and sea lanes of communication (SLOC) a matter of prime national concern.

These development-related factors will dove-tail with those affecting India's national security *vis-à-vis* threats that could emanate *via* the sea. They can be from state actors or non-state actors. Thus, India's maritime security forces will have to be geared to neutralizing multiple levels of likely maritime threats ranging from great powers, major regional powers as also from non-state actors acting on their own or as proxies for some adversary state actor. The study evaluates all these three types of threat to India's maritime security.

India, that is aspiring to play the role of a major regional maritime power, will also be required to fulfil certain associated obligations. Basically, they revolve around India's willingness as also its capability to contribute to the overall security of the waters around it, especially in times of peace, within the framework of existing international law, clauses of UNCLOS-III as also various resolutions of the UN and the IMO, besides politico-military understanding at bilateral and multilateral levels. India's geographical location in the north-central part of the Indian Ocean, that places it in a dominating position *vis-à-vis* major SLOC between the Indian Ocean Region and the Asia-Pacific, helps it to fulfil that obligation to the best of its ability.

The study examines the changing regional and international environment in the post-Cold War period and evaluates various challenges posed by activities of the great powers, major regional powers and non-state actors to India's maritime security as also possible responses to those challenges.

The nature and credibility of responses will depend upon India's overall maritime security capability today and as it is expected to evolve over the next few years. Hence, an attempt is made to examine in some details India's maritime security capability under several inter-related heads like sub-surface warfare, naval-air arm, surface combatants, amphibious warfare and force projection capability etc. These are discussed in some details keeping in view the fact that even well-informed public in India is often not aware of these details. Such a detailed analysis, it is hoped, will help them to position India's policy options in proper perspective.

Another point that is sought to be underlined is that capabilities of the Navy, the Coast Guard and even of the Air Force need to be synergized, wherever found compatible, so as to maximize the effectiveness of the totality of India's capability in that field without parcelling that into isolated and sometimes competing sectors. The need to synergize their roles and capabilities becomes all the more relevant in the context of new concepts like revolution in military affairs (RMA), net-work centric warfare (NCW) and advances in C_3I, especially in the IT sector. The application of NCW cannot be limited to one service alone but also needs to be made relevant in the context of related aspects of all the services so as to justify a truly national response to a given challenge.

No country, not even the Sole Super Power, can hope to ensure its maritime security in isolation since seas have no real barriers and no limit. Hence, cooperation at regional as also at international level has become an important facet of strengthening maritime security of each of the states. India, that had been isolated till late eighties, has been able to break out of that isolation. It has enlarged the area of maritime cooperation with almost all great powers and majority of the regional powers. While its maritime diplomacy has evoked favourable responses in the Bay of Bengal, extending up to the Asia-Pacific Region, as also along the African littoral and island republics in the Indian Ocean Region, India has not been able to forge similar structures of maritime cooperation in the Arabian Sea and the Persian Gulf; an area of prime strategic significance from the point of view of India's maritime security. A combination of factors like the adversary relationship with Pakistan, Iran's growing isolation, the near monopoly of US-led coalition in the region under the formula of CENTCOM's exclusive zone of influence, as also relative maritime inactivity of GCC states, with the exception of Oman, have combined to thwart India's efforts to build structures of bilateral and multilateral cooperation in the sphere of maritime security. That area should be the thrust of India's maritime diplomacy in the years to come.

When one looks ahead, one finds that the threat from non-state actors will be of increasing importance for India. As India develops its maritime assets it will offer more and more targets to non-state actors. While regional and international cooperation to contain that threat will help, the country needs to further strengthen the maritime dimensions of its homeland security, *vis-à-vis* the sea-borne threats posed by non-state actors.

This calls for a totally new approach. It cannot be done either by traditional sea-based deterrence like the Navy and the Coast Guard even when they work in tandem, or by land-based security agencies like the state police and port authorities. Since the area that needs to be sanitized overlaps the coast, even the hinterland, and the adjoining seas, counter measures also need to evolve a mechanism that coordinates the role of multiple security agencies on land and on the sea. Such an effort is possible only when one ceases to look at the problem in the context of a land-based threat or a sea-based threat but to think of it as a combined threat. India will need to develop that new mindset if it has to effectively secure the homeland from sea borne threats posed by non-state actors.

There is no doubt that India has awakened from its deep slumber and rediscovered its maritime heritage. For the first time in centuries, India, as a united, independent and technologically developing state, is seeking to assert its role as a major maritime actor both in the field of economic development as also in the context of its obligations to help promote peace and stability in the region. India needs to develop its maritime capability to be able to play both these roles effectively. Equally important is the new change in regional and international mindset. More and more powers, both in the Indian Ocean Region as also beyond it, are prepared to accept India's new role and to help it attain the capability to play its part.

It will not be wrong to say that mindsets are changing not only in India but also around it. That is a good starting point to chalk out a maritime strategy for the years to come.

New Delhi K.R. Singh

1

ORIENTING TOWARDS A NEW STRATEGIC ENVIRONMENT

OVERCOMING THE COLONIAL HANGOVER

India is an Indian Ocean power. This is not only a geographical but also a historical fact. Pandit Jawaharlal Nehru, in his address to officers and sailors of INS Mysore in March 1958 had said, "History has shown that whichever power controls the Indian Ocean has, in the first instance, India's sea-borne trade at its mercy and, in the second, India's very independence. [1]

This mindset, at that time, reflected the hangover of the long period of colonial and imperial dominance from 1498 till 1947. That was partly due to the continental (land power) mindset of major states like the ex-Bahamani kingdoms, the Vijayanagar Empire, and the inability of small coastal states in the Konkan and the Malabar to match the financial power and technological challenges posed by the Europeans. This mindset ignored the maritime history of Indians before the entry of the Europeans. Today, India is a modern industrially developing, strong and united nation. Nehru had no way of anticipating the strides that India would make in the subsequent decades in reasserting its traditional maritime role.

Today, India is a strong regional maritime power able to reassert its historical position. Today, it can deny to foreign maritime powers what could not be denied during the era of maritime colonial dominance. Moreover, as a central regional power in the Indian Ocean, India has shown its willingness to help secure major sea lanes of international importance in its adjoining waters for users of those SLOCs. Details of these sea lanes and their importance for global peace, security and prosperity need no elaboration. Thus, in the five decades since independence India's self-image about its maritime role and future status has undergone a sea change. Others have recognised it. Indian mindset must also reorient itself to this major change in India's geo-strategic perception of itself as an emerging maritime power.

CHANGING ENVIRONMENT IN THE INDIAN OCEAN REGION

The Indian Ocean has an area of approximately 73.6 mn sq km, with a coastline of about 66,526 km. It is surrounded by three continents; Africa, Asia and Australia. The Indian Ocean Region comprises of 36 states; six of them being island states. Strategic environment in Indian Ocean Region has been reconfigured since the end of the Cold War, more so after the collapse of the Soviet Union. It has removed the Soviet fleet from the Indian Ocean. The region has now become a NATO lake dominated by US-led coalition from among the NATO members and its non-NATO allies like Australia, Japan, South Korea, etc. Navies of other major non-regional powers like Russia and China have yet to make a visible and sustained presence in the region.

The strategic environment continues to be in a state of flux and is undergoing significant modifications at regional level due to policies pursued by US-led coalition and the local response, particularly by non-state actors. The growing threat from these non-state actors, or the terrorists, has also highlighted the need for strengthening maritime dimensions of homeland security at the level of state (province) *per se* as also in cooperation with other likeminded state actors or partners. Indian maritime security agencies have, therefore, to respond to these multiple challenges.

Though forces of the NATO members were present in the Indian Ocean Region during the period of the Cold War they were not operating as a single cohesive force or as an extension of the NATO in the Indian Ocean. It was clear during the 'tanker war' phase (1984-1988) of the Iraq-Iran war when warships of NATO members offered protection to their flag vessels only. Even operation of forces of the NATO members during the Kuwaiti crisis of 1990-91 was under the auspices of the UN and legitimised under various resolutions of the Security Council.

Gradually, Indian Ocean witnessed the emergence of US-led coalition supported by a few NATO members. This was especially true after Operation Enduring Freedom in Afghanistan following the events of September 11, 2001. NATO legitimised its presence under the slogan of war on terrorism, as is evident from its presence in Afghanistan, Iraq and in various choke points under regional maritime security initiative (RMSI). This coalition of NATO members is also joined by some non-NATO allies like Australia, Japan and South Korea. Pakistan, through a non-NATO ally has as yet no real maritime role.

Indian Ocean has now become a NATO (and allies) lake dominated by USA. Previous 'alliance' membership has been replaced by 'interest' partnership. This has made strategic environment very fluid and multifaceted and has given opportunities to states to join the partnership that suits their national interests. As the *Annual Report*, 2005-2006 of the Ministry of Defence puts it, "Progress towards a truly multi-polar world, with India as one of the poles, has been slow but steady." [2] This concept is totally at variance with the traditional concept of non-alignment that India was pursuing till recently.

INDIA'S GEO-STRATEGIC LOCATION

Regional environment needs to be analysed in the context of India's geo-strategic location and interests. As viewed from India's geo-strategic perspective, Indian Ocean can be sub-divided into at least four major zones; the Bay of Bengal and its natural extensions like the Andaman Sea and the Malacca Straits, Central Indian Ocean Region, the Arabian Sea and its natural extensions like the Persian Gulf, Bab-al-Mandeb and the Red Sea, and West Indian Ocean Region that includes the African littoral and small island republics. India has specific interests in each of these zones.

Indian interests in the Bay of Bengal are determined not only by the growing ties with states of South-East Asia and the Asia-Pacific Region and by its relations with immediate neighbours like Bangladesh and Myanmar but also by the island chain of

Andaman and Nicobar. Though separated from the mainland, they are valuable economic assets for India due to the living and non-living resources in their vast exclusive economic zone (EEZ) and continental-shelf. These islands also dominate the sea lanes between the Indian Ocean and the Asia-Pacific. Andaman and Nicobar Islands are, therefore, bound to emerge as the focus of India's maritime strategy in the Bay of Bengal and the Andaman Sea in the years to come.

Earlier, India had hesitated to militarily strengthen these islands lest it caused concern among states of South-East Asia. Many had voiced that concern in late eighties. India assiduously cultivated regional powers and has been able to overcome decades of mistrust. Today, India is accepted as a reliable and friendly regional partner by majority of these states. That gives India a political and diplomatic base to neutralize possible threats to its security emanating from that region or from other parts of the Asia-Pacific. It will not be wrong to say that these regional partners constitute the first line of defence for India just as India constitutes their strategic partner.

Central Indian Ocean Region, that includes Sri Lanka and the Maldives, is of crucial significance for India for three main reasons. It connects the major SLOCs of the Indian Ocean. It also connects Indian littoral of the Arabian Sea and the Bay of Bengal. Finally, developments in this region not only have a direct bearing upon India's domestic polities; particularly in its southern states like the Tamil Nadu and Kerala but also are a major cause of terrorism in this zone. Over the years, India has succeeded in evolving a calibrated formula to manage the threat through the mechanism of close cooperation with the neighbouring states like Sri Lanka and the Maldives without directly involving great powers; a matter of some diplomatic success that is often ignored by strategic community.

India's approach to security in the Arabian Sea and its natural extensions like the Persian Gulf, Horn of Africa, Bab-al-Mandeb and the Red Sea is governed by different sets of variables. They include, apart from the long standing rivalry between India and

Pakistan, energy security and SLOC protection, future of large number of Indian expatriates in the GCC states, potential of developing the North-South corridor linking India *via* Iran to Central Asia and Russia, and finally the interrelated issue of overwhelming foreign military presence and popular defiance that is often fuelled by Islamic radicalism. This has its fallout upon India's domestic environment and erodes its policy of secularism. Thus, India's strategic approach towards the Arabian Sea zone is bound to differ in many ways from that of many members of the US-led coalition.

West Indian Ocean Region comprises of the African littoral, island republics of Mauritius and Seychelles, French overseas possessions like the island of Reunion, and the island of Diego Garcia with its strategic Anglo-American base facilities. India has not intruded deep into this zone except for close ties with small island republics of Mauritius and the Seychelles with which it has special security-related understanding. Ships of the Indian Navy did occasionally visit Diego Garcia in the fifties but no such visit has taken place since the island was ear-marked as an Anglo-American base in mid-sixties. Though India and France are seeking to forge close strategic understanding, Reunion still seems a far off place for the Indian Navy.

India has always been close to East African states and its relations with South Africa have improved following the end of the apartheid regime there. At the moment, India is very close to the island republics of Mauritius and the Seychelles and is sharing with them its maritime know-how. The presence of people of Indian origin there is also an additional bond. It remains to be seen as to when India develops equally close relation with states of the African littoral as a consequence of the new spurt in India-Africa cooperation.

THREAT FROM NON-STATE ACTORS

India's maritime security is now being evaluated not only from the point of the role played by state actors in the context of global and regional environment but also from the point of view of maritime threat to homeland security. This threat is also linked to global and regional environment and the role of non-state actors. Indian decision makers were aware of the threat long before the West took serious note of it. In that context, *Annual Report*, 1990-1991 of the Ministry of Defence had noted that there were certain developments that had cast their shadow on the security environment of our region. "Terrorism, religious extremism and ethnic chauvinism have fomented separatist tendencies. In many cases they have received support from external sources, aggravating the problem and complicating the search for political solution." [3] The view was reiterated in 2005 as well. "India is closely monitoring the rise of Islamic fundamentalism as well as the increasing incidents of terrorism and political violence with its attendant repercussions on the security of India." [4] These non-state actors, especially the terrorists, are also evolving their own coalition at global and regional level. Thus, maritime dimension of terrorism has emerged as a new focus of maritime security of India. To that extent, India's response to its homeland security also merges with the perception of this new threat and the responses at global and regional level. Increasingly, India's focus on maritime security is being driven by this consideration though conventional threats are not ignored.

While India has initiated moves to meet this threat at national level, steps are also being taken to cooperate at regional and global level to confront it. *The New Indian Express* of August 23, 2005 quoted an official as saying that three top-level exercises scheduled between September-November 2005 with USA, Russia and France would focus upon the Navy testing indigenously developed methods to destroy terrorist bases, rescue hostages, intercept transport of weapons of mass destruction (without joining PSI !) and even liberate a country from terrorists. In the joint exercise to be held with the ships of USA near Goa, the focus was to be on engagements with "rogue vessels", and on procedures to deal with biological and chemical threats. In the joint exercise with ships of the Russian Navy in the Bay of

Bengal, the focus was to be on liberating a third country from a terrorist takeover. In November, Indian ships were to exercise with those of the French Navy in the Gulf of Aden and aim at debilitating renegade vessels and escorting a seized ship, apart from working on protocol issues to deal with such situations. [5]

These developments since past two decades if not more have confronted India with new challenges in terms of fast changing geo-strategic environment and diversification of threat, especially in the context of dominant presence of US-led coalition in India's immediate neighbourhood as also the growing challenge from maritime terrorism.

While India needs to cooperate with like-minded states in meeting these sets of maritime challenges, it also needs to reassess its own maritime strategy and how it can utilize its fast expanding maritime assets to confront these challenges. This exercise will help India plan a more viable and long term strategy for its maritime security not only in the context of state actors but also in neutralizing the threat being posed by maritime terrorism; a challenge that needs to be taken seriously while chalking out future maritime security strategy.

Notes

1. Roy, Vice-Admiral Mihir K. "India at the Cross Roads in the Indian Ocean", in Mathew K.S. ed., *Mariners, Merchants and Ocean Studies in Maritime History*, Manohar Publishers, New Delhi, 1995, p. 465.

2. Ministry of Defence (MoD), *Annual Report* 2005-2006, New Delhi, 1991, p. 2.

3. MoD, *Annual Report* 1990-1991, New Delhi 2001, p. 2.

4. MoD, *Annual Report*, 2005-2006, New Delhi, 2006, p. 8.

5. *The New Indian Express*, August 23, 2005, Quote in *Strategic Digest*, 35(9). September 2005, p. 1267.

2

EVALUATING THE CHALLENGES

GREAT POWERS IN THE INDIAN OCEAN

While intentions and, therefore, priorities might change, policy options are influenced primarily by the capability that a state or a group of states possesses. Moreover, capabilities that are being planned also give an indication of what could be the possible intentions of a given coalition of states. This is especially true of the Indian Ocean Region which has been witnessing rapid transformation not only in the roles of great power but also in their capabilities since the end of the Cold War. The end of the Cold War and more so the break up of the USSR saw the virtual elimination of the Soviet/Russian Navy from the Indian Ocean at least for a decade and the simultaneous increase in the military presence of US-led coalition particularly in the areas marked as zone of operation of the CENTCOM.

US-LED COALITION

It will not be wrong to say that the US-led coalition, despite occasional criticism from some European members like France and Germany, has been dominating the region, with or without express UN sanction, at least since the Kuwaiti crisis of August 1990. That dominance is not only being retained but efforts are also being made to further consolidate it in the context of likely conventional war against middle powers like Syria and Iran, as also against non-state actors under the broad framework of war on terrorism. This also includes protecting friendly regional regimes in Bahrain, Iraq, Qatar, Kuwait, Oman, etc. against regional as well as domestic threats. Other great powers like Russia and China have yet to enter the Indian Ocean Region militarily and are not likely to do so for some years to come. Hence, it will be useful to evaluate the possible challenges, direct or indirect, that the presence of US-led coalition poses to maritime security today and in the years to come.

USA is a non-regional power yet it has laid its claims that the Indian Ocean is of vital strategic importance to its security and that of its allies. This stance has been maintained since the beginning of the Cold War and is put forward to justify its large military presence in this region. Vice-Admiral SCS Bangara, in a talk at the University of Calicut on January 18, 2005, said that USA, the only Super Power in the so-called uni-polar world, functions under compulsions and a self-centred philosophy of national interest, to justify all its actions whether they are right or not in your perceptive. [1] Some strategists, however, do not see it as a threat to India. According to Admiral VS Shekhawat, "A substantial US naval presence in the Indian Ocean is a reality in the foreseeable future, as it has been in the past, and is not necessarily against India's interests." [2]

USA's military role also needs to be analysed in the context of its capability to project force overseas, at least since World War II. That capability has not only been maintained since the Cold War, but efforts are now being made to reconfigure it in the context of new threat perceptions.

Present US naval capability needs to be traced at least to the demands of World War II. During World War II, US naval policy and associated capability was dictated by the need in the European war theatre to help protect the SLOCs against the threat of German submarines and the need to launch and sustain a vast amphibious operation across the English Channel to carry the battle to the main land. In the Pacific, USA aimed to neutralize the powerful Japanese Navy as also to launch amphibious operations across long distances to occupy strongly defended islands in the Pacific. These military objectives meant that USA had to develop a strong navy not only with three dimensional capability; surface, sub-surface and air but also a large amphibious warfare capability with associated logistic support systems.

During the Cold War period, these capabilities were upgraded to provide for direct US participation in NATO operations in Europe as also to dominate the Pacific and provide protection to South Korea, Japan and Taiwan. To this capability to wage conventional war was added the new requirement of using ocean as a part of the overall nuclear strategy. Combination of submarine-launched ballistic missiles (SLBN) and nuclear-powered submarines (SSBN) became a part of strategic triad and the most effective aspect of the second strike capability in the context of global nuclear strategy.

US presence in the Indian Ocean during the Cold War period can thus be analysed in the context of using the ocean for the possible deployment of SSBN-SLBM. This possibility had dominated the entire debate in the seventies in the context of declaring Indian Ocean as a zone of peace free from nuclear rivalry. Whether or not USA deployed the median range (2,500n.miles) Polaris A-III and the Poseidon-armed SSBNs in the Indian Ocean has still not been finally answered. However, deployment of SSBNs armed with long-range SLBMs like the Trident in far away Indian Ocean would have been superfluous. Interestingly, some of these Ohio-class SSBNs are being modified for covert operations and as a platform for cruise missiles. They could be deployed in the Indian Ocean.

By the time long-range SLBMs were being introduced, US strategy in the Indian Ocean had started taking a new turn. USA gradually began to replace UK as the custodian of the Western interests in the region, especially in the Persian Gulf. That aimed at the security of the oil supply as also of the regimes that facilitated free flow of oil to the West. While the end of the Cold War put an end to the global nuclear dimension of US strategy, the developments since the Kuwaiti crisis of August 1990 pushed USA and its close allies deeper into the region.

In the post-Cold War period, there is no super power rivalry, and hence no strategic threat from state actors at the global level. Thus, the focus is upon possible threats from regional powers and now increasingly from non-state actors or the terrorists. Access to oil and protection of regimes that can ensure free flow of oil remains the focus of that strategy. To that has been added the new dimension of SLOC protection *vis-à-vis* threats from non-state actors.

US naval strategy in the Indian Ocean Region formulated during the Cold War era failed, in the post-Cold War period, to protect Western interests. Hence, it had to be restructured in the light of new experiences. US naval strategy of force projection based primarily upon periodic deployment of US taskforce and pre-positioning of ships carrying war material in selected areas did not prevent Iraqi forces from overrunning Iraq in one night. The Kuwaiti crisis, therefore, offered some valuable lessons, the most important being the need for adequate on-the-spot presence of army and air force besides that of the navy to forestall similar situation. Hence, after 1991 USA, UK and France maintained their military presence in frontline bases in the GCC states. That itself became a pretext for the rise of radical Islamic opposition, especially in Saudi Arabia.

The second lesson was that the NATO powers did not have the capability to inject men and material into the Indian Ocean quickly and in sufficient number. It took them months to transport men and material by sea and by air before they could launch military operations against Iraq in 1991. The third lesson or rather the spin-off of the Gulf War of 1991, was the application of the concept of revolution in military affairs (RMA), of network centric warfare (NCW) as also of the use of precision-guided munitions (PGMs). While these things had been evolved in the context of Cold War adversaries in the European theatre, they were employed with devastating effect by NATO powers against a middle power of the South. This equation of RMA, NCW and PGM was further improved upon after 2001 with the new role of Special Forces in Afghanistan and Iraq. Most of the deficiencies of 1990-91 have been removed and a more rapid pace of deployment was proved in operations against Afghanistan in 2001 and against Iraq in 2003.

US-led coalition had to further modify its force projection strategy in the context of Operation Enduring Freedom in

Afghanistan when a land-locked country was targeted. This operation saw a mix of sea-to-littoral move as also air-to-land bridge to bases in Central Asia and Pakistan as also greater role of Special Force and PGM. Operation Enduring Freedom also saw a reversal of political role by the USA in the ongoing civil war in Afghanistan between the Taliban who were previously supported by the West, and the forces of the Northern Alliance who were backed by anti-Taliban coalition that included Russia and Iran. It will not be wrong to say that while USA provided the cutting edge of modern technology the ground offensive and defeat of the Taliban and al-Qaida combination would not have been possible without the manpower and conventional weapons provided by the Northern Alliance and its supporters like Russia. The strategy to destabilize the regime in power by provoking and exploiting a civil war was also pursued in Iraq with equally disastrous results for that country.

Iraq war of 2003 did not offer new military lessons. It only showed that USA and its close partners like Australia and UK had further improved upon their capability in the context of RMA, NCW, PGM and use of Special Force as also advances in technology related to C^4ISR (command, control, communication and computer processing besides intelligence collection, surveillance and reconnaissance). The euphoria of easy success in conventional war in Afghanistan combined with the aggressive policy of the new US administration even ignored the wishes of its NATO partners against pursuing a unilateralist agenda. The conventional forces of Iraq were easy to defeat. The Baathist regime was overthrown but the coalition forces were unable to replace it with a viable alternate regime. Not only USA had to beg for more political and military support from its NATO allies and other partners but it has got sucked into a iong and bitter low intensity conflict that is showing no sign of ending. One wonders if USA has learnt the lessons of its wars in Afghanistan and Iraq. The question whether modern facilities designed to fight and win a conventional war between states can help win a low intensity war still remains unanswered.

US military planners are evaluating the lessons of the wars especially in Afghanistan and Iraq, as also the follow-up war on terrorism so as to further strengthen their capability for military intervention if that option has to be pursued. USA and its allies are also taking into account the growing reluctance of some of their erstwhile regional allies to support their military operation and to provide them with suitable base facilities. Even pro-US regime in Saudi Arabia showed its reluctance to permit USA use of its base facilities during wars in Afghanistan and Iraq, primarily due to popular opposition to US policies. Though USA enjoys facilities in other GCC states like Kuwait, Bahrain, Oman, Qatar and UAE they too could be withdrawn in future under popular pressure.

USA and its allies are, therefore, developing two interrelated capabilities; how to project credible force directly from the sea to the littoral even if these bases are denied in the neighbourhood, and how to combat terrorism from the sea itself. In other words, USA is developing a force projection capability against state actors as also non-state actors in a situation of non-cooperation by neighbouring state actors.

For USA, the capability to project force directly from the sea to the littoral is nothing new. It had pursued that strategy in the Pacific during World War II against Japan. But these operations were conducted with the help of US bases that were relatively nearer to the mainland America. Force projection across the Pacific or the Atlantic into the Indian Ocean world pose different sets of challenges. Efforts are being made to overcome them. New concepts like sea basing, littoral warfare, lily pods etc. are being introduced to give shape to the new maritime force projection strategy of sea to the littoral.

Admiral Joy Johnson examined the new thrust on sea to littoral operations and said that it would be the key in shaping peace and stability of a troubled world. He added that US littoral operations can encompass most of the earth's land mass, more than fifty percent of its population and most of the capitals and cities. "If we accept the challenge of a new age and grasp its opportunities, our future sea power will take on a whole new dimension. [3]

Since the end of the Cold War, USA has shifted its emphasis from ocean focused strategy to littoral focused strategy. This shift of focus and the new challenges in the Indian Ocean have led USA to evaluate new concepts like sea basing and littoral warfare. One purpose of sea basing is to facilitate ship-to-shore manoeuvre by housing equipment and support for a brigade-size force capable of assaulting an objective 200 miles inland from a fleet of ships and specialized sea-based platforms. [4] In August 2003, soon after the Iraq War II, the Pentagon called upon the services to develop technologies and strategies to take advantage of America's ability to base military forces at sea. [5]

Sea basing facilities can range from a modest collection of ships carrying equipment and necessary provisions, amphibious war group and a taskforce based around aircraft carrier for additional support if necessary, to a large mobile offshore platform capable of handling even tactical air transport aircraft and off-loading even heavy armour and artillery into lighter vessels, if need be, in adverse sea conditions.

According to Jane G. Dalton, US sea basing envisaged a system of systems, a flolitta of ships serving collectively as a staging and sustainment area from which ground forces can launch attacks ashore in a non-permissive environment, sometimes referred to as 'forcible entry operations'. Though no one knows exactly what the sea basing will look like in any detail, it will probably consist of a network of ships that would support artillery fire, air support, supplies and a secure home for troops fighting on land. The primary components of the sea bases would include the Maritime Pre-positioning Force-Future (MPF-F) cargo ships, the next generation destroyers (DDX), the littoral combat ship (LCS) and the amphibious assault ship, in conjunction with existing guided-missile cruisers and destroyers, aircraft carriers and submarines. The MPF-F cargo ship is being designed to replace today's logistic force cargo ships and would act as a floating logistic centre. It would probably be as large as an aircraft carrier, and accommodate heavy lift helicopters and operate cargo planes as large as Air Force's C-130. It would also be able to move supplies and equipment to those aircraft and other ships while at sea. Another report claims that MPF-F will be directly involved in combat operation and replace big deck Tarawa-class amphibious assault ship. Thus, it will be a fighting logistic ship with flight deck big enough to send hundreds of Marines ashore in rotor craft and launch Joint Strike Fighters. [6]

According to *Jane's Defence Weekly*, sea basing will also involve new types of smaller amphibious craft. These Transformable Craft (T-Craft) would have a speed of 40 knots, carry four to ten M1A1 tanks, and land high and dry on the beach. Their range is estimated to be 2,500 n.miles. An intermediate transfer station, to help move people and material from large ships to smaller vessels, is also being envisaged. [7] Such a mobile offshore base would require an effective defence against naval and air challenges, especially mines, submarines and anti-ship missiles. Thus, it will require a sea shield as also sea strike capability. New ships, UAV's and missile systems are being proposed to fulfil these roles.

According to *Jane's Fighting Ships 2005-2006* US Navy is inducting large (14,264 ton) new multipurpose destroyers after 2010. They will be equipped with highly sophisticated air defence system. They will have 155 mm gun with a range of more than 100 km, and SSM that will be equipped with GPS guidance system. USA is also building small littoral combat ships for neutralizing hostile submarines, fast attack craft as well as to perform the role of mine-counter measure ships. These will operate near the littoral and control offshore waters and provide protection to amphibious warfare vessels as also auxiliaries.

Since the emphasis is upon swift response, there are proposals to form expeditionary strike group (ESG) that could provide for rapid response even without the support of carrier battle groups. It is envisaged to be built around an amphibious ready group of US Marines, which will be supported by surface warships and submarines for mission specific roles. These ESGs are designed to combat threats at lower level, especially in the context of war on terrorism.

Related to these responses is another strategy that envisages the ability of US to project force across the world at short notice but with minimum overt presence in the area of interest. General James Jones, Commander of the US European Command, had envisaged creation of a set of 'lily pads'; small and lightly staffed facilities for use as jumping off points in a crisis. These warm bases would be outfitted with supplies and equipment to rapidly accommodate far larger forces. These small, expandable bases, would be linked like spokes to a few larger heavy infrastructure bases. At the margin, virtual bases would be established by negotiating a series of access rights with a wide range of states. Much more equipment would be pre-positioned at land and sea with the increased focus on specialized units for rapid base construction. [8]

Apart from various strategic options as discussed above, USA is also improving its capability to project force in the Indian Ocean in the light of its past experience. Thus, Navy has no serious plans to alter its carrier fleet for some years to come except to replace a couple of ships that would be decommissioned in due course. USS Kitty Hawk is expected to be replaced by USS H.W. Bush in 2008. USS Enterprise is likely to be replaced by the new design CVN-21 in 2014-15. Given the present low level of threat from state actors the existing fleet of eleven carriers is deemed sufficient to project US power across the oceans.

Instead of adding to the carrier fleet USA is reconfiguring its large amphibious ships so as to operate vertical take off and landing (VTOL) aircraft like Sea Harrier so as to act as small aircraft carrier that can provide air support in circumstances where the presence of large taskforce built around an aircraft carrier is not required. Already large amphibious warfare vessels, like the Wasp class (40,532 tons), are being reconfigured to carry six to eight Sea Harrier jet fighters as well as 42 helicopters including attack helicopters. If need be, the mix can be altered to include more Sea Harriers. In future, these aircraft are likely to be replaced by F-35 Joint Strike Fighter (JSF). Seven such vessels are operational and the eighth of the class will join in 2007. Five Tarawa-class (31,967 tons) amphibious warfare ships are also equipped with Sea Harriers and V-22 Osprey till-wing aircraft. New San Antonio-class ships that are being built will carry V-22 Osprey tilt-wing aircraft that have a longer range as also higher speed and payload. They will be more effective in projecting power from the sea to the littoral. Thus, these 'aviation heavy' amphibious ships will also act simultaneously as smaller and cheaper aircraft carriers. [9]

USA is also increasing its sea-based capacity to use Tomahawk cruise missiles for 'first strike' in conventional war. Towards that end it is converting four of its large Ohio-class SSBNs. Its SLBMs will be replaced with 154 Tomahawk cruise missiles. The Ohio-class submarine will also be able to launch covert operation. Number of cruise missiles will be reduced to 126. Instead, locked chambers will provide access to dry dock shelter and the new Advanced SEAL Delivery System. [10] Indian Ocean will automatically be the area of their deployment. USA is also building ten new Virginia-class SSNs. All are expected to be ready by 2014. These are Tomahawk-specific and are likely to replace old Los Angeles-class SSNs. There are report of plans to rearm the long range strategic missiles like the SLBM Trident as also land-based ICBMs with conventional multiple high explosive warheads. About 24 Trident missiles are proposed to be so converted. Each missiles would be able to carry 100 independently targeted conventional warheads. [11]

EUROPEAN PARTNERS

Coalition partners of USA are also improving upon their existing maritime force projection capability. Of them, UK is the most reliable partner. Weakness of British force projection capability was revealed even during the Kuwaiti crisis of 1990-91 when British participation was hampered by the lack of attack carriers and modern amphibious warfare capability. The Strategic Defence Review of 1998 marked the transition from the Cold War strategy to force projection strategy. Attempts are being made to recast the Royal Navy so as to enable it to play an effective role in expeditionary operations in the littoral and for power projection ashore. The Naval Strategic Plan 2000 sets out the route map to implement that strategy in the next 15 yeas. [12]

While several ships are being decommissioned, orders are being placed for new ships. They include two medium-size Queen Elizabeth-class attack carriers of about 65,000 tons each, capable of operating about 35 aircraft that would include the STOL variant of F-35 and helicopters. These new ships are scheduled to be operational by 2012-15 and will enhance UK's littoral warfare capability. Till then the small aircraft carriers with Sea Harriers would be retained.

Experience during the Kuwaiti crisis of 1990-91 had revealed the weakness in amphibious warfare capability. That led to the construction of the Oceàn, a 21,785 ton LPH. It was employed during operations in Afghanistan in 2001 and Iraq in 2003. If necessary, one of the small carriers could also be re-rolled as helicopter carriers. UK will also induct two new Albion-class LPD. They will replace HMS Bulwark. There are proposals to build two Bay-class LSD of 16,180 ton each. They will also have flight decks for helicopters. Six new roll-off (RO-RO) transport ships of 20,000 ton each have also been inducted as also two new large fleet tankers. These new ships are going to greatly enhance UK's sea-lift capability.

UK is also ordering six new Type 45 destroyers. The first is likely to be commissioned by 2009. It will have improved anti-air warfare capability. [13] UK might acquire the long range 155 mm gun as also land attack missiles that are being developed by USA for these ships. These additions will substantially enhance UK's maritime force projection capability by 2010-2015.

Among the European powers, France had always maintained an autonomous presence in the Indian Ocean Region that could, if and when necessary, cooperates with US-led coalition. Next to UK, France also has a limited force projection capability. It operates a nuclear-powered medium attack carrier, Charles De

Gaulle, that took part in 2001 operations against the Taliban but kept out of Iraq War in 2003. France might acquire one more carrier in future though funding might be a problem. The French Navy has a six-year procurement programme for the period 2003-2008. That includes capital intensive ships like one SSBN, two SSN, besides two destroyers and four multi-purpose frigates. They might be armed with the SCALP long-range cruise missile now under development. The French Navy already operates two Foudre-class LSDs and proposes to acquire two new Mistral-class LSD/TCDs. Its old helicopter carrier *Jean d' Arc* is expected to serve till 2010. France has a number of auxiliaries to support a modest amphibious force.

Other states in Europe are also modifying their naval strategy from the earlier role of containing the Soviet Navy in the Baltic Sea, the North Sea and in the Mediterranean to one of supporting US-led operations in the Indian Ocean Region. They were already well equipped for what is now termed an littoral warfare. Some states are now improving upon their capability. The Visby corvette of Sweden is a good illustration of the new trend in European design of littoral combat ship. It is not only designed around the stealth technology but also makes extensive use of carbon-fibre reinforced plastic. The material not only provides for high strength, low weight, low radar and magnetic signature but also about fifty percent reduction in weight. That allows for greater payload or higher speed and longer range. [14]

Some European states are now acquiring vessels that would support force projection strategy. Italy is adding one small multi-purpose aircraft carrier of 27,000 tons. Beside 18-20 aircraft it will also carry a few tanks as also some transport vehicles. It will also be equipped for command and control role. Denmark is constructing two frigates and two combat support ships. The Netherlands is also enhancing its force projection capability. Its second LPD is to be commissioned in 2007. It is a large 16,680-ton platform configured for expeditionary and amphibious operation as also a joint task group headquarter afloat, besides humanitarian and disaster relief operations. [15] These new acquisitions by European powers also dovetail with European Union's Rapid Reaction Force whose zone of operation covers the Mediterranean as also the Arabian Sea region.

USA's coalition partners in the Asia-Pacific region are also modifying their naval capability for the new role. Of them Australia and Canada, the backbone of the so-called Anglosphere, have been actively involved in support of USA in the Indian Ocean since the Kuwaiti crisis of August 1990 and have participated in all operation since then. Historically, USA has had strategic identity of interests only with countries of the White Commonwealth such as the UK, Canada and Australia or with alliance partners like post-WW-II Germany and Japan. [16]

Of them, Australia's role as an Indian Ocean powers has been more crucial. According to Admiral V.S. Shekhawat, because of America's extremely close ties with Australia, its military and political actions have to be interpreted through the global and regional objectives of the USA. [17] This close partnership has earned for Australia the title of America's deputy sheriff in the region. Australians object to it. They would rather prefer to be seen as alliance partners (ANZUS) and coalition partners in war on terrorism.

Australian Navy has been acquiring ships that would enable it to participate in force projection role. Tabruk, a heavy-lift ship, was commissioned in 1991. It is likely to be replaced in 2010. In 1994, USA had transferred two medium-size amphibious warfare ships. Each of them is capable of supporting battalion-size troops (about 450) along with supporting artillery and armour as also four helicopters. Fleet replenishment ships and oil tanker have been inducted to enable ships of the Royal Australian Navy to operate far away from the shore.

There are proposals to upgrade these facilities. Under the 10-year plan, by 2013, Australia will strengthen the air warfare capability of its surface vessels like destroyers and frigates with US help. Two new LHDs, estimated to cost US$ 1.5 bn are expected to enter services by 2012. These will replace the existing ex-US amphibious warfare ships. The new LHDs will be able to transport 1,000 personnel and 150 vehicles including tanks and other armoured vehicles, as also provide landing spot for six helicopters. [18] Australia is thus gearing up its navy so as to play a more effective role in the US-led coalition in the Indian Ocean Region.

Canada has also been active in US-led coalition and has operated its naval vessels in the Indian Ocean Region since the Kuwaiti crisis of 1990. The constant deployment of its surface combatant in far away region means that the Canadian Navy will be needing replacement for existing surface combatants. There are proposals to build new warships to progressively replace three Iroquois-class and 12 Halifax-class ships. The first ship of this type is expected to join by 2019. In the meanwhile there are proposals to refit and upgrade the Halifax-class ships with upgraded Sea Sparrow missiles and associated radar and command/control system. [19] Canada is also going to acquire three new 28,000-ton vessels for sea-lift and afloat support role.

Among the Asian partners, Japan is destined to play a major role in the years to come for two main reasons. Japan is fast breaking out of its post-World War II operational limitations that had restricted its naval activities to within 1,000 miles of its coast. Also, during the Cold War, Japan's major contribution as US ally was to help monitor and if possible neutralize Soviet Pacific Fleet. Now, focus has shifted to cooperate with US-led coalition in the so-called war on terrorism.

Under article 9 of the Japanese constitution Japan had renounced for ever the use of war as a means of settling international dispute. By implication, it means that Japan cannot enter into collective security arrangement or deploy its military forces abroad to fight a conventional war. Mr. Fukhushiro Nukage, Japan's Defence Minister, in his address to the Royal United Service Institution (RUSI), London on January 11, 2006, said that though the constitution recognizes the right of self-defence as an inherent right of a sovereign state but it is interpreted in such a restrictive manner as not to allow it to exercise the right of collective self-defence. There are efforts to amend the constitution. A commission was established in 2000 for both the houses of the Japanese Parliament (Diet). It was reported that opinion in both the houses was divided. Amendment will need two-third majority in both the houses as well as a majority in the national referendum. [20] Both are not easy to obtain.

Japan has been reorienting its defence strategy from deterrence oriented to response oriented steps. The anti-ballistic missile defence was an illustration of the change. Japan's National Defence Program of December 2004 highlighted the need to cooperate with international community. Japanese Defence Minister also reiterated that alliance between USA and Japan was indispensable not only for ensuring Japan's security but also for the maintenance of peace and stability in the Asia Pacific region. He also stated that cooperation with international community was a secondary mission for Japan's Self Defence Forces. "We are now considering upgrading those tasks to a primary mission." [21] Upgrading the status of the Defence Agency to that of a full-fledged Defence Ministry also reflects the new thrust in Japan's naval strategy in future.

Japan's dependence upon USA has further increased in the context of South Korea's testing of long-range Taepodong-2 missiles as also its allegedly covert nuclear weapon programme. Following the missile tests by North Korea in July 2006, Japan has decided to accelerate its anti-missile defence programme with US support. In the interim period USA has dispatched to Japanese port the Arleigh Burke-class destroyer whose Aegis weapon system is capable of tracking and engaging short range ballistic missiles.

Japan's entry into overseas operations has been a slow process. In 1991, after the Kuwaiti crisis, it was involved in mine clearing operations in the Gulf. It joined UN-led peacekeeping operations since 1992. It was involved in disaster relief operations after the Tsunami. After the events of 9/11 and following Operation Enduring Freedom, Japanese SDF has provided fuel and water to vessels of eleven coalition partners. These operations would have ended by April 30, 2005 but were extended by six months. [22] Japan also posted 600 defence personnel in Iraq to perform humanitarian role after 2003. Japan is participating in several exercises related to Proliferation Security Initiative (PSI), including maritime interdiction exercise hosted by Japan in 2004.

Since the Maritime Self Defence Force cannot operate overseas freely, Japan has projected its Coast Guard as an instrument of its maritime diplomacy in South and South-East Asia. However, its proposal of 1999 for formation of a 'regional' coast guard to combat piracy in South China Sea and in the Malacca Straits was turned down. Japan's constitutional constraints also limit its support in fight against piracy. It cannot provide financial assistance even for the purchase of patrol boats to regional powers like Malaysia and Singapore. Its contribution is, therefore, limited to financial and technological assistance for providing navigational safety and pollution control. India has, therefore, emerged as a viable and valuable partner in the context of regional maritime security especially after Indian maritime forces apprehended MV Alondra Rainbow in 2000. [23] Japan's Coast Guard has been interacting with Indian Coast Guard since then.

Japan has a powerful navy comprising of submarines, destroyers, frigates and auxiliaries and maritime patrol craft. It also has been strengthening its amphibious warfare capability. During 1998-2003, it acquired three large Oosumi-class amphibious warfare ships of 8.900 tons each. It is also building large surface combatant vessels. Though classified as destroyers, at least four of the Kongou-class destroyers (7250-9585 tons) can be easily classified as cruisers. Reportedly, two modified Kongou-class destroyers have been ordered. They will be designed as command vessels and will even carry V-22 Osprey tilt-wing aircraft. Thus, Japan is also gearing up to play a more proactive role in the Indian Ocean in the years to come. It has also succeeded in preparing the diplomatic base for the same through its active role in support of anti-piracy operations in the region. Cooperation in SLOC protection will be the next logical step.

Unlike USA, Japan has succeeded in retaining a low profile lest it reminds states in South-East Asia of its role during World War II.

OTHER GREAT POWERS

Russia: The Soviet Navy that graduated from a coastal sea denial role of World War II to one with global reach by late eighties once again shrunk to a shadow of its former self following the disintegration of the USSR. While the end of the Cold War had removed the rationale for a large three dimensional navy with global presence, the financial collapse as well as political disintegration of USSR forced Moscow to write off a large part of its navy. Even relatively new vessels that were amongst the most sophisticated that were ever built were either decommissioned or mothballed and allowed to rust in naval dockyards. Though Moscow had retained some strategic submarines as a part of the triad of what can now be called credible minimum strategic deterrence *vis-à-vis* USA, the Russian Navy had shrunk in size. It seemed as if the regime in Moscow had given up naval ambition and had reduced Russia to the status of a land power.

Russian Navy, however, witnessed a revival by the beginning of the millennium. That was reflected in two documents; Foundations of the Russian Federation Policy in the Areas of Naval Activities for the Period Till 2010, and the Naval Doctrine of the Russian Federation for the Period Till 2020, approved in 2000 and 2001 respectively. [24] The new regime gave preference to modernising and strengthening strategic-nuclear part of the triad. Hence, new improved Bulava SLBM as also GLONASS satellite navigation system for greater accuracy of the long-range missiles including PGMs were given priority. Conventional forces were given lower priority.

Russian Navy has been able to salvage some of the warships of the 'Soviet' period to recreate a navy till such times when more funds can be earmarked for new vessels. At the moment Russian Navy operates about 13 SSBNs for strategic deterrence, 35 SSNs most of whom can launch long range cruise missiles that can be armed with nuclear warheads, 13 conventional submarines, one large aircraft carrier, five large missile cruisers, 19 destroyers, 44 frigates, one Ivan-Rogov-class LPD and 21 LSTs. These are distributed among the three fleets in the North Sea/Atlantic Ocean, the Pacific Ocean and the Black Sea.

As noted earlier, Moscow began to give greater attention to the Navy under the new leadership of President Putin. He reasserted the decision during his annual address to the Federal Assembly on May 10, 2006. He said that steps were afoot to modernize Russia's defence forces between now and 2020. Naval shipbuilding has got underway again, and Russia is building new vessels of practically all types. He specifically mentioned the construction of two nuclear-powered submarines to be armed with new Bulava missile system. These were the first such submarines to be built since 1990. [25]

There is no doubt that pending the decision on new naval policy, Russian shipyards were building sophisticated warships like conventional submarines capable of launching SLCM, destroyers and frigates and virtually rebuilding the old aircraft carrier for the Indian Navy. These shipyards are now ordered to build warships for the Russian Navy as well.

Keel has been led for the new Admiral Gorshkov-class frigate in February 2006. There are plans to construct five more vessels. This frigate reportedly will be more advanced than the Talwar-class frigate built for the Indian Navy. It will feature modular design and will incorporate stealth features. A design for a destroyer, as a follow up of the Sovremenny-class destroyer, is being finalized. Already one Stregushechiy-class large corvette is operational. Two more are to be built by 2006-2008. The Russian Navy is proposing to acquire several smaller corvettes and patrol craft for adjacent waters. Beside the construction of the SSBN, Russian Navy is also building new Lada-class (Amur-class) conventional submarine as replacement for similar submarines that are getting old. These submarines are likely to be deployed in the Baltic Sea. [26] There are also reports that Russia might build new aircraft carriers. Reportedly soon after Rosoboronexport clinched the Vikramaditya deal with India, Deputy Defence Minister M. Aleksei Moskorsky disclosed plans for two or three aircraft carriers, probably nuclear powered, to be built between 2015-2017. Funding for them has been included in the draft Weapons Programme 2006-2015 that is under evaluation. The first ship will be deployed in the Pacific while the second might replace admiral Kuznetsov in the Northern Fleet. [27]

Russian Navy has come out of its shell and is conducting exercises in all its neighbouring waters, including the Indian Ocean. It is still too early to say if and when the Russian Navy will be operating in a sustained manner in the Indian Ocean Region. Its position in the Black Sea is not very secure. Present government of Ukraine is opposed to extending the Russian Fleet Agreement beyond 2017. Such a move is likely to seriously affect Ukraine's domestic stability. Already, majority of people in the Crimean Peninsula are opposed to the presence of the NATO troops there. The population is also likely to resist removal of Russian naval presence from there. Though under pressure in the Black Sea, Russia is now keen to re-establish its naval presence into the Mediterranean. It has sought facilities for two naval bases in Syria at Tartus and Latakia. The reason given is that it will help curb maritime terrorism. The NATO is already active in that area.

It should not be forgotten that the Black Sea and the Mediterranean Sea are important in the context of Russia's SLOC *vis-à-vis* the Pacific. The SLOC traverses the Indian Ocean. That SLOC will acquire greater significance once the North-South corridor connecting Russia/Caspian Sea/Arabian Sea *via* Iran becomes viable. It should also not be forgotten that unlike the Cold War era, the Russian Navy is developing common interests *vis-à-vis* navies of the US-led coalition especially in the context of war on terrorism and is a partner in Proliferation Security Initiative (PSI).

Geopolitical realignments also cannot be ruled out. Though Russia and USA may have common objective of confronting terrorism there are signs of growing tension on three main counts;

expansion of NATO in former Soviet territory, attempt to control oil and gas resources of Russia and also of Central Asia, and NATO's threat of using sanctions against Iran. China will support Russia on the last two issues. It is possible that these issues might force Russia to once again deploy its navy in the Indian Ocean Region. It will be no surprise to see a greater Russian (and Chinese) naval presence in this region by 2010 when Russia is expected to start building new warships.

China: China's naval strategy needs to be analysed in the context of its overall maritime strategy. China is determined to emerge as a major maritime state. In 1996, China formulated 'Ocean Agenda 21' that aimed at development and utilization of all its maritime assets and resources. In 1998, a White Paper was issued on Development of Chinese Marine Programme. The focus was on building a large merchant marine and hence on construction of hundreds of large and medium shipyards along the Chinese coasts. This is also reflected in the massive naval build up of China. According to Admiral VS Shekhawat, Shanghai alone has more shipyards building warships than in the whole of India. [28] China's naval strategy will be driven by its overall maritime strategy, merchant marine and vast sea borne overseas trade including energy resources. Hence, the Pacific Ocean as well as the Indian Ocean is bound to be the focus of Chinese maritime/naval strategy. Changes in Chinese naval strategy since the eighties point in that direction.

Chinese naval strategy underwent a basic shift from the previous policy of sea denial in the coastal and offshore waters to sea control of its offshore waters that extend deep into the South China Sea. The shift in focus of the Chinese Navy or PLAN was the result of influence of strategists like Admiral Lieu Huaqinq, Commander-in-Chief of the Chinese Navy between 1982-88. The first objective was to assert Chinese presence up to the first island chain stretching from the Kurile Islands near Japan to the Ryuku Island, Taiwan, the Philippines and even Borneo. [29] This zone was also referred to as the green waters. Beyond that was the second island chain stretching from the Alaska in the north up to

Australia. It included Marina and Guam Islands. This zone constituted China's 'blue waters' and extended deep into the Pacific Ocean. [30] This was an ambitious move and had to be achieved by 2020. [31] Thus, China's priorities seem to be to consolidate its presence first in the green waters and then extend it to the blue waters. That capability, which it hopes to attain by 2020, would also enable it to project itself in the Indian Ocean Region. Its naval strategy will also be seen as a major challenge by Japan and USA since China would be able to influence their SLOC connecting the Pacific and the Indian Ocean.

China is fast modernising its navy to suit its new strategic-nuclear as well as conventional roles. China has one Xia-class SSBN. It was refurbished by 1998 and is expected to be in service till 2010-11. China is hoping to build new type 094 SSBN that would be armed with advanced SLBMs by 2020. *Jane's Fighting Ships 2005-2006* reports that China is constructing two new conventional submarines that are likely to be completed by 2007. Like the Russian Kilo-class submarines these will be able to launch SLCMs. They are likely to replace the Song-class submarines. It is also reported that these submarines might have air independent propulsion (AIP) capability. It is uncertain if these submarines are based upon the Russian (Lada) Amur-class submarines.

In the meanwhile, China is seeking Russian expertise to construct new SSNs. These are believed to be based upon Victor III-class of Russian SSNs. First of this class of SSN was expected to be operational in 2006 and three more were exported to be completed by 2010. These are likely to replace the Han-class SSNs in operation at present. The SSNs, along with modern conventional submarines including twelve Kilo-class submarines armed with SS-N-27 anti-ship missiles, ordered from Russia, will provide the Chinese Navy a credible underwater capability in the green waters.

China has been building modern Jiangwei-class frigates as well as Luda, Luhu and Luhai-class destroyers. But these were deemed to be inadequate. Hence China ordered four large

Sovremenny-class destroyers from Russia. All of them were in operation by 2006. Chinese surface vessels lack long-range SAMs. That is bound to restrict their zone of operation closer to land-based air support. There are reports that China wishes to strengthen its large surface combatant force. According to *Jane's Defence Weekly*, China, after receiving four Soveremenny-class destroyers from Russia, is proposing to order two more larger destroyers. [32] *Jane's Fighting Ships 2005-2006*, however, claims that China is constructing two new destroyers of about 7,000-tons each. They are likely to be armed with Grumble vertical launch anti-air missiles with the range of 100 km. These ships are expected to be ready by 2007. If and when completed these ships will provide the Chinese task force an adequate air umbrella even without the presence of an aircraft carrier. That will enhance China's blue water operational capability.

There is some debate about China acquiring an aircraft carrier in the near future. Though China has been purchasing decommissioned aircraft carriers like the Australian Melbourne-class and ex-Soviet Kiev-class and Minsk-class ships yet it has not given the indication of its desire to build one. It did buy the large half-finished aircraft carrier Vayag from Ukraine allegedly as scrap. It has not been completed as an operational aircraft carrier so far but according to Admiral VS Shekhawat it is believed to have been repainted in Chinese markings. China is procuring the wherewithal to make her operational by 2010. It may be used in a training role until China is ready to fully enter carrier-borne naval aviation. [33] Since the Chinese Navy has a 'blue water' objective it will seek to acquire a new medium attack carrier may be by 2010. But even the laying of the keel of such a ship would have been reported. After the decision to acquire an aircraft carrier is taken it will take at least five to seven years for the carrier to be commissioned and at least three more years for the Chinese Navy to integrate it in its overall naval operation. Thus, there is no likelihood of China operating on aircraft carrier, if it at all wishes to do so, before 2015.

Is the question of acquisition of aircraft carrier linked to the possible deployment of Chinese Navy in the Indian Ocean? An aircraft carrier does give a state certain power projection capability. There is no doubt that China is going to depend increasingly upon SLOC in the Indian Ocean for its energy security as also for its growing trade. According to Lee Jae-Hyung, China's oil import is likely to expand from 1.4 million barrels a day (mbd) to 3 mbd by 2010. China believes that it could guarantee the safety of the SLOC in South-East Asia and Indian Ocean through close cooperation with Myanmar, Pakistan and Iran. [34] China has helped to upgrade Myanmar Navy and ports. It is also building a modern port at Gwadar in Pakistan. There are reports that it is keen to construct bunkering facilities on the southern coast of Sri Lanka. [35]

Experts tend to differ on the question of Chinese naval deployment in the Indian Ocean in the years to come. According to Admiral VS Shekhawat, a major or permanent Chinese naval presence in the Indian Ocean is unlikely in the near term in the absence of a clear strategic objective and the inability to sustain prolonged deployment. [36] According to Srikant Kondapally, China have plans to acquire two aircraft carriers, two SSBNs, Six SSNs, eighteen modern destroyers and thirty frigates by 2020. However, according to him, it is difficult to conceive of China deploying its naval forces 'permanently' in the Indian Ocean till about 2045. [37] It is difficult to predict what might happen four decades hence or what China might hope to achieve by stationing its force permanently in Indian Ocean region by 2045. By them, even USA might have opted out of its strategy that is conceived of in the context of energy security based upon dominating regional oil and natural gas resources as also the related SLOCs. It will, however, be wrong to presume that Chinese would let matters rest till they have a capability to dispatch a taskforce based around an aircraft carrier.

The question thus gets linked to the overall Chinese strategy in the context of the Indian Ocean Region, Is it powers projection? If so, against whom and for what purpose? Is it for SLOC protection? Can China ensure it by deploying taskforce in the region since that action might generate hostile response among several littoral states and thus defeat that purpose. Or, will China mark its presence at a low level and seek to project itself as a power interested in contributing towards enhancing peace and stability in the region and thereby securing its political and economic objectives; namely acceptance as a great power whose views need to be counted while deciding the future of the region, and also to ensure its energy security. China's policy as also that of Russia in the context of Iran's nuclear fuel enrichment programme can be a pointer in that direction.

This role can be performed even if China dispatches a modest taskforce that includes a heavy destroyer as the command ship, two or three other large surface combatants, fleet replenishment ships and may be one SSN. China has been cultivating its own allies over the past decades among the littoral states like Myanmar, Bangladesh, Sri Lanka, Pakistan and Iran. China is also trying to come closer to major GCC states like Saudi Arabia. It might also be able to obtain political support from the members of the Shanghai Five that includes Central Asian states and Russia. Landlocked states of Central Asia would also develop a strategic interest in peace and stability in the Indian Ocean for their own economic interests like alternate trade route as also export market for their energy products. Thus, China, if it plays its cards well, can emerge as a major actor in the Indian Ocean Region even without deploying a large taskforce. These developments need to be evaluated before India decides upon its long-term policy in the context of Indian Ocean Region.

REGIONAL POWER: PAKISTAN

During the Cold War era, Pakistan was seen as a counterweight to India. This was reflected in transfer from USA to Pakistan of large number of warships armed with sophisticated equipment and missiles like six Gearing class destroyers armed with, Harpoon missiles, ASROC anti-submarine rockets, and eight Brook and Garcia - class frigates.

The end of the Cold War, that also coincided with the return of the Russian SSN Chakra after completion of three year lease period, marked a shift in US policy towards Pakistan. Brook and Garcia - class frigates that were on lease were recalled. There was no replacement for the Gearing - class destroyers. That forced Pakistan to acquire six Type 21 frigates that were being decommissioned by the British Navy in the light of its reduced commitments following the end of the Cold War. Pakistan could, with great difficulty, acquire three P-3 Orion maritime patrol aircraft from USA. It lost one and did not get its replacement for some time. In the meanwhile Pakistan had been upgrading its ex-British Type 21 Tariq-class frigates by fitting equipments from old US warships and SAMs from China to retain some surface warfare capability, especially ASW, vis-à-vis the Indian Navy that remains its prime adversary.

Of late, Pakistan has been trying hard to enhance its naval capability. It has ordered four Jiangwei II (E-22P) class frigates from China at the cost of US$ 600 mn. These 2,250-ton ships are likely to be armed with eight anti-ship missiles each of Chinese origin, one HQ-7 (Chinese version of French Crotale) short-range SAM, as also two RBU-1200 anti-submarine rocket launchers. They are expected to carry two helicopters each. As per the deal that was finalized during the visit of Admiral Muhammad Afzal Tahir, Chief of Pakistan Navy, to China, three of these frigates would be built in China and the fourth will be constructed at the Karachi Shipyard. The first frigate is likely to be delivered in 2008 and the last in 2013.

The *New Indian Express* (Kozhikode) of May 24, 2006 also reported that Pakistan had struck a deal to buy four naval vessels from Greece during the visit of Pakistan's Prime Minister Shaukat Aziz to Athens. There were also reports that Pakistan was earlier seeking transfer of Oliver Hazard Perry-class frigates from USA. This was revealed by Admiral Shahid Karimullah to journalist in September. [38] Probably, USA did not want to send wrong signals to India. The deal with Greece could be the compromise.

Pakistan has also added two fast attack craft armed with anti-ship missiles. These were built at Karachi Shipyard. Marsun

Shipyard in Thailand provided technical support reportedly based on a modified German design. These ships, Jurrat and Kuwwat, of 250 tons each have a top speed of 32 knots and are armed with Chinese C-802 anti-ship missiles. [39] These ships are an improvement upon the Jalalat type of fast attack craft built in 1990s with Chinese assistance.

Pakistan has invested its rather limited funds that are earmarked for the Navy to acquire modern submarines from France. Three modified version of Agosta-class submarines, Agosta 90 B, were ordered in early nineties. The first of its class, Khalid, was built in France and commissioned in 1999. The second and third were to be built at Pakistan Navy's Dockyard at Karachi. The second submarine, Saad, was commissioned in late 2003. The third, Hanza, is under construction and would employ the MESMA module for air independent propulsion (AIP). [40] Pakistan Navy thus became the first navy to experiment with the new system that will enable it to generate power by using oxygen and ethnol to drive turbine and generate electricity to turn the propeller and thus extend its underwater operational capability for a considerable longer period as compared to submarines powered by battery alone. The two submarines constructed earlier would also get converted to the new AIP system during their major refits.

It is reported that Pakistan Navy has finally decommissioned four Daphne-class submarines. It needs replacement not only for them but also for two old Agosta-class submarines. Richard Scott quoted *La Tribune* to the effect that following the signing of the Scorpene deal with India the French company DCN has commissioned work on initial design of the new Merlin-type conventional submarine for Pakistan. Pakistan, had ordered three Agosta 90B from DCN in 1994. The last would be delivered in 2006. Though Pakistan would prefer DCN for the supply of more submarines in future it is also approaching German HDW and Spanish Navanti for the same purpose. [41] *Defence News* of February 27, 2006 also reported that Pakistan was seeking three new submarines from DCN. France has cleared Armaris to offer three submarines to Pakistan. Pakistan might also opt for German 214 class design. The total cost was estimated at US$ 1.0 to 1.2 bn. [42] Pakistan has also built three midget submarines capable of launching two torpedos as also undertaking covert sabotage operations. Pakistan had also obtained three mine countermeasure ships from France. Now that Pakistan is going to operate Gwadar port as also Jinnah naval base besides Karachi it will need more of the same.

Till recently, Pakistan's naval-air capability depended upon a few old Mirage fighter bombers configured to launch Exocet anti-ship missile as well as Atlantic and Orion maritime patrol and ASW aircraft similarly armed. Pakistan's naval-air capability was getting eroded. Its Atlantic fleet was getting old and needed replacement. Reportedly, they will be removed from service by 2007. One of its three Orion aircraft had crashed. It seemed that Pakistan's naval-air arm, an important component of its naval strategy, would be seriously eroded. However, its newly acquired status as a non-NATO ally in the war on terrorism paid dividends. Once again Pakistan began to receive military-related aid from USA.

Defence News of December 6, 2004 reported that Pakistan was offered the choice between new E-2 Hawkeye AEW 2C aircraft at US$ 1.6 bn or used E-2 upgraded at half the cost or eight surplus P-3 Orion at US$ 970 mn. Other items included ship-based Phalanx close support weapon systems for US$ 155 mn. US White House was seeking to push US$ 3.5 bn aid package for Pakistan through the Congress as a part of 2005 Foreign Operations Appropriation Bill. [43] According to *Jane's Defence Weekly* of September 7, 2005, eight surplus P-3C Orion aircraft were provided cost free to Pakistan, allegedly for border security role. US-based Lockheed Martin was to upgrade the avionics. The value of upgrade was not reported. [44] Pakistan's Deputy Chief of Naval Staff, Rear Admiral Muhammad Shafi, had said that the first batch of these aircraft had been received by Pakistan. [45]

Pakistan did not opt for US E-2 Hawkeye aircraft but was

proposing to acquire an undisclosed number (reportedly eight) of Saab 2000 turboprop aircraft as platforms for Ericsson AEW & C systems. That was to counter India's plans to acquire Phalcon system from Israel. Pakistan's proposal was suspended following the earthquake in 2005 but foreign donations and grants helped to reduce economic pressure. Reportedly, China has agreed to offer AWACS based on An-12 to Pakistan. Pakistan had also plans to acquire Gripen fighters from Sweden but the option was given up after USA agreed to transfer large number of F-16 aircraft. [46]

Over the years, Pakistan's naval strategy has not changed much. According to a paper presented by Commodore S. Shekhar and Commander N.R. Ravi in 1989, in the event of hostilities, the PN's objective would appear to be 'sea denial', operating in defensive parameters around home waters. "The first perimeter would consist of recce-in-force and free-wheeling interdiction using the Atlantic and Mirage aircraft. The second perimeter would consist of capital ships and ASW helicopters to maintain a protective AS barrier and to engage the remnants of the force that had penetrated the first perimeter. This perimeter is also expected to ensure a cordon-sanitaire long enough to allow the PN submarine force, mainly the Agosta-class submarines, to escape and enter deep waters of the Arabian Sea where they will mount disequilibrating attacks on Indian shipping, ports and naval vessels. A third perimeter would provide the innermost cordon of the citadel defence with ASW armed Sea Kings, missile craft and shore missilery. [47] Interestingly, things have not changed much even now except that Pakistan has acquired a new naval base.

Navy had remained the neglected arm of Pakistan. Yet, it had succeeded in utilizing its limited funds to fashion a robust sea denial capability based upon missiles like Harpoon and Excocet that can be launched by aircraft, surface vessels as also submarines. Surface vessels also give it a limited ASW capability near its coast. Missile-armed submarines also provide it with a capability to threaten adversary even beyond the radius of action of its sea denial strategy of about 200 n.miles from its shore.

It will be important to speculate upon the impact of new

global thrust on war on terrorism upon Pakistan's naval capabilities. Pakistan has once again become a 'frontline' ally of the NATO allegedly against the forces of Islamic militancy as symbolized by al-Qaeda and the Taliban. Earlier, in the eighties, it was a frontline state against the Soviet in Afghanistan. As in the past, today also, Pakistan is deriving political, economic and military benefits for its support to the US-led coalition. Increasingly, Pakistan Navy's role in counter-terrorism is being emphasised. It is reported to have participated since 2004 in the Coalition Maritime Campaign Plan, originally premised on interdicting militant movement by sea but since then expanded to cover transnational criminal activities.

According to Robert Karniol it is the only regional navy contributing forces and was set to assume overall command of the 'Multilateral Taskforce 150" in April (2006). He also wrote that Pakistan Navy was proposing to acquire four corvette size ships, preferably locally build, for the new role. According to him, lifting of US sanctions, has allowed Pakistan Navy to obtain several long-delayed systems including Vulcan-Phalanx Block II close-in weapon, RGM-84/UGM-84 Harpoon Block II missiles, Atlas heavy torpedo for Agosta-class submarines and eight Orion maritime patrol aircraft for US$ 970 mn. All of them will be updated by 2009. [48]

USA seeks to justify these arms transfer on the basis of a new principle. General Peter Pace, Chairman of the Joint Chiefs of Staff of the USA Military, when asked about US response to test of Agni III by India, said that it would not destabilize the region. According to him testing of Agni III or sale by US of F-16 to Pakistan should not destabilize the region since stability of nations was increased when they had confidence in their defensive capabilities. [49] Is the new policy based upon balanced force accretion, instead of the earlier policy of balanced force reduction, a way to ensure regional stability? Such a policy will only encourage qualitative and quantitative arms race in South Asia with its unpredictable consequences.

Unlike the Cold War era, Pakistan Navy, as far as USA is

concerned, has lost its role as a counter to Indian Navy. Rather, it has acquired a new role in the context of war on terrorism. This role has become all the more important for USA since it is not sure about the political and military support from important Gulf states like Saudi Arabia as well as in the context of increasing belligerent role of the new regime in Iran. That makes the Pakistan Navy a major regional actor in the northern part of the Arabian Sea and in the Gulf of Oman. These are vital areas in CENTCOM's zone of influence.

By contrast, Indian Navy has emerged as a preferred partner in the new strategy in the Indian Ocean that revolves around SLOC protection in and around the waters surrounding the Indian land mass and the island chains in the Arabian Sea and the Bay of Bengal. Hence, though Pakistan is emerging as an active partner in war on terrorism, that cooperation, for geographical reasons alone, is largely confined to sea around its littoral in a part of the Arabian Sea.

The future role of Pakistan Navy will also be determined by its capabilities in the years to come. Unless Pakistan is able to retain the support of large hearted partners like USA and China on a long term basis Pakistan Navy by 2015-2020 will comprise of a maximum of six modified Agosta-class (or its near equivalent) submarines, a few midget submarines, four Chinese frigates, three aging mine counter-measure ships (unless new ones are added) and a few large missile armed patrol vessels. Its naval air arm will once again be degraded and the surplus or second-hand Orion C-3 aircraft that are being handed over now will need replacement. Such a mix, designed primarily for a sea denial role will further limit Pakistan ability to play a meaningful role in SLOC protection or even in combating maritime challenges posed by non-state actors. As admiral VS Shekhawat had noted, Pakistan does not have the industrial capability or the financial resources to be a major sea power. The sea denial capability of its navy will only constrain Indian Navy's operation in the Arabian Sea. [50] Admiral Arun Prakash, however, has a different view. According to him, Pakistan, as a traditional rival, will not go away in a hurry and "will have to be countered by the possession of necessary military wherewithal-conventional as well as nuclear". [51]

NON-STATE ACTORS

Beside the present and future force projection capability of great powers and medium powers or state actors, the role of non-state actors also needs to be taken note of in the context of threat to maritime security and stability in the Indian Ocean Region. Their activities range from armed robbery on board ship to hijacking and piracy, illegal fishing, illicit transfer of arms, drugs, personnel, and WMD-related material, and finally armed attack on shipping that might include suicide attack using boats loaded with explosives. Scenarios are also being built of terrorists using containers for illegal transfer of men and material, employing ships under flag of convenience and even hijacking tankers and CNG carriers for attack on valuable installations or for causing ecological damage. Increasingly, this threat is being taken seriously and Indian Ocean is emerging as its prime arena in the context of war on terrorism.

Martirr Murphy, however, questions these assumptions. He argues that lack of necessary skill and the practical difficulties facing terrorists in attempting to operate in the maritime sphere may render many of the nightmare scenarios, feared by government and port authorities, unlikely. He says that port is a large area and hard to destroy though explosion might cause death and destruction. He also says that crude oil is difficult to ignite as the case of French oil tanker Limburg hit by terrorists proved. [52] Also, several oil tankers were hit during the Iraq-Iran war in the Gulf without causing great explosions. Such voices are often lost in the wilderness because all great powers, many of the minor and small powers as also the UN have made terrorism as the basis of the primary threat in the post-Cold War period. Having lost an adversary, they have discovered a new one. The new Cold War is a war against non-state actors.

Unlike state actors, it is difficult even to identify these non-state actors or assess their capability for conducting covert operations. However, one can divide them into two major heads; groups that have been so identified, and others that remain anonymous. The LTTE has long been identified as indulging in acts of maritime violence that are increasingly being recognised even in the West as acts of terrorism. The EU members who earlier had protected and indirectly supported LTTE activities have now blacklisted it as a terrorist organisation. But several other groups are still anonymous. Most of them are designated under the broad-band of *al-Qaeda* network thereby giving that organization credit for acts that it might not even have planned. Surely, transfer of arms and explosives to Indian coasts *via* the Arabian Sea as also Bay of Bengal was not the handiwork of *al-Qaeda*, though one can point a finger at ISI of Pakistan and related agents in that context.

Acts constituting threats to maritime security can be divided into two broad categories; those that are not directly linked to acts of violence like illegal fishing, and others that are directly linked to acts of violence like piracy, illegal transfer of arms, WMD-related material, taking of hostage, hijacking of ships etc. While some of these acts have global ramification others target only a few states. Hence, steps to counter this threat rests upon a three-tier strategy; strengthening maritime dimension of homeland security, promoting regional cooperation, and finally global action. Of the three, primacy needs to be given to strengthening homeland security. Unless a state has a robust and effective framework of homeland security it cannot participate effectively in regional and global efforts to contain the new threat posed by non-state actors.

Notes

1. Bangara, Vice-Admiral SCS, "Security in the Indian Ocean Region: A Naval Perspective", in Nambier, E.K.G. and Suryanarayana, V. eds., *Lectures in Maritime Studies*, Publications Division, University of Calicut, 2005, pp. 72-73.

2. Shekhawat, V.S., "Approach to Sea Power", *Seminar*, (562), June 2006, p-45. Shekhawat, V.S., "Approach to Sea Power", *Seminar*, (562),

June 2006, p-45.

3. Johnson, Admiral Jay, "Anytime, Anywhere, A Navy of the 21st Century", *Proceedings of the US Naval Institute*, 123(11), November 1997, pp. 48-50.

4. Hondrix, Jr., Lt Commander Henry (US Navy), "Exploit Sea Basing", *Proceedings of the US Naval Institute*, 129 (8), August 2003, p. 61.

5. Lowe, Christian, "Amphibious Operations, Attack Platform: Sea-basing Would Make Reluctant Allies Irrelevant", *Armed Forces Journal*, March 2004, p. 26.

6. Dalton, Jane G., "Future Navies-Present Issues", *Naval War College Review*, 59(1), Winter 2006, pp. 18-19.

7. "US Seeks Prototypes to Test Sea Basing Concepts" *Jane's Defence Review*, 42(37), September 14, 2005, p. 20.

8. Campbell, Kurt M. and Ward Celeste, "New Battle Scenarios", *Foreign Affairs*, 82(5), September-October 2003, p. 97.

9. Koch, Andrew, "US Navy: Marines Eye Path to Smaller Carrier", *Jane's Defence Weekly*, 41(5), April 14, 2004, p.5.

10. Posen, Barry R., "Command of the Cosmos: The Military Foundations of US Hegemony", *International Security* 28(1), Summer 2003, p.11; *Strategic Digest*, 34(12) December 2004, pp. 1756-57 and Sykora, Captain Charles D. (US Navy), "A Transformation Limited by Legacy, Command and Control", *Naval War College Review*, 59(11), Winter 2006, p. 44.

11. Brown, Nick and Glassborow, Katy, "US Navy Looks For Global Strike Capability", *Jane's Defence Weekly*, 43(5), February 1, 2006, p. 30.

12. Scott, Richard, "Royal Navy Poised to Perform Another Rebalancing Act", *Jane's Naval Intelligence*, 109(3), April 2004, pp. 26-28.

13. *Jane's Navy International*, 111(2), March 2006, p. 9.

14. *Defence News*, October 10, 2005, *Quoted in Strategic Digest*, 35(11), November 2005, pp. 1546-1548.

15. *Jane's Defence Weekly*, 43(21), May 24, 2006, p. 12.

16. Shekhawat, Admiral V.S. (Retd.) "Maritime Dimensions of India's Security: The Future", *Indian Defence Review*, 15(4), October-December 2000, p.69.

17. Ibid., p. 69.

18. *Jane's Navy International*, 111(2), March 2006, p. 33.

19. *Jane's Defence Weekly*, 43(18), May 3, 2006, p. 10.

20. Nukage, Fukushiro, "Japan's Defence Policy: Basic Principles and New Initiatives", *RUSI Journal*, 151(1), February 2006, pp. 17, 19.

21. Ibid., p. 18.

22. *The Hindu*, April, 24, 2005.

23. Chopra, Rear Admiral Rakesh "The Maritime Dimensions of Energy Security", *Journal of the United Service Institution*, 134(557), July-September, 2004, pp. 381-82.

24. Patrushev, Vice-Admiral V.V. (Retd.) "Will Russia Have Aircraft Carrier?" *Military Thought*, 12(2), 2003, p. 162.

25. *Strategic Digest*, 36(g), June 2006, p. 629.

26. Ivanov, Henry, "Austere Deterrence", *Jane's Defence Weekly*, 43(18), May 3, 2006, p. 29. and Karnozov, Vladimir, "Debut for Project 677 Submarine", *Asia-Pacific Defence Reporter*, 31(6), July-August 2005, p. 41. Ivanov, Henry, "Austere Deterrence", *Jane's Defence Weekly*, 43(18), May 3, 2006, p. 29. and Karnozov, Vladimir, "Debut for Project 677 Submarine", *Asia-Pacific Defence Reporter*, 31(6), July-August 2005, p. 41.

27. *Asia-Pacific Defences Reporter*, 31(9), December 2005, January 2006, p. 31, and Hiranandani, Vice-Admiral G.M., "The Russian Àircraft Carrier Perspective". *Defence Watch,* 5(11), July 2006, p. 26.

28. *Asia-Pacific Defences Reporter*, 31(9), December 2005, January 2006, p. 31, and Hiranandani, Vice-Admiral G.M., The Russian Aircraft Carrier Perspective. *Defence Watch,* 5(11), July 2006, p. 26.

29. Kondappally, Shrikant, "China's Naval Strategy", *Strategic Analysis*, 23(12), March 2002, p. 2043.

30. Downing, John, "China's Evolving Maritime Strategy" Part I, *Jane's Intelligence Review*, 8(3), March 1996, p. 130.

31. Cheng Li, "China in 2000: A year of Strategic Thinking", *Asian Survey*, 41(1), January-February 2001, p. 78.

32. *Jane's Defence Weekly*, 43(2), January 11, 2006, p.14.

33. Shekhawat, V.S., "Approach to Sea Power", *Seminar*, (562), June 2006, p. 45 and Hiranandani, Vice-Admiral G.M., "The Russian Aircraft Carrier Perspective". *Defence Watch,* 5(11), July 2006, p. 25.

34. Jae-Hyung, Lee, "China's Expanding Maritime Ambition in the Western Pacific and the Indian Ocean", *Contemporary South-East Asia*, 24(3), December 2000, p. 253.

35. *The Hindu*, June 1, 2005, quoted in *Strategic Digest*, 35(7), July 2005, p. 970.

36. Shekhawat, V.S. "Approach to Sea Power". *Seminar*, (562), June 2006, p. 46.

37. Kondapally, Srikant, "Chinese Navy in the Indian Ocean", *Journal of Indian Ocean Studies*. 8(1-2), August 2001, pp. 85-7.

38. *Jane's Defence Weekly*, 42(36), September 7, 2005, p. 8.

39. *Jane's Defence Weekly*, 43(19), May 10, 2006, p. 18.

40. *Jane's Defence Weekly*, February 6, 2002, quoted in *Strategic Digest* 32(3), March 2002, pp. 533-34.

41. Scott, Richard, "DCN Launching Design Work for Pakistan Submarines", *Jane's Defence Weekly*, 43(3), January 18, 2006, p. 4.

42. *Strategic Digest*, 36(4), April 2006, p. 452 and 36(7), July 2006, pp. 880-81.

43. *Strategic Digest*, 35(4), April 2005, pp. 429-30.

44. *Jane's Defence Weekly*, 43(36), September 7, 2006, p.8.

45. *Strategic Digest*, 36(3), March 2006, p. 348.

46. Bokhari, Farhan, "Islamabad Backs Swedish Deal", *Jane's Defence Weekly*, 43(22), May 31, 2006, p. 7.

47. Shekhar, Commodore S., and Ravi, Commander N.R., "Factors Affecting the Choice of a Propulsion System for the Indigenous Submarine Building Programme", in Eastern Naval Command, *Compedium of papers, Defence Oceanology Seminar*, Visakhapatnam, December 14-15, 1989 (Memeograph copy in IDSA Library, New Delhi), p. 72.

48. Karniol, Robert, "Plugging the Gap", *Jane's Defence Weekly*, 43(12), March 21, 2006, p. 32.

49. Dikshit, Sandeep, "US Stand Facilitated Missile Test", *The Hindu*, July 10, 2006.

50. Shekhawat, Admiral V.S., (Retd.). *Indian Defence Review*, 15(4), October-December 2000, p. 68.

51. Admiral Arun Prakash, "Indian Maritime Doctrine", in Nambier, E.K.G and Suryanarayana, V., eds., *Lectures on Maritime Studies*, Publications Division, University of Calicut, 2005, p. 30.

52. Murphy, Martin, "Maritime Terrorism: The Threat in Context", *Jane's Intelligence Review*, 18(2), February 2006, p. 20.

3

RESPONSE TO MARITIME CHALLENGES

ASSESSING CHALLENGES IN POST-COLD WAR PERIOD

Changing politico-military environment since the end of the Cold War has projected two distinct sources of threat to nation's maritime security. While the threat from state actors persists, the new threat from non-state actors has also started posing serious challenges not only to individual states but also to international peace and security. Both these challenges need to be analysed separately so as to design appropriate counter measures.

India's response to present and future politico-military presence and related capability of various state and non-state actors in Indian Ocean Region will depend upon a combination of military preparedness as well as diplomatic measures designed to suit every individual case separately over the given period. These would range from great powers to middle powers as also different types of non-state actors. Hence, over a period, India will need to evolve a mix that will ensure an effective and credible deterrence specific to each type of threat.

In that context, India's military capability to neutralize challenges in Indian Ocean Region becomes significant in defining India's maritime strategy. India's regional and even global policy will be determined, among other things, by its capability to play a meaningful role in the Indian Ocean Region. Its voice will be heard only if it has the necessary capability. Hence, if India wishes to play its desired role as a major regional power it has no option but to develop that credible maritime capability.

THREAT FROM STATE ACTORS

The nature of maritime threat is different from that posed by a land power. Unlike threats to national security from landwards, which always originates from neighbours, threat from the sea are different to predict and prepare for because of the nature, reach, flexibility and mobility of naval forces. This is true not only of state actors but also of non-state actors. "An inimical distant naval power, if it gains access to bases in the Indian Ocean can rapidly alter the strategic balance against Indian interests, even if it does not have the resource of a super power. History has shown that nations having a substantial interest in the seas need to have capability to protect them against threats which may seem nebulous in tranquil times. Times change, as do national interests. Threat perception, therefore, needs to be kept up to date." [1]

USA: While seeking to assess India's maritime security in the years to come it is important to understand the dramatic changes in regional and global strategic environment since the end of the Cold War era so as not to seek a continuity of policy when the environment has altered. During the Cold War era, though USA had a strong naval presence in the Indian Ocean, it was not primarily directed against India. USA, during the Cold War era, did act indirectly by promoting Pakistan in its anti-India policy politically, economically and even militarily through arms transfer. In December 1971, during the Bangladesh conflict, USA dispatched a taskforce led by USS Enterprise. It was at best a political and a diplomatic gesture of support to its alliance partner. USA had to pay a political price. Perception in the Ministry of Defence changed drastically.

The *Annual Report* of the Ministry of Defence, 1970-71, published before the Bangladesh conflict, while discussing the maritime situation in the Indian Ocean Region, said that it had become a subject of speculation and at times of acute controversy in the recent past. "Of interest to us is the fact that these developments may result in increased tensions in the area and have a bearing on the national fortunes of the countries washed by the Indian Ocean". [2] By contrast, the *Annual Report*, 1972-73, said, "There have, however, been some unfavourable developments. The appearance of the VII Fleet in the Indian

Ocean during the December conflict has inevitably given rise to some misgivings." [3]

The Enterprise syndrome continued to affect Indian perception and continued to be listed as a 'matter of concern' to India as to other littoral and hinterland states of the Indian Ocean. [4] That perception had not altered even in 1986 which heralded the beginning of the end of the Cold War. As per the *Annual Report*, 1986-87, the military presence of extra-regional powers and their search for military bases in the region was seen as a part of their interventionist motives and efforts to support friendly and displace unfriendly littoral regimes. [5]

The Enterprise syndrome was evident even in 1990 when K. Subramanyam suggested the following parameters for India's naval security doctrine. They included, among other things, adequate submarine capability including nuclear-powered submarines armed with long-range guided missiles to raise the cost of any external power attempting coercive diplomacy against India. He argued that India should have observation satellites, including an ocean surveillance satellite, and maritime reconnaissance and strike capability to forestall a threat to our installation and to avoid surprise attack against India. [6]

It look some time for this mindset to change even after the end of the Cold War as was evident from the Indian response to war against Iraq in 1991. Attempt to defreeze the situation after 1995 had a setback following the Pokhran II of 1998. It will not be wrong to say that the events of September 11, 2001 and the rising international tide against terrorism was a major turning point. Both, India and USA, began to see each other as partners to combat the new threat. Also, India's geographical centrality and willingness to join international efforts in defeating terrorism helped to establish India's credentials as a positive factor in the newly evolving strategic environment in the region.

USA too had stopped playing the old card of seeking to contain India by backing Pakistan even though Pakistan was also a favoured non-NATO ally in fight against al-Qaeda and the Taliban along the frontiers of Afghanistan and Pakistan. India enjoys another major advantage over Pakistan. While the West trusts the regime in Pakistan, as it does regimes in several other Islamic states, it is reluctant to trust a large section of the public in those countries. In India, not only the regime but also the majority of the public is seen as partners in this war on terrorism.

Despite the rhetoric of restructuring the world order in the post-Cold War period, perception of Indian strategic thinkers has not altered greatly. According to Admiral V.S. Shekhawat, countries of concern to India will be Pakistan in the short and medium term, China in the long term and the USA as a variable permanent presence for the foreseeable future. He also added that USA was unlikely to intervene in India without risking a major political and military confrontation. He noted the forward movement in Indo-US relations. But, harking back to the Enterprise syndrome, he said that USA was willing to risk that in 1971 when it attempted to intervene on behalf of Pakistan with the USS Enterprise Task Force in the Bay of Bengal. He also added that while US intentions may keep altering, its substantial naval capability in the Indian Ocean is likely to be a permanent feature and requires to be taken strategic note of.

Given the history of US self-perceptions as an indispensable nation, self-assumed role of globecop, the only Super Power with a global maritime reach as well as the tendency to script strategic scenarios to further US long term objectives, it cannot be presumed that Indian and US interests will not come into conflict in the region. He also argued that US fascination with Pakistan as a key player in Central Asia and the Gulf and counterweight to India, suggests that US policy could in future revert to one of support to Pakistan. Should this extend to overt or covert military support to any of the frequent Pakistani misadventures against India, it will have to be by sea and will need to be countered at sea. It follows that India will need to field a navy which will have to be reckoned with by any outside intervening power. [7]

Almost similar views were expressed by Vice-Admiral S.C.S. Bangara. Addressing a group of scholars at the Calicut University on January 18, 2005, he said that one must be prepared to face the unexpected. The presence of extra-regional powers in the Indian Ocean Region would influence India's security options and freedom of operations. He suggested that India needs to build capabilities to deter multinational forces from interfering in India's national activities. "We need to carry out surveillance and establish presence in our areas of interest to know what they are doing. We need to engage them so that they do not do anything contrary to our interests. If the Navy can help in maintaining our foreign policy free from any external pressures it fulfils a very important military and diplomatic role." [8]

Though there is a new understanding between India and USA in the post-Cold War era, there are also serious reservations about the US doctrine of unilateralism and of seeking solution through the use of force. This combination along side USA's ever increasing capability for force projection across long distances is seen as a potential source of threat to stability in the Indian Ocean Region. Also, the dramatic turn that US administration is capable of taking with the change of regime in Washington, fails to inspire full confidence whether any long-term arrangement can be worked out with USA. Hence, there will always be the element of unpredictability. That, in turn, will justify India's quest for minimum credible deterrence even *vis-à-vis* great powers in the years to come.

China: Unlike USA, that is across the Pacific or the Atlantic, China is a next door neighbour of India as also of other regional powers like Myanmar, Bangladesh and Pakistan. China and India as large regional powers, and as immediate neighbours, are also likely to compete for importance in their respective neighbourhood. Attempt to evolve a policy of peaceful co-existence in the fifties was shattered in 1962. China also tried to encircle India by supporting Pakistan and Bangladesh politically and through arms supply in the seventies and the eighties. Unlike Indo-American relation, Sino-Indian geopolitical relations have not as yet undergone basic restructuring except that China is showing willingness to restart the process of peaceful coexistence by trying to improve economic relations, through cooperative efforts in the field of energy security and by initiating a process of confidence building and better border management. It remains to be seen as to what extent would China promote these alternatives or would continue to pursue its previous policy of seeking to contain India *via* Pakistan and Bangladesh. At the moment, it seems that China is continuing to pursue a two track policy of retaining its option *vis-à-vis* Pakistan while seeking closer cooperation with India; a policy not much different from that of USA.

There have been three basic changes that China has taken note of since the end of the Cold War and more so after the disintegration of the USSR. The first is that the Russian Federation is no longer a threat to China. Rather, the two can jointly work to manage the immediate neighbourhood in Central Asia. That would in turn ensure energy security as well as help contain the threat of radical Islam. Secondly, China's booming economy and growing dependence upon imported fuel will make it depend upon access to oil and gas fields in South-West Asia as well as a secure SLOC. Pakistan can play only a limited role in both these respects. India, by contrast, can play a more decisive role either as a partner or as an adversary. Lastly, China, despite efforts at political detents and close economic linkages, still believes that USA is the primary adversary. Consequently, will China be prepared to trust India because of India's growing strategic contacts with USA in particular and the West in general. China will like to keep its options open *vis-à-vis* Pakistan, Sri Lanka, Bangladesh, Myanmar and even Thailand as alternate to India. Thus, despite the growing entente between India and China, India will have to ensure a military capability, especially sea denial, in case China assumes a hostile posture in the context of its Indian Ocean strategy in the years to come. Will that drag India into confrontation with neighbours like Myanmar, Bangladesh, Sri Lanka or even Iran? Thus, India's China policy will also influence India's regional policy, especially in the Bay of Bengal and even in the Arabian Sea.

Pakistan: Though Pakistan continues to treat India as its primary adversary, Pakistan is no longer the prime focus of Indian maritime strategy, at least since the end of the Cold War, for two main reasons. While Pakistan Navy had been starved of funds and equipment, Indian Navy had increased the gap both in quantity and in quality. Hence, though Pakistan Navy is treated with respect as a competent adversary its overall capability to pose a serious threat to India is limited now only to its fleet of submarines armed with long-range anti-ship missiles and the fleet of P-3 Orion maritime patrol craft similarly armed. Though India might not succeed in repeating 1971, Pakistan Navy too will be contained within its coastal waters and will find it increasingly difficult to operate freely in waters further away. Its underwater capability, however, needs to be taken seriously and India will be well advised to improve its ASW capability both qualitatively as also quantitatively. This has become all the more important now when India's development strategy is being geared not only to an expanding maritime trade but also to the protection of its ports and hundreds of off-shore oil and gas platforms.

Maritime threat posed by Pakistan would take a more serious turn if it were to join with a great power like China against India. India's steadily growing maritime force will be able to counter even that combined threat because Pakistan, cornered in one part of the Arabian Sea, cannot ensure the SLOC security between its ports and the Malacca Straits. Also, in such an eventuality, international configuration might favour India. US-led coalition that includes Japan as also some of the ASEAN states would not like to see Chinese dominance in areas of their primary strategic concern. Both Pakistan as also China would be aware of it and would factor that in their maritime strategy in the years to come.

NON-STATE ACTORS

While the degree of threat from state actors can be assessed with some certainty, it is very difficult to assess the threat *vis-à-vis* the timing, place, as also the level of violence that is posed by non-state actors. Also, while the military capability of state actors can be located and targeted, it is difficult to locate and neutralize the capability of non-state actors. Hence, constant vigil and a robust and operational structure of homeland security that is able to sanitize the coastal waters at least up to a distance of 200 n.miles from the coast if not more has acquired primacy in the context of India's maritime security. Equally important in the context of India's maritime security is the degree and extent of cooperation in this context with regional state actors as also with others who are affected by the new threat.

There is no doubt that the Navy and the Coast Guard do play an important role in containing the threat from non-state actors. But, multilateral cooperation is indispensable for a comprehensive strategy to combat the new maritime challenge. It is equally important to strengthen India's own homeland security.

While decision makers in India are becoming aware of the need for creating a mechanism for ensuring homeland security from maritime threats, yet few effective measures have been taken in that context. Also, while India has understanding with several of its close maritime neighbours in Indian Ocean Region in the context of promoting cooperation to enhance maritime security, yet effective regional cooperation is hampered due to constraints of international law which are further compounded by sensitivities on the touchy subject of national sovereignty. Till these constraints are overcome in practice, India needs to strengthen its own homeland security so as to counter the threat from non-state actors.

MARITIME OBJECTIVES AND NAVY'S ROLE

Over the years, Indian Navy has been attempting to define a role for itself. As years passed by the role began to be perceived more sharply. Navy's role is determined primarily by the national objectives as perceived by the elite. According to Admiral Arun Prakash, India's national objectives lie in ensuring a secure and stable environment which will permit the economic development and social uplift of its masses, so that country can ultimately take its rightful place in the international comity of nations. "Within this overall objective our primary maritime interest is to ensure national security and provide insulation from external interference, so that the vital tasks of fostering economic growth and undertaking development activities can take place in a secure environment". [9]

The Navy would be shaped taking into account the polarization of forces and the current and future maritime capabilities in our region, and in the light of the full spectrum of conflict from low intensity warfare to strategic deterrence. According to Admiral Arun Prakash, India would maintain a capable maritime force which would have the reach, endurance and sustenance to safeguard our maritime interests in areas in the Indian Ocean Region. It will essentially be formed around the core of two aircraft carriers, with necessary escorts, and adequate submarines and aviation component and a logistic train. He said that India would foster self-reliance, and added, "We are determined that in consonance with India's ancient maritime tradition, this will be a force for peace, friendship and good-will, which will reach out to extend a helping hand wherever needed in our maritime neighbourhood. [10]

Indian Ocean space has always been the 'area of interest' for the Indian Navy. Admiral Madhavendra Singh defined it as, "It extends all the way to the choke points that afford entry into the North Indian Ocean. The accompanying map covered almost the entire Indian Ocean Region stretching from the Cape of Good Hope to Western Australian coast line and from the Southern coast of Indonesia and the Andaman Sea to Persian Gulf and the Red Sea. [11]

According to Vice-Admiral S.C.S. Bangara, "We are actively deployed in our areas of interest to respond to crises. This not only signals intent to maintain stability but also displays a capability to contribute towards it." He added, "We are ready to provide military assistance, if required in the region, as directed by the government of the day." Vice-Admiral S.C.S. Bangara also listed some of the missions of the Indian Navy. They included establishing a presence to advertise our interest in regional stability and show our capability to contribute towards it.

"Being ready and able to deploy at short notice to potential hot spots by itself could be an insurance against forces that promote instability". Presence also enables the Navy to carry out surveillance in our areas of interest and to monitor what is happening there–an important peacetime activity. Second mission deals with proactive engagement with other multinational forces in the region. The intention is not only to understand their methods of operation and their capabilities but also to show them our capabilities and abilities to protect our national interests. "The potential for deterrence that the Navy has can only be showcased to extra-regional powers in the Indian Ocean Region by actively engaging them". The third reason is the need for interoperability and to be ready for multinational crisis response and joint exercises under a multinational/UN banner. Yet another mission is power projection so as to send calibrated signals to different audiences. These signals could be of friendship, technological ability, interest or coercion, depending upon the circumstances of the case. Finally, disaster relief and assistance is also an important mission. [12]

Indian naval strategists have been debating over three interrelated issues; the role of the Indian Navy, appropriate strategy, and related weapons mix. Some enthusiasts had advocated even in the sixties that Indian Navy should be strong enough to dominate the SLOCs in the Indian Ocean from the Cape of Good Hope to the Malacca Straits. It was rather a tall order at that time and was probably produced as an argument to seek more funding for the Navy.

More reasoned arguments centred around the role of aircraft carrier and large surface combatants in the context of India's naval strategy. There was a strong lobby that opposed the deployment of aircraft carrier by the Indian Navy. PVR Rao argued that unlike the US Navy, Indian Navy would not be asked to launch an amphibious operation against a hostile coast. He said that for defence of India's coastline against enemy attack, land based aircraft can be equally effective. He even argued that cost of building airfield and maintaining them would be far less than the cost of an aircraft carrier. [13] Brigadier N.B. Grant called an aircraft carrier not only a white elephant but also a sitting duck. [14] Vice-Admiral Subimal Mookerjee argued that the Navy needed to be reengineered around submarines and shore-based long range multipurpose aircraft in support. "Most cost effective ways to stymie coercive and interventionist actions are missiles and submarines". [15] It is interesting that these experts were advocating for a large maritime power like India a naval strategy that Pakistan had already perfected. It only shows that not only civilians but also service personnel can have a 'continental' mindset and hence limited view of maritime and, therefore, of naval strategy.

It was probably Admiral R.H. Tahliani who, as early in 1981, sought to define Indian Navy's role. According to him, the navy could have four roles; global, ocean going, contiguous and coastal. He rejected coastal navy role for India. He also said that only Super Powers can hope to have a global role. He advocated that Indian Navy should be between a contiguous navy and an ocean-going navy. [16] Probably that option prevailed. Weapons mix since the eighties corresponds to that role. That role will prevail till the Indian Navy does not acquire nuclear-powered submarines equipped with medium to long-range cruise missiles and/or ballistic missiles capable of being armed with nuclear warhead.

In the light of changing regional and global environment Indian Navy is also modifying its roles as also its rationale. As per Admiral Arun Prakash, rational for the Indian Navy is that it is the primary enabling means by which the state ensures the use of the sea for its own purposes, while at the same time ensuring that others do not use it in a manner prejudicial to its interest. According to Admiral Arun Prakash, it has four major roles or operations; military, diplomatic, constabulary and benign. Under military operations he lists besides the conventional roles like sea control, sea denial and blockade, low intensity maritime operations (LIMO); a response to the new challenge posed by non-state actors. [17]

One illustration of awareness of maritime affairs is that the Navy has now started looking beyond 'naval' doctrine to 'maritime' doctrine. An internal Indian Navy study, Strategic Defence Review: The Maritime Dimension-A Naval Review, May 20, 1998, stated, "The Indian Navy must have sufficient maritime power not only to be able to defend and further India's maritime interests, but also to deter a military maritime challenge posed by any littoral nation or a combination of littoral nations of the Indian Ocean Region, and also to be able to significantly raise the threshold of intervention or coercion by extra regional powers. [18]

Indian Navy came out for the first time with a 'maritime' doctrine which was revealed on April 24, 2004. [19] Admiral Arun Prakash, Chief of the Naval staff, while inaugurating the Chair for Maritime Studies, University of Calicut, on October 16, 2004, dealt with main concepts like doctrine and strategy and their interface as also the vision for the future. He concluded, "In general the Doctrine attempts to convey that the India Navy can be the catalyst for peace, tranquillity and stability in the Indian Ocean Region, across a range of conditions and circumstances that one can imagine in *peace time*. [20]

Capability of Indian Navy is designed to fit multiple roles and challenges, both existing as also anticipated. According to Admiral Arun Prakash the order of battle of the Indian Navy is not configured on the basis of perceived threats to our security but on the basis of capabilities existing in our neighbourhood and the likelihood of emergent challenges. This is true for our adversaries as well as for countries not having an adversarial posture towards us for the present. The underlying premise is that if a capability is available or is being developed by a country with which we share boundaries or interest, it could have a bearing on our security, should circumstances or intentions change over time." [21] Geoffrey Till, quotes Admiral V.S. Shekhawat, "National naval forces should, therefore, be seen more as an insurance against the unpredictable than as a requirement against perceived geostrategic threats in the region. [22]

MARITIME SECURITY: NEED FOR SYNERGY

Comprehensive maritime security of any country cannot be ensured by any single organization however powerful it might be. Therefore, there is need to synergise roles of concerned sectors like the Navy, the Coast Guard and the Air Force so as to avoid duplication of efforts as also to prevent inter-services ill feelings if not rivalry. At the moment, the Navy and the Coast Guard as well as the Navy and the Air Force have developed that synergy.

According to Air Vice-Marshal (Retd.) H.S. Ahluwalia, Indian Air Force coordinates maritime air operations with the Navy through a Maritime Air Operation Head Quarters co-located with Western Naval Command in Mumbai. IAF aircraft dedicated to the maritime strike role are exercised through periodical exercises with both Western and Eastern Naval Fleets. He suggests that there will be need for greater synergy when the Navy begins to operate Mig-29 aircraft onboard the aircraft carriers, and when Su-30 aircraft with refuelling capabilities are armed with air-launched version of BrahMos anti-ship missile.

Air Vice-Marshal HS Ahluwalia suggests the need for formulating a joint doctrine for such operations. The doctrine should encompass the roles of all types of fighters and support aircraft that would enhance the effectiveness of the operation and incorporate adequate flexibility for use of aircraft that may not, at the outset, be earmarked for naval support roles. He feels that hostile maritime situation, in Indian context, will take place not far from land-based air forces and, therefore, there is the need to ensure availability of necessary air support for naval operations. [23]

Synergy is also needed to ensure a comprehensive package for maritime security *vis-à-vis* non-state actors. Hence activities of the Navy the Coast Guard and Air Force also need to be coordinated with security-related agencies of other concerned sectors like the Border Security Force, port authorities, the customs and immigration, ONGC, fishery departments and state's marine police that are existing or are bound to be formed sooner than later. Contribution of civilian maritime programmes like shipping, ship-building and repair, fishing vessels especially deep sea fishing vessels etc. also need to be dovetailed in the overall framework of maritime security both in times of peace as also in times of national emergency.

Notes

1. Shekhawat, V.S., "Approach to Sea Power", *Seminar*, (562), June 2006, p. 45.

2. Ministry of Defence (MOD), *Annual Report 1970-1971*, New Delhi, 1971, p. 21.

3. MOD, *Annual Report, 1972-1973*, New Delhi, 1973, p. 8.

4. MOD, *Annual Report, 1976-1977*, New Delhi, 1977, p. 2.

5. MOD, *Annual Report, 1986-87*, New Delhi, 1987, p. 1.

6. Subrahmanyam, K., "Naval Security Doctrine for India", *Strategic Analysis*, 12(11), February 1990, p. 1144.

7. Shekhawat, Admiral V.S. (Retd.), "Maritime Dimensions of India's Security: The Future", *Indian Defence Review*, 15(4), October-December 2000, pp. 66, 69-70.

8. Bangara, Vice-Admiral S.C.S., "Security in the Indian Ocean Region : A Naval Perspective", in Nambiar E.K.G. and Suryanarayan, V., eds., *Lectures on Maritime Studies*, Publication Division, University of Calicut, 2005, pp. 78-79.

9. Admiral Arun Prakash, "India's Maritime Doctrine", in Nambiar, E.K.G. and Suryanarayan, V., eds., *Lectures on Maritime Studies*, Publication Division, University of Calicut, 2005, p. 24.

10. Admiral Arun Prakash, "Maritime Challenges", *Indian Defence Review*, 21(2), January-March 2006, pp.49-62.

11. Singh, Admiral Madhvendra (Retd.), "Modernization of the Indian Navy: 2020", *Indian Defence Review*, 20(4), October-December 2005, p. 48.

12. Bangara, Vice-Admiral SCS, *Collection of Maritime Studies*, Calicut University Press, 2005, pp. 77-9.

13. Rao, PVR, *Defence Without Drift*, Bombay 1970, p. 172.

14. Grant, N.B. "Does India Need More Aircraft Carriers?" *Indian Express*, December 12, 1986. Zutsei, Amer, "Navy's Blue Water Obsession", *Journal of the United Services Institution*, 119(497), July-September 1989, pp. 269-74 and Debey, Amitab, "*Indian Defence Review*, 6(3), July 1991, p. 159.

15. Mookerjee, Subimal, "India's Defence Expenditure": A Holistic Approach", *Journal of the United Service Institution*, 125 (522),

October-December, 1995, p. 458.

16. Tahliani, Admiral R.H., "Maritime Strategy", *Journal pf United Service Institution*, 111, (462) July-September 1981, p. 230.

17. Admiral Arun Prakash, *Lectures on Maritime Studies*, 2005, pp. 26-8.

18. Roy-Chaudhury, Rahul, "US Naval Policy in the Indian Ocean", *Strategic Analysis*, 22(9), December 1998, p. 1326.

19. For a brief review see Vice-Admiral Mihir Roy, "Indian Maritime Doctrine: A Synopsis", *Defence Watch*, 3(12), August 2004, pp. 15-6.

20. Admiral Arun Kumar, *Lectures on Maritime Studies*, 2005, p. 28.

21. Ibid., pp. 289.

22. Till, Geoffrey, "Security Concerns in the Indian Ocean: Making Waves?" *RUSI Journal*, 142 (3), June 1997, p. 17.

23. Ahluwalia, Air Vice-Marshal (Retd.) H.S., "IAF in Maritime operations", *Indian Defence Review*, 20(3), July-September 2005, pp. 31.2.

4

INDIA'S MARITIME SECURITY CAPABILITY

An analysis of India's maritime security capability over the years and its projected growth shows that it has been slowly but steady enhancing in quality while retaining its quantitative core. This is reflected in India's maritime security capability in 2005-2006 and the possible projections for the near future (See table at the end of the chapter). India's maritime capability can be broadly analysed under the following heads: subsurface vessels, naval-air components and surface vessels of various types, besides precision-guided munitions (PGMs) and the command, control, communication and intelligence (C_3I) systems. In view of the recommended synergy of various sectors an attempt has been made to combine the overall potential of related services in India while analysing and evaluating this capability.

SUB-SURFACE CAPABILITY

India's sub-surface fleet of vessels comprises of sixteen old and not so old conventional submarines. They include two F-class vessels, INS Vela and INS Vagli. INS Vela, acquired in 1973, had a refit in 2001. Though decommissioned from active role they will remain in operation reportedly as test bed for analysing other systems. Thus, Indian Navy operates in effect 14 submarines.

Of the four Shishumar-class submarines, two were acquired from Germany in 1986 while remaining two were constructed in the Mazagaon Dock Yard Ltd, Mumbai in 1992 and 1994. Of them, INS Shishumar has been refitted and others may also be refitted if their service life has to be extended pending induction of new submarines of the Scorpene-class.

India acquired more sophisticated submarines from USSR/Russia. Two of the Kilo-class submarines were acquired in

1982. Eight more were acquired at regular intervals between 1986-2000. These are large ocean-going conventional submarines and are reportedly very quite during their underwater operations. When delivered, the Kilo-class submarines were equipped with torpedo only. However, the last of the class, INS Sindhushastra, commissioned in 2000, was armed with sea-launched cruise missile (SLCM). Subsequently, as and when Kilo-class vessels were sent for refit to Russia, they were updated with SLCM capability. Reportedly five vessels have been so updated.

The refit costs about US$ 80 mn per submarine. It includes new sonars and associated systems that can automatically track twelve and engage four targets. Two of the six tubes are configured for launching the Klub (SS-N-27) SLCM anti-ship missile. Bharat Electronics Limited and Indian Navy's Weapon Engineering and Electronic System Engineering has not only developed an Indian sonar but also the Pachendriya fire control system. INS Sindhughosh has been fitted with these systems. Remaining Kilo-class submarines will also have those systems during their refits. [1]

The SLCM capability gives the Kilo-class a much desired surface strike capability. SS-N-27 anti-ship missiles have a maximum range of 180 kms. Through the missile cruises at a speed of Mach 0.7 yet it accelerates to Mach 2.5 when approaching the target. That speed, as also 450 kg warhead, makes the modified Kilo-class submarine a very effective subsurface platform for sea denial role. Pakistan had acquired that capability in late eighties when it refitted its Daphne and Agosta-class submarines to launch the Harpoon missiles. Modified Agosta-class submarines can launch the French Exocet missile.

As noted, many of the submarines of the Indian Navy are getting old and though being refitted and updated will need replacement if the necessary strength has to be retained to operate effectively in the vast ocean space around the Indian subcontinent. Modern submarine construction is restricted to only a select few states. Russia has a programme and at one time there were reports that India was interested in Project 677 Lada or the Amur class conventional submarine. Germany's Type 214 was out of the picture because of the allegations of financial kickbacks during the previous deal. By the time the court had disproved the charges negotiations with the French company on the Scorpene deal were far advanced. Thus all attention was focused on the Scorpene deal. Though the French Navy does not operate them Chile and Malaysia have ordered two each. Despite criticisms India decided to acquire that submarine. The HDW had argued that Type 214 was not only superior but also 20-30 per cent cheaper. [2]

The Scorpene deal was the result of Project 75 that was finalised by the Naval Submarine Design Bureau and approved by the Ministry of Defence in 1997-98 as a part of its 30-year submarine building plan. The aim was to boost indigenous capacity and revive the submarine building in the Mazagaon Dock Yard Limited, Mumbai. As per Project 75, negotiations began in 1999 with Thomson CSF (now Thales). Armaris is the joint venture of Thales and French ship builders DCN International. Reportedly, Amur-class Russian submarine was briefly considered but in essence negotiations were conducted only with the French company. The project was finalised at the level of Ministry of Defence in 2002 though contract was not signed.

Military Balance, 2002-2003 noted that Indian Defence Minister, George Fernandez, announced in February 2002 that India would not lease, as was proposed in late 2001, two nuclear-powered submarines from Russia but instead acquire six French Scorpene diesel electric submarines. [3] The proposal was to acquire six submarines and have an option to build 24 more to reach the figure of 30 as envisaged in Project 75. The estimated cost at that time was US$ 330 mn per submarine. [4]

The project was stalled due to objections from the Congress Party-led opposition at that time. Edurdo Faleiro of the Congress Party, who was also a member of the Parliament's Standing Committee on Defence, alleged that Thales was involved in a shady deal while selling La Fayatte-class frigates to Taiwan in

2002. He also argued that the deal would further delay indigenous effort at self-reliance. The matter was reportedly scrutinized by the watch-dog agency, Central Vigilance Commission, which cleared it.

The Congress-led United Progressive Alliance came to power following the election and the Congress-led government, now in power, revived the issue. Shri Pranab Mukherjee had sought the waiver of the escalation clause that was a part of the earlier deal. Under that clause Government of India had to pay Rs. 2 crore per day as penalty for delay in concluding the contract. Since price negotiation had ended almost 18 months back Government of India, under that clause, had to pay almost Rs. 1,000 crore for the delay. Pranab Mukherjee also wanted the French company to sign the integrity clause that gives the guarantee that no middlemen were involved in the deal. He also said that deal might not be renegotiated if the company revised the escalation clause. [5]

The Paris-based Armaris agreed to wave US$ 1.6 bn penalty and the deal was worked out during the visit of Indian Prime Minister Shri Manmohan Singh to Paris and during his meeting with French President Jacques Chiraq on September 12, 2005. Reportedly, the deal was also linked to French support for the civilian-nuclear power deal being negotiated between India and USA. The deal was finally signed in New Delhi on October 6, 2005. Under that agreement the first submarine is to be delivered after seven years, i.e. by 1212. Others would follow after an interval of one year each. All the six submarines are expected to be delivered by 2018. The estimated cost is between Rs. 15,000 crore and Rs. 18,789 crore.

Indian Navy is reportedly satisfied with the Scorpene submarine. It embodies stealth technology and has sophisticated sensors as also weapon systems. The Scorpene is a large ocean-going submarine with a displacement of 1,668 tons (dived). Though other details are still speculative it is reported that first three submarines would have only diesel-electric power plant while the succeeding three might carry additional air independent propulsion (AIP) system; not necessarily French MESMA

System. [6] Besides the 21" torpedo it can also launch the Exocet MM-40 anti-ship missile which has an estimated range of 180 km and is capable of using GPS terminal guidance system. [7] However, according to *Defence News* of October 17, 2005, Scorpene would be armed with Exocet SM-39 missile. The Ministry of Defence had placed the order with European MBDA for the same. SM-39 is launched enclosed in VSM (*vehicle sous marine*), a self propelled and guided container that can manoeuvre before surfacing so as not to reveal the exact position of the submarine. Once in air SM-39 leaves the VSM and proceeds to the target. [8] Reportedly the missile can also have land attack capability. The company has reportedly offered to transfer technology for production of the Exocet missile at no additional cost though additional funds would be needed for any direct sale of missiles. [9]

These submarines will be built at the Mazagaon Dock Yard Limited, Mumbai. The Navy has paid US$ 137 mn for initial training and for buying equipment for the production of the Scorpene. Some technical experts have been sent to open office at Cherbourg in France to facilitate the implementation of the deal.

Before the ink had dried on the contract, the BJP-led group, that had earlier regulated the deal, began to accuse the Congress-led government of corruption and of the role of middlemen in the deal. Though some objections had been raised at the time of the signing of the deal [10] the criticism became more vocal in March 2006. BJP-led opposition group asked for the termination of the contract. Defence Minister Pranab Mukharjee not only refuted the charges but also said that the government had even reduced the total cost by Rs. 300 crore. [11] The opposition also named Abhishek Verma as the alleged middleman who, in turn, threatened to sue some of these leaders. Some groups like Citizen's Forum Against Corruption and Transparency International India etc. also filed public interest writs in the Supreme Court by March end seeking a probe by CBI in the alleged charge of corruption.

One hopes that the controversy does not further delay the submarine acquisition schedule. These Scorpene submarines are to replace ex-Russian F-class submarines and at least two first batch of HDW submarines from Germany. Two of the ex-German submarines and eight of the Kilo-class submarines received in the eighties will also need replacement by 2015. According to Admiral Madhvendra Singh, Mazagaon Dock Yard Ltd. cannot deliver these extra ten submarines. Hence a second submarine line needs to be opened so as to supply submarines at the rate the Navy needs them. Either Germany or Russia can be contacted for the same. He also argued that with the government having opened the doors of defence production to private industry it would be best if a suitable private sector company was given this responsibility." [12]

NUCLEAR POWERED SUBMARINE (ATV)

The most exiting aspect of India's sub-surface warfare programme is the so-called advance technology vessel (ATV) or the nuclear-powered submarine. Even after decades of work, the project is nowhere nearing completion. The ATV project was reportedly conceived of around 1977. If so, it must have been a bold vision because India had just acquired its first conventional submarine from USSR and was hard pressed even to pursue a civilian nuclear programme, leave aside nuclear weapon programme, after Pokhran I of 1974. The inability to develop an indigenous underwater platform left India with no alternative but to obtain, on a three-year lease, a soviet SSN that was about to be scrapped. It was renamed INS Chakra.

One does not know if Indians took the programme seriously but USA and its supporters did so. Apart from spreading reports of India's 'hegemonic' designs USA also supplied Pakistan with eight Brook-Garcia class frigates configured for ASW operations. They were withdrawn, much to Pakistan's chagrin, soon after INS Chakra was returned to USSR in 1991. According to Admiral J.G. Nadkarni, INS Chakra played an important role in offering Indians training in maintaining and operating nuclear powered submarine. [13] The experience must have been fruitful because work, at least on the reactor, made faster progress. According to Rahul Bedi, who had interacted with Dr. M.R. Srinivasan, former Head of Atomic Energy Commission and Secretary of the Department of Atomic Energy, the reactor was being designed by scientist from BARC. Navy and the DRDO were working on the design of the submarine. [14] According to *Jane's Fighting Ships,* 1997-1998 (under India), the fabrication of ATV was to start in 1997 probably at Visakhapatnam and the project was to be completed by 2004. Russian participation was also indicated. But, after the disintegration of USSR, the extent of Russian participation would have been drastically restricted. No wonder the project got delayed for years.

It was revived after the visit of Prime Minister A.B. Vajpayee to Russia. There were also reports that, pending the construction of ATV, India would acquire on lease one or two Akula-class SSNs. [15] *The Hidustan Times* of February 22, 2002 reported that submarine crew from the Indian Navy were being trained in Russia for the past one year on Akula-II SSN. [16] There were reports that India would acquire on lease an unfinished Akula SSN. The construction had been halted in 1995 when 85 per cent work had been completed. *Defence News* of March 4, 2002 had even said that the submarine was being built for delivery in 2004 as a part of 3-year lease contract for US$ 300 mn. There were talks of obtaining another SSN on lease. [17]

There was no transfer of SSN. However there were press reports that Russia had agreed to help India build its own ATV. That coincided with the report that the test reactor for ATV was tested on land. It had reached criticality in October 2004 and had become fully operational by December 2004.

Russia's cooperation was acknowledged, and subsequently retracted, by Indian Defence Minister Pranab Mukherjee when he had visited Russia to attend the two-day session of India-Russia Intergovernmental Commission for Military Technical Cooperation. He first acknowledged it but soon denied it while on his way back. [18] He reportedly told the Indian media persons that when he talked about ATV he had the Russian Amur-class conventional submarine in mind and not the nuclear powered submarine. [19] As if to reconfirm the report of Russian help, the *Hindu* quoted *Kommersant* of Russia about the lease of two project 09710 Shehuka-B SSNs under a US$ 1.8 bn contract for ten years as still under consideration and that Russia had resumed the construction of two vessels whose work was frozen in 1990s. It also reported that 200 Indian Navy personnel were undergoing training in October 2005 at a submarine training centre at Sosnovij Bor near St. Petersburg. [20]

Indian ATV programme is slowly taking a final shape. The prototype 100 Mw nuclear reactor had used enriched uranium, reportedly with 20 per cent enrichment, supplied by Rare Earth Materials Project at Ratnahalli near Mysore. Now, work is on to construct a larger reactor, reportedly a 190 Mw pressurised water reactor (PWR), and to integrate it with other components of the submarine which is likely to be built at Visakhapatnam. Optimists believe that it will be commissioned by 2010-2012. [21] If so, that will hopefully coincide with the commissioning of first of the Scorpene-class submarines. According to Mark Farrer, Indian ATV will be about 6,000 tons. Reportedly, it will be an evolved Akula-class submarine powered by 190 Mw nuclear power plant and will have VLS tubes. About four to six such submarines are proposed to be built. It could be armed with Sagarika SLCM under development since 1990 by Aeronautical Development Establishment, Bangalore. [22]

Since the ATV will be basically SSN, it will be armed, besides torpedo, with SLCMs. One does not know if the missile will be launched from torpedo tube or will the submarine have a vertical launch capability. There were press reports that experiments were going on to use a pontoon fixed at a depth of ten meters as a test bed for the missile. [23] It is too early to say if the experiment was for SLCM or SLBM. Names of several missiles are mentioned; like the Sagarika. It is supposed to have a range of 300 km and is powered by ram-jet engine. BrahMos or the Klub missile in use in the Kilo-class submarine could also be used.

It is possible that with the experience gained with the SSN India may decide to pursue the option of using nuclear power plant rather that diesel-electric and AIP combination for its future sub-surface vessels. That will give Indian SSNs the advantage of long endurance and sustained sub-surface operation at high speed over long distances. This will make the SSN a better platform for hunter-killer role as also strike role. Interestingly navies of USA, France and UK have long abandoned using conventional submarines and construct only SSN.

Once India gains enough experience with SSN, it can proceed to the next big leap of constructing SSBN armed with medium range SLBM. This submarine will have to be at least fifty per cent larger than the SSN if it has to launch 3,500 km range SLBM. India will also need time to perfect its submerged launch ballistic missile with adequate range. The most reliable missile Agni A1 with 700 km range is considered inadequate as SLBM even if it acquires a submerged launch capability. Hence, one can agree with Vice-Admiral RB Suri that India will have to wait till 2020 for its SSBN/SLBM. [24]

For a better understanding, the concept of sub-surface warfare and related systems need to be analysed under three major sub-heads; the platform *per se* (submarine), the power plant that can be conventional diesel-electric alone or augmented with air independent propulsion (AIP) system, or a nuclear-reactor, and finally weapons that include different types of torpedo, submarine-launched cruise missile (SLCM) and ballistic missile (SLBM). Their warheads can be conventional high explosive or even nuclear. Over the years, Indian Navy has been graduating steadily towards greater sophistication in all these different facets of subsurface warfare programme.

The first stage was the purchase of F-class submarine armed with torpedo. The HDW submarine from Germany was a qualitative improvement. That was followed by the Kilo-class submarine. The second stage was reached when the Kilo-class submarine was modified to launch long range cruise missiles

(SLCM). The Scorpene-class submarine if and when inducted will be a further modification if it is equipped with AIP system. It will give it increased underwater endurance as also mobility. That advantage and the long-range SLCM will make it a deadly platform for sub-surface operation at least closer to the coast where it can be provided protection against hostile ASW operations.

The nuclear propulsion frees the submarine from dependence upon atmospheric oxygen for its operation and thus it can cruise at high speed under water for a longer period of up to three months. Its role will, however, be greatly determined by the weapons that it is capable of operating. If it is built to launch only torpedo and SLCMs it is only an upgraded version of conventional submarine with AIP system, though with the added advantage of longer under water endurance and reach. To be a part of the strategic nuclear triad, it has to be equipped to launch intermediate to long range ballistic missile armed with nuclear warhead. Thus, SSBN armed with SLBMs alone can be a part of the strategic triad. Does the ATV project, as it is conceived of today, qualify under that head?

Indian Navy has long since asserted that it wished to develop a nuclear-weapon capable submarine as a part of its contribution to the strategic nuclear triad. Some have reported that the Sagarika missile is being developed for that role. It is not certain if it is a ballistic missile or a cruise missile or is nuclear capable. Also, what is its range? A credible SLBM has to be a ballistic missile with a range capable of reaching the main centres of the adversary. But no such missile is in sight at the moment. The Navy has been experimenting with the Dhanush, a naval version of short-range Prithvi missile. There is as yet no report that the larger and more easily deployable Agni A1, a single stage, solid fuel, nuclear warhead capable ballistic missile with a 700 km range has even been considered for the short-range SLBM role.

Reportedly, Agni III is to be the basis of India's SLBM programme. It is a large missile. This 16 metre high, two-stage missile, weighs about 48 tons. It has, however, the desired IRBM range of 3,000 to 3,500 km. Its first test was unsuccessful. Hopefully the defect would be rectified and the land-based version of the missile would be operational in due course of time. However, the submarine-launched version of Agni III and a suitable large platform of about 9000-ton displacement for the same will take lot more time to be perfected.

In this context one can raise another point. Does India need a nuclear-powered sub-surface platform (SSBN) as a base for its SLBM programme? USA, USSR, China needed them because these platforms had to travel long distances to their areas of deployment across the seas, at least during the early years when their SLBMs had short and medium range of 2,500 n.miles and less. Once the SLBMs acquired the inter-continental range most of these SSBNs were deployed nearer to the shore and protected against hostile anti-submarine operations. India, unless it wants to engage USA or European States in a nuclear confrontation, does not need to operate its sub-surface strategic force too far away from the coast. Thus, an intermediate or a medium range SLBM with 3,000 to 3,500 km range will be adequate to act as a part of the sea-based second-strike capability. The platform also need not be deployed far off from the coast.

Thus, while India pursues its SSN capability, which is what ATV really amounts to at present, it can simultaneously design a larger submarine with AIP capability besides conventional diesel-electric power plant, as a platform for its SLBMs. By the time a suitable missile is finally identified and tested for underwater launch, the platform will be ready. India can test both the prototype platform as also SLBM and when both are ready India can substitute nuclear power reactor for the conventional diesel/AIP power plant to pave the way for a truly SSBN/SLBM programme.

NAVAL-AIR ARM

India's overall naval-air capability needs to be rated in the context of the synergy between the Air Force, the Navy and the Coast Guard. This capability relates to different roles like strike, anti-submarine warfare (ASW), electronic warfare (AEW), search and rescue (SAR), maritime reconnaissance (MR) etc. For better understanding, naval-air capability is divided into land-based and sea-based aircraft, both fixed/wing and rotary wing.

When one examines these roles in the context of land-based fixed-wing aircraft, long-range strike role deserves special notice not only because it extends India's maritime reach deep into the adjoining waters but also because it is a good illustration of close cooperation and synergy between the Navy and the Air Force.

At the moment this role is performed by eight Jaguar deep-penetration strike aircraft operated by the Air Force. These are equipped with special radars and each are armed with two air-to-surface Sea Eagle missiles. One expects that when the air-launched version of the BrahMos missile becomes operational, newly acquired Su-30 aircraft will be armed with it. The radius of action of Su-30 can be further extended by mid-air refuelling. That will give India a credible deep penetration maritime strike capability extending into the sea up to about 1,000 km from the coast. By the time this combination is ready, by about 2008-10, India's space-based reconnaissance and communication capability either on its own or in cooperation with Russia will result in far greater accuracy of the missile.

The Indian Space Research Organisation (ISRO) has begun work on a Rs. 1,200 crore project that received the green signal from the government in May 2006. The project, Indian Regional Navigational Satellite System (IRNSS) is to be developed indigenously and is likely to be implemented over India in the next five to six years. IRNSS would consist of a constellation of seven satellites and a large ground segment. All systems, including user receivers, would be built in India. The first satellite would be launched in 2008-09. Three would be placed in geo-synchronised transfer orbit (GSO) while the remaining four would be in geo-stationary orbit. All satellites would be identical and weigh 600 kg each. When ready it will replace the GPS system in use in India at present.

In terms of its civilian application, the system will help track vehicle on land and also on water and identify where they are at any given point of time. It might also have its military uses. To ensure a more dedicated long-range satellite-guided missile system as also other uses India is seeking access to Russia's GLONASS global navigational satellite system. Under a bilateral agreement signed in 2004 India and Russia will jointly launch navigational satellites to make GLONASS fully operational by 2007. [25] India was negotiating for participation in EU's Galileo programme of a similar nature. It decided to opt out. One possible reason could be security. China is actively engaged in this venture.

There were reports that India was interested in acquiring medium range supersonic bomber Tu-22 M armed with air-to-surface missile (ASM). Now, one does not hear of that. Su-30 and BrahMos ASM would in future perform that role. The air-launched version of BrahMos, with Su-30 as launch platform, is expected to be tested by 2007. At the moment Su-30 can carry only one missile but the capacity can be increased to three if the airframe is strengthened. Additional funding for the air-launched version of BrahMos was sanctioned in December 2005. [26]

At the moment, Indian Navy depends for long-range maritime patrol (LRMP) and anti-submarine warfare (ASW) operations upon Tu-142 and Il-38 land-based aircraft. Tu-128 LRMP/ASW aircraft are large four-engined planes. They have long endurance and can help monitor a given maritime zone for hours. India operates eight of these aircraft that are located at INS Rajali in Arakkonam. Reportedly, Government of India has given permission to the Indian Navy to replace these aging aircraft in due course of time. Indian Navy operates five Il-38 May medium-range MR/ASW aircraft. Like Tu-142, they were also acquired from USSR. Two of them were lost in accident and were replaced (on lease) by the Russian Navy. They are located in Goa. According to Rear-Admiral Sunil K. Damle, all five aircraft would be sent to Russia for refurbishing and upon return rebased in Arakkonam. [27] Thus, very soon there will be a gap in long-range MR/ASW capability when eight Tu-142 are withdrawn from service without a suitable replacement.

Flight International of October 11-17, 2005 had reported that USA had offered India in 2004 up to ten refurbished P-3 Orion aircraft. USA was also offering them to Pakistan. New Delhi wanted to test two of these aircraft for three years before selecting a new maritime patrol aircraft. [28] US Defence Department informed the US Congress that it had approved the sale to India of logistic support worth US$ 133mn for two Orion P-3C aircraft that it proposed to lease to India. The Pentagon also said that these two aircraft would replace two Il-38 aircraft. [29]

Indian Navy was offered P-3B model to be upgraded to P-3C standard. Reportedly, the question was discussed on May 27, 2004 during the visit of US delegation led by Ed. Ross, Director for South Asia Defence Security Cooperation Agency. No price was indicated. The deal faced major hurdles after the transfer of these aircraft to Pakistan was confirmed. Admiral Arun Prakash was quoted by *Aviation Week and Space Technology*, December 6, 2004, as saying that India might rethink buying upgrades of ex-US Navy P-3B if Washington went ahead with the sale of P-3 aircraft to Pakistan. [30] The US offer was again derailed on financial ground. Naval Head Quarters reportedly communicated to the Defence Ministry that the investment needed to lease and maintain two P-3 Orions in India would be economical only if the Navy planned to purchase the entire fleet of Orions later. It needs to be noted that P-3 Orion is already a closed chapter for US Navy and is likely to be replaced by P-8 that is under development. [31]

Indian Navy is searching for a new platform in the light of its long term requirements. Many other manufacturers are interested in the deal. They include the French Falcon 900 MPA as also Atlantic ATL-3, Russian Il-38, Brazilian Embraer, beside the Lockheed P-3 Orion. Reportedly, Boeing has also offered eight P-8A MR aircraft under direct military sale. It is still under development in USA.

Admiral Madhvendra Singh suggests that India would need 30 LRMP aircraft for surveillance of the Indian Ocean. The present fleet of Dornier and Islander is adequate for surveillance near the coast.[32] In the light of India's requirement for medium and long-range MR/ASW aircraft for its Navy as also for the Coast Guard, India needs to develop its own version of land-based MR aircraft, if necessary in collaboration with others who can share platform and other systems. Indian Navy has rejected the ship-based E-2 Hawkeye 2000. Six of them were offered. Indian Navy would prefer a land based AEW&C aircraft. There is proposal to deploy this system or board aircraft like the Embraer EM-145 and Saab 2000. [33]

India's requirement of maritime reconnaissance near the coast is met today by Dornier 228 that has been configured for that role. It has a search reader, FLIR (forward looking infra-red device), cameras and search light. It is unarmed and is designed for reconnaissance over India's EEZ. Though Navy also operates it, it is the main-stay of the Coast Guard which reportedly operates about 20 of these aircraft.

Now that the Coast Guard is also enlarging its zone of operation, it is searching for a larger platform. According to *Flight international* of January 4-10, 2005, India is reviewing responses from several companies for two new MR aircraft. The deal is worth US$ 55 mn. All the big firms including HAL are interested. This platform has to be twin-engined with the speed of 180-405 km per hour, an endurance of eight hours and a range of up to 3,700 km. It should be able to have short take-off and landing capability, i.e., ability to operate from small airfields. Besides the role of MR, fishery protection and SAR, it is also expected to serve as a command and control platform. It should be able to operate in all weathers and its search radar should be capable of providing a 360° coverage. [34]

India's programme to acquire three Phalcon-type airborne early warning systems for the Indian Air Force has been long delayed. Indian Air Force had developed its first generation version of AWACS based upon an Avro airframe. Unfortunately, the aircraft met with an accident and the project was stalled, reportedly for political reasons. Though the platform was lost, the details of the systems and the necessary software would still be available with the Air Force. If the Navy, the Air Force and the Coast Guard coordinate with HAL and other agencies to develop a prototype of AWACS suitable for MR/ASW role also it might not replace the role of the advanced AWACS as demanded by the Air Force but it will surely give the Navy and the Coast Guard an indigenous base to further update the system over the years. Since the focus is on war or terrorism and maritime surveillance such a capability will provide an adequate base for incremental qualitative upgrade over the years.

According to *Annual Report*, 2005-2006 of the Ministry of Defence, the Government had sanctioned in 2004 for an indigenous airborne early warning and control system (AEW&C System). Rs. 1,800 crore was sanctioned. A time frame of 78 months was given for the user trial. It was proposed to have one prototype and two operational aircraft. The System was reportedly to be based on an executive jet. It is not clear if it is a new project or a continuation of the old one. K. Tamilmani, Director of the Centre of Air-Borne Systems (CABS), that is developing the AWACS, said during his speech at the 29th Annual Science Festival organized by the Bangalore Science Forum that the prototype would be ready by 2007 and the AWACS will fly by 2010. [35] It will be useful if the views and requirements of the Air Force, the Navy and even the Coast Guard are taken into account while designing the system so that duplication can be avoided and economy of scale can be achieved.

UAV

Unmanned aerial vehicles (UAV) are being increasingly used for reconnaissance and even for strike role as is clear from US operations in Afghanistan and Iraq, and Israeli operations in Occupied Palestine and the Lebanon. Indian armed forces too have been using it since a few years. Though India has been experimenting with indigenous UAV called Nishant for some years it has relied more upon UAVs imported mostly from Israel. Indian Navy too had been preparing to induct it and had been training since past three years. Indian Navy formally inducted them and a UAV Squadron, INAS 342, was commissioned in Kochi on January 6, 2006 by Admiral Arun Prakash. It operates two types of UAVs, Searcher and Heron. Both are from Israel. The inherent advantages of UAV will lead to their greater use and at least one UAV fleet will be deployed in due course of time in each of the naval bases. The Coast Guard and the BSF will also use them.

The Army is the primary customer for Indian Nishant and the Cabinet has approved 12 units for the Indian Army. The Coast Guard too has shown interest in the Nishant and has sought modifications to suit its requirements. Nishant is a large UAV with a wing-span of 6.4 metres. It can fly for five hours with a payload of 300 kg. Its optimum attitude is 13,000 feet. The payload comprises of TV, camera, laser range finder as well as laser designator etc. It needs a 10-member crew to operate. [36]

There is no doubt that because of their inherent advantages like lower production and maintenance cost (as compared to manned aircraft), absence of pilot that not only reduces danger to the life of the pilot but also enables the UAV to loiter for longer period since there is no human fatigue, multiple modes of search that include radar and infrared, ability to control the machine from the ground base etc, UAVs will be increasingly relied upon to monitor maritime zones near the coast. They will therefore, play an important role for the Navy, the Coast Guard as also for various other agencies involved in homeland security *vis-à-vis* maritime threats. Thus, UAVs will plug a crucial gap in maritime reconnaissance especially closer to the coast.

Given the long coast line as also innumerable vulnerable islands both in the Bay of Bengal as also in the Arabian Sea, and the new threat posed by non-state actors, India's security forces will soon be operating large number of UAVs. Not only the maritime forces but also land forces like the Army and the BSF will be increasingly relying upon them for collecting real time intelligence data. Hence, India will be acquiring large number of UAVs in the years to come. Not all of them can be imported. India will have to think seriously about their domestic production to cater for different customers. Since UAVs will be more economical for small maritime states also, Indian UAVs can find foreign market. Developing suitable UAVs can even be a way of promoting regional maritime cooperation between India and some of its regional maritime neighbours or even countries like Japan that are interested in SLOC protection.

HELICOPTERS

Helicopters are employed by the Navy, the Coast Guard as well as agencies like the ONGC. Though they are often based on board large surface vessels they are also deployed on land to support operations on sea. Unlike the Navy, the Coast Guard and the ONGC have more helicopters based on land. They perform various roles like MR, ASW, ASV, AEW, SAR, commando operations as also ferrying men and material to fixed platforms on the continental-shelf.

Though almost all helicopters can be used for MR, special equipment are required for more dedicated rolls. Helicopters for ASW operations have besides radars, dunking sonars, sonoboys, depth charges or torpedoes. Indian Navy operates Sea King Mk 42B, Ka-28 Helix A, ALM Dhruv and even light Chetak (armed only with torpedo) for this role. India had relied heavily upon Sea King Mk 42A for strike role and had armed it with Sea Eagle ASMs. Now that strike role is being undertaken by the Jaguars. In future, MiG-29M operating from new aircraft carries will be entrusted with that role. Helicopters also serve a useful purpose as airborne electronic warfare (AEW) platform. Ka-31 helicopter carries radar antenna that can be folded beneath the fuselage. Medium helicopters like Sea King Mk 42C are also used to deploy commandos in vertical lift operations.

Over the years these helicopters have improved in their performance. While Ka-25 made way for Ka-28 and Ka-31, Chetak is being replaced with ALH Dhruv. Dhruv may also replace some old Sea King helicopters used for ASW role. Reportedly about 12 Ka-28 helicopters are due for mid-life update. About 16 Sea King helicopters are getting old. Sea Kings had also faced spare-shortages following Pokhran II. They need replacements. As a result of the sanctions Indian Navy's fleet of 16 Sea King MkB and four Sea Kings MkC, acquired in 1985-86, were grounded for lack of spares. Navy was forced to strip some of these helicopters for spares so as to provide essential spares for others. Though sanctions were lifted in 2001 US cleared the spares for delivery in 2003. Seven of the Sea Kings that had been so stripped were refitted under a contract to Augusta Westland and the HAL.

Medium helicopters like Sea King and Ka-28 and even Ka-31 will need replacement between now and 2020. While Dhruv can be a replacement for some in ASW role yet it is not large enough for long-range operation or for a longer loiter time role. Hence, India will eventually need replacement for about 27 Sea Kings, 12 Ka-28 and 9 Ka-31 helicopters; a total of about 48 helicopters. Even if Dhruv replaces some of them, India will need about 40 of these medium size helicopters for the Navy. ONGC's fleet of helicopters also needs replacement. Moreover, the Army and the Air Force will also need replacement for their medium helicopters like Mi-17 and assault helicopters. Hence, it demands an indigenous solution as a long-term policy. Reportedly IAF has plans to buy 70 Mi-17 helicopters. [37] The Navy has sent proposals to eight overseas suppliers for outright purchase of 16 helicopters at a cost of US$ 600 mn to replace the fleet of Sea King Mk 42. It has also option for eight more helicopters. [38]

Acquiring them from abroad might seem an easy way out. But it is a question of large domestic market as well as promoting self reliance to the extent possible. The experience of ALH Dhruv should encourage India to plan for a medium-lift helicopter that can be configured for use by the Navy, the Army, the Air Force as well as by the Coast Guard and the ONGC for their specific roles.

SURFACE COMBATANTS

Indian Navy and the Coast Guard operate surface combat platforms of several types. These can be listed as aircraft carriers, destroyers, frigates, corvettes and large patrol vessels capable of operating helicopters, besides smaller patrol craft, mine-counter measure vessels, amphibious warfare ships and auxiliaries. Over the years, India has been building more and more ships in its own dockyards as also improving their firepower related capabilities. Stealth technology is being incorporated in the fighting ships now under construction like the Kolkata-class destroyer and the Shivalik-class frigate. Of these, the aircraft carrier, destroyer and frigates have attracted attention of other navies.

Aircraft Carrier: Indian Navy, since its inception, had set the goal of operating aircraft carriers. The wish was granted when it formalized the deal to acquire a half-finished light aircraft carrier, HMS Hercules, from UK. The decision was announced on July 28, 1956 though the deal was finalized in 1957. The ship was finally completed and commissioned in March 1961 as INS Vikrant. It was designed to operate Sea Hawk fighters, Alize ASW aircraft and Alouette III helicopters. It was a relatively small escort carrier. It was under repairs during the 1965 war. But it played a crucial role in 1971 operations, despite the mechanical handicaps like reduced power due to boiler problems. Despite its age as also small size it was not only retained but also given costly refits periodically so as to allow the Indian Navy to retain the aircraft carrier capability and related operational experience. During the major refit in 1979-81, old and obsolete Sea Hawks were replaced by Sea Harriers. The Sea King helicopter replaced the Alize ASW aircraft. During the next major refit, the ship was given a ski-jump capability so as to enhance the performance of Sea Harriers.

There was a limit beyond which the service life of INS Vikrant could not be stretched and a replacement was eagerly sought. The British Navy was disposing of the aircraft carrier HMS Hermes that had taken part in the Falkland war of 1982. It was commissioned first in 1959. It was purchased by India in 1986, and refitted, modernized and recommissioned as INS Virat in May 1987. More Sea Harriers and Sea Kings were added, INS Vikrant was retained for some time to credit the nation with a two-carrier capability. This false notion ended when INS Vikrant was finally decommissioned.

INS Virat, when acquired, was also an old ship and needed frequent refits. More important was the question of spares for the Sea Harrier aircraft and Sea King helicopters. Their spares were not available from Britain because many of those components were of US origin and had come under sanctions following Pokhran II nuclear tests. Though sanctions were subsequently lifted the Navy still needed extra aircraft not only as replacement for old Sea Harriers but also for use in new aircraft carrier INS Vikramaditya and in the ex-US LPD that is being acquired.

According to Admiral Madhvendra Singh Sea Harriers are proposed to be phased out by 2015 when the naval version of light combat aircraft (LCA) Tejas is expected to be ready. [39] According to Rear-Admiral Sunil Damle, India might acquire eight ex-British Sea Harrier FA2 aircraft. Deal is likely to be finalized by 2007-2008. It was reported in October 2006 that the deal was off because UK was removing vital components like Blue Vizen fire control radar before the sale. In the meanwhile the Sea Harriers are to undergo refit and upgrade that will include a new radar from Israel, Rafael Derby air-to-air missile, helmet-mounted sight etc. The upgrade will take 18 months and would enable the aircraft to operate for ten years more. [40]

Since INS Virat was also aging fast, Indian Navy needed replacement not only for INS Vikrant but also for INS Virat. Once again, there was a heated debate on the question of relevance of aircraft carrier for India. Indian Navy, however, continued to insist upon retaining the capability. Since no comparable ship was available in the market at that time India decided to construct one indigenously. Steps in that direction, at the design stage, were taken by 1988-1989 after the government had agreed in principle to provide necessary funds for the programme. But confusion prevailed till mid-nineties largely due to limited funds as also the likely role of the new aircraft carrier. It was during this period that India was offered a new option. The erstwhile powerful Soviet Navy was being virtually disbanded and some of its aircraft carriers were available.

Negotiations for the acquisition of Admiral Gorshkov, a ship named after the father of modern Soviet Navy, began in 1994 and, as is the usual practice, dragged on till January 1999 when the then Defence Minister, George Fernandez, said that an agreement had been arrived at on the subject. But, several more hurdles had to be crossed before the final deal could be signed. Reportedly, Russia was willing to sell the original ship for US$ 200 mn. Subsequently it agreed to transfer it 'free' if India agreed to the condition that it be refurbished and retrofitted in Russia. The Navy did its technical evaluation and gave its recommendations. The next stage was negotiations on the cost of refit and the type and cost of aircraft that would operate on board that ship.

Jane's Defence Weekly of January 29, 2003 reported that George Fernandez, during his Moscow visit to attend the Indo-Russian Inter-Government Commission for Military Technical Cooperation, not only agreed on the deal but also asked for transfer of four Tu-22 supersonic bombers armed with air-to-surface missiles as well as two Akula-class SSNs. The price continued to be the primary hurdle in finalizing the deal. [41] The Cabinet Committee on Security cleared the deal on Admiral Gorshkov on January 17, 2004 and it was finally signed on January 20, 2004. [42] The ship was to be refitted at Sev Mash Enterprise, Severodvinsk. The cost of refit is estimated to be between US$ 625 and US$ 740 mn depending upon what modifications are included in the final calculations.

According to Vice-Admiral S.C. Chopra (Retd.), the refitted Gorshkov, to be commissioned as INS Vikramaditya, would incorporate a new system for launching and recovery of fixed-wing aircraft like MiG-29K. The system, called short take-off but arrested landing (STOBAL), was experimented by the Soviet Navy in its aircraft carrier Admiral Kuznetsov. It will be incorporated in Admiral Gorshkov during its refit. Under that system the aircraft is launched with a 'hold back' device that helps the aircraft to acquire full thrust before rolling for take off. The take off is assisted by a 14 degree ski jump. Recovery of the aircraft is by the traditional method of a tail hook picking up one of the several arrester wires along the angled portion of the deck. To facilitate this system, the deck of the ship is cleared off of most of the weapons and related systems that were in the ship before the refit. [43] This will allow the new aircraft carrier to operate more capable aircraft like MiG-29 that have supersonic speed, longer range and greater weapon carrying capacity than the Sea Harrier. That will offer the new aircraft carrier an 'attack' capability that INS Virat lacks. It needs to be underlined that British aircraft carriers operating Sea Harriers were not employed during any of the major wars fought in the Persian Gulf region between 1991 and 2003.

The role of the aircraft carrier depends upon the capability of the aircraft that it operates from its deck. Reportedly Indian Navy had evaluated two aircraft, French Rafael and Russian MiG-29, for its new ship and opted for MiG-29 series. Indian Air Force already operates MiG-29 in the role of interceptor fighter and hence it was a familiar aircraft. Though it did not have a naval version, Russians promised to deliver it by the time the ship was being refitted, i.e. by 2009. Price was negotiated. Russians reportedly wanted US$ 33 mn per aircraft which Indians thought was high. Initial order was for 16 aircraft that included four MiG-29 KuB aircraft, a two-seat combat capable trainer. To encourage price reduction, number of aircraft to be acquired was increased by 16 more so as to equip the indigenously built air defence ship. The cost for 16 aircraft, that also included flight simulator and other related equipment, is estimated at about US$ 700 mn.

MiG-29 is a modern aircraft capable of supersonic speed and long range. As an interceptor it can track 10-12 targets and simultaneously engage up to four of them at a distance of 110-120 km. It can also be armed with air-to-surface missile for strike role. Beside fixed wing aircraft, the new aircraft carrier will also be carrying ASW helicopters like Ka-28 and Ka-31 airborne early warning (AEW) helicopters. INS Vikramaditya, when commissioned in 2009, will be based in the newly constructed naval base at Karwar.

The acquisition of the aircraft carrier from Russia as also the new forward role that is being defined for the Indian Navy in the Indian Ocean, seem to have tilted the balance in favour of the construction of an aircraft carrier or air defence ship, as it is being designated, at the Kochi Shipyard. Russians have also promised to help in its construction. Since the new ship, to be named INS Vikrant, will have role comparable to that of INS Vikramaditya, its configuration as also aircraft and sensors etc. are likely to be similar.

It was reported in 2004 that the government had promised to release Rs. 3,000 crore towards its construction. It will be built at the Cochin Shipyard Limited. Cutting of steel began on April 11, 2005 and the new vessel is likely to be launched in 2009. It will be commissioned at the earliest by 2012. India has already ordered MiG-29 K aircraft for the new carrier. It will also have complement of ASW and AEW helicopters. Thus, by 2012, Indian Navy will be fulfilling the long cherished dream of operating two modern aircraft carriers. Since the gestation period of an aircraft carrier is long, about 15 years, Admiral Madhvendra Singh has suggested that the acquisition of a successor to INS Vikramaditya be approved now so that the replacement is available by 2020. [44] It needs to be noted that INS Vikramaditya (ex-Admiral Gorshkov) was a Soviet era ship and will need replacement after 2020.

After India receives INS Vikramaditya by 2009, Indian Navy can operate two carrier battle groups. Each will have one aircraft carrier, two destroyers, two or three frigates/large corvettes, one or two attack submarines and a fleet replenishment vessel. While INS Vikramaditya will operate MiG-29 aircraft, INS Virat will continue to operate Sea Harrier aircraft. INS Virat is expected to retire after INS Vikrant, being built in Kochi, is commissioned by 2014. There are reports that once INS Vikrant is launched, Cochin Shipyard would began construction of another aircraft carrier so that Indian Navy will always have the capability to operate two carrier battle groups at any given time. If so, a long desired goal will be achieved.

Destroyers: Indian Navy had acquired, during the early years of its formation two light cruisers and a few destroyers of World War II vintage. Indian Navy must be given the credit for giving a long life to the scraps of the British Navy. Only Bangladesh Navy and may be the Myanmar Navy can beat that record. It was only in the eighties that Indian Navy was able to acquire modern destroyers from USSR. India opted for modKashin-class destroyers. With a gas turbine power plant, modified SA-N-2 Styx anti-ship missiles, SA-N-1 SAM system, torpedo launchers and an ASW helicopter on deck, it added a great punch to the fire power of the Indian Navy. Three of these R-class destroyers were obtained between 1980-83 and two more in 1986-87. These were periodically updated. One of these was reported to be fitted with BrahMos SSM. Others may also be so equipped.

By mid-eighties India had acquired some experience in the construction of Nilgiri-class and Godavari-class frigates. Indian Navy decided to construct a series of three destroyer. The keel of the first, INS Delhi, was laid on May 4, 1987. The ship was launched in February 1991. Unfortunately, the programme got delayed because the USSR, a major supplier of parts, was disintegrating. It was some time before the new state, the Russian Republic, was salvaged and the pipeline for supply of military equipment rebuilt. As a consequence, INS Delhi could be commissioned only by the end of 1997. Once the things were streamlined the second and the third destroyer of the series rolled out at an interval of two years each.

For a country that had not built a major surface combatant till 1960s it was a credible achievement. Indian naval designers had succeeded to put into a modest 6,700-ton destroyer, 16 (four quads) SS-N-25 anti-ship missiles with an active radar homing up to 130 km, two SA-N-7 SAM launchers, two Barak anti-missile missile systems, one 100 mn rapid fire gun, four torpedo tubes, two A/S mortars besides providing space for two helicopters. The gas turbine engine gives it a maximum speed of 32 knots.

By the time the first of the series was being built Indian naval planners were busy designing a more modern destroyer that would incorporate stealth technology. The new destroyer, INS Kolkata, was launched on March 31, 2006 at Mumbai. It is likely to be armed with 16 BrahMos anti-ship missiles with a range of 290 km. The stealth design will also mean that the ship will incorporate vertical launch mode for its long-range SAM, probably improved Barak. The new destroyer will also carry several systems developed in India like the Nagin towed sonar. INS Kolkata is likely to be commissioned by 2010. Two other sister ships will follow by 2015. Thus, India will be able to replace three of the R-class destroyers that it had acquired in early eighties.

Frigates: While destroyers provide the lead, frigates are the backbone of modern conventional navy. India had acquired a mix of old and new frigates from UK. That source dried out by mid-sixties and India had to rely either upon its indigenously built Nilgiri-class and the Godavari-class frigates or seek them from the USSR. Thus, India acquired the Petya-class frigates from USSR. Though small, the size of a large corvette, they were a great improvement upon the WW II vintage British frigates and even the new Khukri-class ASW frigates that were acquired from UK. They helped to fill a crucial gap till India could build more frigates on its own.

India began the construction of frigates by building under licence the British Leander-class frigates. The keel of the first ship, INS Nilgiri, was laid in 1966 in June 1967, missiles fired from a small Komar-class patrol craft of the Egyptian Navy sank an Israeli destroyer near the Egyptian coast. The supremacy of the missile over gun was thus established. But India continued to build the Nilgiri-class ships. Of them, the last two, Taragiri and Vindyagiri, are believed to have improved performance and are likely to be retained for a longer period.

Nilgiri-class frigates were followed by the indigenously designed Godavari-class frigates. They were slightly bigger than the Nilgiri-class and were armed with four Styx anti-ship missiles, one SAM launcher besides ASW weapons. It had provisions for two helicopters. Three of this class were commissioned between 1983-85.

Lessons learnt during that construction were incorporated when India opted to build the follow on Brahmaputra-class frigates (Project 16A). As had happened with the Delhi-class destroyers, the keel of the first ship of this class was laid in 1989 but the project had to await the restructuring of the Soviet-Russian state systems. Needless to say its construction was delayed beyond 2000. It is a larger vessel of about 4,450 tons and is armed with 16 (four quads) SS-N-25 SSMs, a rapid fire 76 mm gun, four 30 mm AK 650 rapid fire gun system, six (two triple) torpedo tubes, and has provision for two helicopters.

Fast changing technology even left the Brahmaputra-class far behind in the race. India, therefore, once again opted for the purchase of new frigates from Russia. Three new frigates (modified Krivek-class) were ordered and all three were delivered between 2003-2004. This Talwar-class frigate was probably one of the most advanced ships of its class at that time. Though compact, with only 3,780-ton displacement, it carries a heavy punch of eight SS-N-27 Navator Klub anti-ship missile with a range of 180 km. Though the missile cruises at the speed of Mach 0.7, at the terminal phase its speed increases to Mach 2.5. The missile carries a large warhead of 450 kg. The Klub missile is launched from a vertical-launch system (VLS). The ship also has a 25 km range SA-N-7 SAM launcher, two Russian anti-missile systems each comprising of twin 30 mn guns and SA-N-11 SAM. It has torpedo tubes and A/S mortars as also modern sonar. It operates one helicopter (Ka-28 or Ka-31).

There were reports that India would order more of these ships. The decision got delayed. In the meanwhile it was decided to incorporate the advance technology, including the stealth technology, in the indigenously designed Shivalik-class frigate. Three of the Shivalik-class frigates have been ordered at the Mazagaon Dock Yard Limited, Mumbai. First ship of this Project 17 was laid in July 2001. It was launched on April 18, 2003 and is expected to be completed by 2008. [45] Others would follow soon after. It is about 4,900 tons and has a top speed of 32 knots. It could be armed with either BrahMos or Klub SSM launchers,

SA-N-7 SAM launchers, two anti-missile systems either a combination of 30 mn gun and short-range SAM or the Barak system, a 76 mm rapid fire gun and ASW rocket launchers. It will operate one helicopter. Reportedly twelve ships of this class are to be acquired over the years.

According to Admiral Madhvendra Singh, Indian Navy will need over the years 40 large surface combatants like destroyers and frigates. One wonders if the Navy can attain that goal. In the meanwhile there is urgent need to replace old ships. One Leander-class frigate has been decommissioned. At least four more will need to be replaced shortly. Three ships of Project 17 will replace first three of the Leander-class frigates. Three Godavari-class frigates will need to be replaced between 2010-15. Thus, there is need to place order at least for six more P-17 frigates to maintain current level of frigates.

Of the five Kashin-class destroyers, three would be 25 years old while two would be 17 years old. These old R-class destroyers would need to be replaced by 2010-20. Three destroyers under Project 15A (Kolkata-class) are on order. Admiral Madhvendra Singh suggests that it would be cost effective to order five of them as replacement for the Kashin-class destroyers.

India would need nine P-17 frigates and five P-15A destroyers between 2005-2020; i.e. one ship per year. It is not possible for the Mazagaon Dock Yard, where these ships are built, to deliver that number. Hence, India will need to place order for frigates abroad. Repeat order for the Talwar-class frigate, that was pending for some time, therefore, became essential. Admiral Madhvendra Singh had suggested that four instead of three ships of that type should be ordered. [46] Reportedly, the Navy is ordering only three of these frigates. Price negotiations have been completed and the Navy was to put up the proposal for this Rs. 3,000 crore deal before the Defence Committee on Security for approval. These new frigates will be equipped with BrahMos missiles as well as several Indian components related to communication and electronic warfare suites as also an indigenous air defence system instead of the Russian Kashtan.

Officials maintain that the Navy was exercising the clause for placing of repeat order when the first deal was signed and hence there was no need for calling of fresh tenders. [47]

Corvettes: Though Indian Navy had inherited corvette size ships on the eve of independence it did not acquire new ships of that type till late seventies. The limitations of the small Osa missile boat and simultaneously the advantage of the anti-ship missile led Indian Navy to acquire a larger platform. Three Durg-class corvettes were acquired after 1977. They were about 660 tons and were armed with four SS-N-2C Styx missiles with a range of 83 km. The ship also had twin launchers for SA-N-4 SAM and carried a 57 mm gun.

Indian Navy preferred a heavier corvette that could operate even under unfavourable sea conditions away from the base. It decided to design one suitable for its requirements. First ship of Project 26, the first of the four new Khukri-class corvettes, was laid down in 1985 and was commissioned in 1988. The last was commissioned in 1991. It was a 1,423-ton ship armed with Styx SSMs and a short-range SA-N-5 SAM. It had a platform that could take a light helicopter.

The success of the Khukri-class corvette, despite its large radar signature, prompted the construction of four more corvettes of about the same size. The Kora-class corvettes, built at the Garden Reach, Kolkata, faced the supply problems that the destroyers and the frigate programmes had faced due to the disintegration of the USSR. But the supply position improved by the middle of the nineties and the first of the Kora-class corvettes was commissioned in 1998. All four ships were ready by 2004. They are armed with 16 (four quads) Zverda SS-N-25 missiles as also SA-N-5 or equivalent short range SAM launcher. The ship also has a helicopter platform but there are no reports of anti-submarine warfare weapons. Thus, like the Khukri, the Kora-class is also primarily dedicated for strike role under all types of sea conditions further away from the coast. They can even replace frigates in a taskforce. There are as yet no proposals for acquisition of more large corvettes, primarily for strike role.

Patrol Vessels: Equally important is the role of large patrol vessels (large corvette size) in the context of maritime security, especially of high value off-shore platforms and for keeping major SLOCs under surveillance. In that context large patrol vessels of the Navy and the Coast Guard perform almost parallel roles. The Coast Guard was the first to introduce this type of vessel. The Vikram-class off-shore patrol vessel (OPV) was introduced in 1979. Nine vessels of this type were acquired to keep large EEZ along the mainland coast as also around the Anadaman and Nicobar group and the Lakshadweep under surveillance. It has a hanger for light helicopter.

In the meanwhile the Navy too decided to acquire large patrol vessels. Three of the Sukanya-class vessels were acquired from South Korea between 1989-1990 and the remaining were built by the Hindustan Shipyard, Visakhapatnam, between 1990-93. One ship of this class has been handed over to Sri Lanka Navy. Reportedly, another ship is likely to be presented to the Coast Guard of Mauritius. Another ship INS Subhadra has been modified as a test bed for the Dhanush (modified Prithvi) short-range ballistic missile. Sukanya class patrol vessel is about 1,800 tons. Keeping in view its role it is armed with only a 40 mm gun besides machine guns. A few years back these vessels were also armed with four RBU-2500 ASW rocket launchers. One does not know if they are also fitted with sonars to enable them to use their ASW weapon effectively. The ship can operate a light helicopter. One ship of this class was detailed to escort high-value American ships during their transit through the Malacca Straits in 2001-02.

Admiral Madhvendra Singh has commented that the Indian Navy has been left with only five operational large off-shore patrol vessels while it needs twelve to patrol the off-shore oil fields and islands as also monitor sea lanes. He also maintains that the Navy needs 28 fast attack craft to patrol inshore and coastal waters of Gujarat, Tamil Nadu and similar other areas. [48]

The Navy is not only acquiring new off-shore patrol vessels but is giving them away to others. In the meanwhile, the Coast Guard is filling the gap by acquiring not only more large off-shore patrol vessels but also taking on the role that the Navy was performing earlier. The question is not who has how many boats; the Navy, the Coast Guard or the State Marine Police that is being formed. What is needed is not duplication of roles and, therefore, of vessels or aircraft but a synergy among various maritime security agencies which alone can result in smooth operation as also maximum utilization of national maritime resources.

Indian Coast Guard has also acquired a modified version of the Sukanya-class vessel. The Samar-class vessel is also built by the Hindustan Shipyard, Visakhapatnam. Four of this class have been commissioned. More are being built. It is a 2,005-ton vessel and has a long range of 7,000 n-miles at 15 knot speed. It is also armed with a more powerful 76 mn Oto Malera gun. It can operate a light helicopter. The Samar-class vessel demonstrates that the Indian Coast Guard has developed the capability to operate far away from the coast and over an extended period in providing protection not only to SLOCs around India but also to some of the island states in the Indian Ocean with whom India is developing close security-related understanding.

Light Force: Corvettes of smaller size are operated by the Navy. As mentioned earlier, India had acquired three Durg-class corvettes armed with Styx SSMs. It also continued to operate smaller Osa-class missile boats primarily for sea denial role near the coastal waters. These fast attack craft armed with missiles were gradually replaced by the Veer-class (modified Tarantula) small corvettes. First five were acquired from USSR while remaining eight were built in India at Goa and Mazagon Dock Yards. These 477-ton vessels were armed with four Styx SSMs. Last two were reportedly to be armed with four quads of SS-N-25 missiles. The vessel also carries a short-range SA-N-5 SAM launcher, one 3" gun and three 30 mm rapid fire cannons. All these vessels were commissioned by 2002 and are based at Mumbai.

Though most of the large surface force like destroyer and frigate are equipped for ASW role Indian Navy has few corvettes that are configured for ASW operations. It had purchased four

Abhay-class (Pauk-class) corvette, of the size of the Veer-class missile corvette, for ASW role from USSR. They were commissioned between 1989-91. Beside the 3" gun and one 30 mm rapid five cannon and short-range SAM it is armed with two twin launchers for torpedoes and two RBU-1200 anti-submarine rocket launchers. It also has VDS for detecting submarines. There were reports that these ASW-specific corvettes would be given a new lease by replacing their power plant. But it seems that option has been given up. The Garden Reach Workshop, Kolkata, has been asked to construct four ASW corvettes. Many more are needed.

India's maritime defence forces also operate off-shore patrol craft of 200-300 tons as also smaller inshore patrol boats of less than 50 tons. Coast Guard, because of its specific requirements, operates more of these boats. Indian Navy operates six of these seaward defence boats (SDB). Now, in the light of threat from non-state actors, new boats are being built that have longer endurance and greater speed. INS Bangaran of that class was commissioned in 2006 at Kochi. It is a 320-ton boat with high speed, better surveillance equipment and is capable of monitoring the shipping near the Laccadive Islands, The Coast Guard, that operates about 22 of the old-fashioned SDBs, is also building new more capable boats. Already the 280-ton Sarojini Naidu-class boat has been inducted. It is armed with 30 mm gun and has water-jet propulsion system that will provide it with greater agility as also speed. Navy's Bangaran-class and Coast Guard's Sarojini Naidu-class boats will gradually replace the old vessels used for monitoring the coastal waters near the mainland and around the various islands.

The Coast Guard felt the need for smaller boats to operate nearer to the shore especially in the sensitive waters between India and Sri Lanka. It acquired eight 32-ton Swallow-class boats from South Korea between 1980-82. Navy also felt the need for a smaller fast attack craft to meet the challenges from non-state actors, especially the LTTE. It purchased two Super Dvora Mk II from Israel and built three more at Goa. This 50-ton boat has a top speed of 50 knots and a range of 700 miles at 42 knot speed. It is armed with a 20 mm gun and two 12.7 mn heavy machine guns and carries sophisticated sensors like surface search radar. Coast Guard is also proposing to acquire replacement for the Swallow-class boats. It already operates some interceptor boats as well as six hovercraft.

CRITICAL EVALUATION

Inadequate ASW Capability: When one analyses surface combatants of the Indian maritime security forces, one finds a certain bias in favour of strike role against hostile surface vessels and may be against targets on the shore. Almost all destroyers, frigates and corvettes, large and small, except those that are dedicated for ASW role, like the Nilgiri-class frigates and the Abhay-class small corvettes, are armed with sophisticated anti-ship missiles. India had acquired twelve Petya-class frigates from USSR in the seventies. The ship was armed with two twin torpedo tubes, two RBU-2500 ASW rocket launchers and two DC racks besides four 3" guns (two twins). All of these ships have been decommissioned. One had sunk in the Bay of Bengal. It is most unfortunate that no attempt was made to replace these light ASW frigates at a time when Pakistan Navy was rapidly improving its sub-surface warfare capability by arming its submarines with SLCMs and also by acquiring three modified Agosta-class submarines and building midget submarines.

Undoubtedly, destroyers and frigates and even submarines are equipped for ASW roles but to detach them from their prime task–operating as a part of a taskforce on the high seas–for ASW and SLOC protection near the coast and ports will be counter productive. Hence, there is urgent need to plug that gap at the lower end of the spectrum. Given the submarine based deterrence from Pakistan today, and from other powers in future, *vis-à-vis* the vast coast line of India that is dotted with several major and intermediate ports as well as sensitive offshore platform in India's continental-shelf, India needs to build a strong ASW capability.

Torpedoes, depth charge and mortars were the normal

weapons used against submarines. The Soviets improved upon that by introducing rocket assisted A/S mortars fired from launchers that could be trained in different directions. These can be fired in a salvo to bracket a designated area where submarine was expected to lurk. The weight of the warhead and the range of the rocket vary. Indian Navy has opted largely for RBU-6000 launchers for its major surface combatants. Each of them has 12 tubes and the warhead is 31 kg. Thus, a submerged submarine up to the range of 6,000 metres or 6 km can be targeted. This system is fitted in the Rajput and Delhi-class destroyers and the Talwar-class frigate. The Shivalik-class frigate may also be so armed.

There is no double that Indian Navy, being aware of the need for enhancing its ASW capability, would be planning a suitable strategy. There are reports that the DRDO in collaboration with Bharat Electronics Ltd. Has perfected an indigenous ASW system that is capable of detecting submarine and launch torpedo or missile against it. But there is enough scope for improvisation even under the present condition. Indian Navy and the Coast Guard between them would have about nine large offshore patrol vessels capable of operating naval version of ALH. Also, both together have more than 25 medium size (200-300 ton) patrol craft. It is possible to give them a limited ASW capability. Larger vessels of the Sukanya-class and the Samar-class can act as platforms for ALH that is configured for ASW role with radar and dunking sonar. They can also act as the command centres. Sukanya-class is already armed with four RBU 2500 A/S rocket launchers. Such provision can be built in the Samar-class vessel also. These larger vessels can be supported by medium size patrol craft that can also have provision for incorporating ASW weapons like rocket launchers, mortars and/or depth charges as well as active sonar for the attack role. Thus, the combination of ASW helicopter carrying vessels and medium-size patrol craft capable of being equipped for ASW role can even function as a mini task force for SLOC protection and ASW operation near the coast. This mini task-force can be supported by Dornian MR as also medium size (Sea King Mk 42B) ASW helicopters operating from bases on the land. Such a step will also lead to a greater synergy between the Indian Navy and the Coast Guard; an essential prerequisite for enhancing maritime security of India in the years to come.

Missiles: Over the decades Indian Navy has been enhancing its fire power capability by gradually inducting missiles best tailored for the role. The induction of the Styx SS-N-2 anti-ship missile on the Osa boat resulted in a dramatic result off the Karachi harbour during 1971 operations. Over the years, improved versions of Styx missiles with longer range, sea skiming capability and improved terminal guidance were fitted to the R-class destroyers, Godavari-class frigates, and Durg, Khukri and Veer-class corvettes. Zvezda SS-N-25 kH-35 Uran anti-ship missile with 130 km range was fitted to Delhi-class destroyer, Brahmaputra-class frigates, Cora-class large corvettes and possibly some of the Veer-class corvettes.

The Talwar-class frigates ordered from Russia had a still more powerful SS-N-27 Klub missile with a range of 180 km. Klub missile has a supersonic speed of March 2.5 at the terminal end and is, thus, very difficult to detect and neutralize. India has already tested the BrahMos missile configured on Russian 3 M55 Onikes/Yakhont (NATO designation SS-NX-26) and there were reports that they would be fitted to one R-class destroyer as a replacement for the old Styx SSM. If successful, other ships would also be fitted with the new missile. Reportedly, the Kolkata-class destroyer being built in India and new frigates ordered from Russia will be equipped with that missile. According to experts, BrahMos is reportedly the best SSM available so far in the world and the company is seeking to market it to other 'friendly' countries.

India also improved the performance of its Kilo-class submarines by providing it with the capability to launch anti-ship missiles while remaining submerged. INS Sindhushastra, acquired in 2000, was originally fitted with the submerged launch cruise missile (SLCM) capability. The missile that can be so launched is the SLCM version of Novator Alf Klub SS-N-27 with active radar homing up to 180 km and with Mach 2.5 speed at the terminal stage. Some other Kilo-class submarines were also modified to launch SLCM while undergoing refit. This has greatly enhanced the strike role of the conventional submarine. The capability to launch conventional torpedo especially for ASW role is retained. All the Scorpene submarines that are to be built in India would also have these capabilities.

Surface vessels beyond the reach of shore-based aircraft need their autonomous anti-air capability. Earlier that was provided by duel purpose main guns as also by a variety of air defence guns ranging from 20 mm to 57 mm. This cumbersome barrage, necessarily of short range, was replaced by guided anti-air missiles or the SAMs. India's first indigenously built frigate, the Nilgiri-class, was armed with short-range Sea Cat SAMs, a modified version of the land-based Tiger Cat missile. The first effective long range SAM was introduced when India acquired its first R-class destroyer from USSR in 1980. It was armed with two launchers for SA-N-1 Goa missile that had a range of 31 km. The indigenously built Godavari-class frigate that was commissioned first in 1983 was armed with SA-N-4 twin launcher. It had a range of 15 km. While many of the small frigates and corvettes like the Khukri-class, Kora-class, Veer-class, etc. were armed with short-range SA-N-5 missiles, larger vessels like the Talwar-class frigates and Delhi-class destroyers are armed with SA-N-7 that has a range of 25 km. It is also a faster missile with the speed of Mach 3. The Kolkata-class destroyer and the new Talwar-class frigates that are being built could also be armed with the naval version of indigenously developed Akash SAM or the Improved Barak.

Surface vessels are increasingly facing the threat of anti-ship missile launched from land based aircraft, surface vessels or even submarines. New systems are being developed to neutralize that threat. Talwar-class frigate is armed with two CADS-N-1 Kashtan, that combines two 30 mm rapid fire guns with short range SA-N-11 missile. India has also opted for the Barak anti-missile missile system from Israel. They have been fitted to seven ships including aircraft carrier Virat, Delhi-class destroyers and may also be fitted to other destroyers and frigates being built in India. India's DRDO and Israel's IAI have agreed to jointly develop the next generation of Barak system. It will have an extended range. The deal is worth US$ 330 mn. [49]

Following the attack by Israeli armed forces on the Lebanon since July 2006, some political parties in India were demanding that India should cut off its weapons-related collaboration with Israel. The charge of kickbacks in the acquisition of the Barak missile as also the objections of the DRDO at that time were also repeated. It is essential that India's long term strategic interests and short-term foreign policy issues be separately dealt with. India had paid a price of the boycott of the Bofors during the Kargil conflict. That lesson should have gone home.

Once the advantages of guided missile were discovered attempts were made to launch them from different platforms. Thus, various versions of air-launched missiles were introduced. India also acquired the Sea Eagle ASM to arm the Sea King helicopter of the Navy as also Jaguar strike aircraft of the Indian Air Force. These have over the horizon range. Unlike the Exocet ASM that had been extensively used by Iraq during the Iraq-Iran 'tanker war' between 1985-88, Sea Eagle has not been tested in battle condition so far. Anyway, it needs a replacement. India is developing an air-launched version of the BrahMos. Once that it ready a suitable platform like the Su-30 can be modified to launch it. There are also reports that MiG-29K aircraft that is to operate from the Vikramaditya and the new Vikrant might be armed with CH-31 ASM that will have anti-ship as also anti-radar capability.

No evaluation of state's capability for maritime security can be complete without taking into account the following four aspects: mine counter-measure system (mine sweepers), force projection or amphibious warfare ships, logistics and supply vessels, and ships dedicated for survey and research of the maritime zone around it.

Minesweepers: Indian Navy had inherited and acquired a few minesweepers from UK after independence. Indian Navy had also acquired minesweepers from USSR. At present Indian Navy operates 12 large (800 ton) Netya II (export version) minesweepers. These Pondicheri-class vessels are equipped with hull mounted high frequency sonar for detection of mines. They are also armed with four 25/30 mn guns, SA-N-5 SAM launcher and two RBU-1200 five tube anti-submarine mortar tubes for self defence. Indian Navy also operates two Mahe-class (Yevgenya-class) inshore minesweepers. These 90-ton ships are maintained at Kochi. Three of this class were paid off in 2003-2004.

India's growing dependence upon maritime trade, growing relevance of energy related SLOCs as also the policy to develop more intermediate ports in the near future means that India will have to greatly strengthen its mine counter-measure capability. Admiral Arun Kumar after taking over as the Chief of the Naval Staff, had said that apart from submarines and fast attack craft, Indian Navy needed more minesweepers. [50]

Though all recognise the urgent need for strengthening India's mine-counter measure capability no serious steps are being taken as yet in that direction. There are reports that eight mine-counter measure vessels would be built at Goa Shipyard with foreign collaboration and equipment. But as yet no concrete steps are being taken to replace the existing fleet whose vessels will need to be retired after 2008. [51]

Is it possible to take some interim measures? During World War II trawlers were converted as minesweepers. One wonders if modern trawlers, while under construction, can also be provided with suitable structures that will enable them to be quickly modified as mine hunters in times of emergency. These trawlers can even be maintained by the fishery department of various states as also by the central government as research/survey vessel or even used for commercial exploitation of fishery resources in off-shore waters. They can even be manned by retired personnel from the Navy and the Coast Guard belonging to that particular area. Thus, they would be familiar with the local waters. In times of emergency these vessels and the personal can be inducted for national duty under the usual rules. This dual-purpose vessel, though not very sophisticated, will help strengthen India's maritime security especially against the growing threat from non-state actors who can resort to use of mines to disrupt normal traffic even in peacetime.

Such a move will have several advantages. It will save the fund starved Navy from investing in large number of minesweepers. Construction of specialized trawlers-cum-mine hunters will generate work in shipyards. These ships, besides helping the fishery department in survey and research, will also keep an eye on unauthorised fishing in the area and thus reduce the burden of the Coast Guard that can then operate further away from the inshore waters. Finally, it will help to actively involve the fishery department in the maritime security of India.

Amphibious Warfare Ships: During World War II Indian troops had been landed along the coast of Burma (Myanmar) by landing ships. Indian Navy inherited several of these landing ships and craft. Most of them were old and could be maintained with great difficulty. Indian Navy, while seeking to keep the tradition, acquired about mine smaller tank landing craft (LCT) from USSR and Poland. Indian Navy did provide support to the Indian Army's effort to land troops along Bangladesh coast in 1971 operations. The joint operation was, to say the least, a fiasco. Reportedly, a few Gurkha soldiers were drowned while moving from the ship to the coast. These vessels also suffered due to lack of spares following the end of the Warsa Pact and the break-up of USSR. About five of them are maintained by the Navy but there is urgent need for their replacement not only because they are getting old but because the requirements for amphibious operations are changing rapidly.

In the meanwhile Indian Navy had acquired six small landing craft of 500 tons each. These Vasco da Gama-class ships have a military lift of 250 tons. They were added between 1980-1987. These are not only slow but have a range of only 1,000 miles at 8 knot speed.

Indian Navy wanted to retain the large amphibious warfare capacity and hence ordered a new large LST to replace the WW II

Magar LST. The new Magar-class LST was commissioned in 1987. The Gharial followed in 1997. They are 5,655-ton vessels and have a range of 3,000 miles at a speed of 14 knots. They have a military lift of 15 tanks, 8 APCs and 500 troops. They also have platform for two medium size Sea King Mk 42C helicopter for assault or commando operations. Gharial carries four LCVP on devits. Reportedly, the Shardul, that was launched in April 2004, is been given a design change. Details are not available but this ship may become the first of the three new amphibious warfare vessels that are being proposed. Airavat another of this type, was launched at Garden Reach Yard in March 2006.

Modern trend is for combining the performance of landing-ship dock and landing-ship helicopter thereby providing a mix of amphibious operation and vertical lift for any given operation. These ships are more suitable not only for force projection but also for disaster management. These ships are important for India because of its own operational requirements in far away islands of Andaman and the Nicobar as also because of the security role that India may be asked to perform in its neighbourhood. India needs at least three of these vessels of about 8,000 tons each, with a range of 3,000 miles. They should be able to operate landing craft capable of ferrying APCs, trucks and jeeps as also equipped with helicopters for vertical lift operations. While the redesigned INS Shardul can be ready by 2007-2008, Airawat can be completed by 2010-12.

According to Admiral Madhavendra Singh since India has no expertise in the construction of such sophisticated ships it was decided to import two used LPD (landing platform dock) in the first instance. He added that reported offer by US Navy for such platform should be made use of while Indian designers and shipyards ready themselves for building the follow on. Force projection capability suggested was a brigade group in LPDs and other ships. [52]

The acquisition of LPDs also needs to be seen in the context of the shift in India's naval operational goals. Admiral Arun Prakash, while addressing the three-day conference of naval commanders on May 2, 2006, said that focus is shifting from autonomous open sea operations like sea control and blockade to a direct linkage with land battle and littoral operations and that operational manoeuvre from the sea can favourably influence the progress of land-air battle. He also said that the LDP Trenton of USA would be inducted into Navy by next year (2007). [53]

For full effectiveness, 'maritime manoeuvre from the sea' relies upon synergy between the Navy, the Coast Guard, the Air Force and the Army. Reportedly, Indian Navy was to hold in the first quarter of 2007 a massive war game exercise in the northern part of the Arabian Sea area of India. Pakistan had been informed of that under Indo-Pak agreement of 1991 on mutual confidence building. Indian Navy was going to pool about fifty warships from the Western and the Eastern Fleet that would have included aircraft carrier, destroyers, frigates and submarines besides other warships. Indian Air Force was expected to offer Jaguars that have been configured for maritime strike role. Army was also to be involved in the exercise. With the induction of Jalashva in 2007 and INS Vikramaditya in 2008, Navy's contribution to these manoeuvres will be further enhanced.

According to one source, acquisition of USS Trenton was initiated after the tsunami disaster when existing facilities were found to be inadequate. [54] According to Vijay Sakhuja, a high level Indian delegation had visited USA to inspect USS Trenton, an Austin-class amphibious vessel. The subject also came up for discussion during the visit to New Delhi of Lt. General Jeffrey B. Kohler, Head of Pentagon's Defence Cooperation Security Agency that oversees US military sales. Reportedly, USS Trenton was to be offered to India at a low price. According to press reports, the Trenton deal was forwarded to the Cabinet Committee on Security for approval. The cost was Rs. 218 crore which included refit and supply of 5-year spares as also training. A sum of Rs. 300 crore was also requested for the acquisition of six Sea King helicopters that would operate from that ship. Though commissioned in 1971, the ship still has 15 years of sea worth life left. USS Trenton was formally decommissioned from the US

Navy on January 17, 2007. It is being refurbished at Norfolk before it is formally handed over to the Indian Navy in May 2007. Already 300 sailors and 27 officers under Commodore H.S. Ahluwalia are in USA and are being trained to operate the new vessel. When it is commissioned in the Indian Navy, it will be renamed Jal Ashva.

USS Trenton was commissioned on March 6, 1971. It received a service life extension in 1988-90. It will be replaced in the US Navy when new San Antonio-class LPD is commissioned. Thus, the ship would have been decommissioned by US Navy if the Indian Navy had not agreed to buy it. According to the data provide by the *Jane's Fighting Ships 1984-1985*, eleven ships of this class were built between 1965 and 1977. The ship is 9,000 tons light and 17,000 tons in full load. It has provision for five to six medium helicopters, docking well for landing crafts beside cargo hold and vehicle garage. It can carry 930 troops besides 473 crew and officers. It also has one LCU, and three LCM besides smaller LCVP. Its LCU can ferry 180-375 tons. LCM can ferry one main battle tank or 80 troops.

There is no doubt that this ship, though 36 years old when it will be acquired, will enable Indian Navy to learn to operate a new type of vessel. It would also offer Indian naval designers and experts in the dockyard an insight into this new type of ship. But, can USS Trenton be a model for the Indian Navy? US Navy, because of its geographic isolation due to the Atlantic and the Pacific, needed such large LPDs for force projection across vast distances from the sea since World War II. Today, the need to project force on the littoral from across the sea in sensitive areas like the Persian Gulf is prompting USA as well as its coalition partners to further augment their force projection capability. Undoubtedly, India too should acquire it but the scale needs to be readjusted to suit India's own strategic needs rather than blindly following what the NATO and its partners plan to do in the Indian Ocean Region. For India a scaled down version of LPD will not only be more appropriate but will also save Indian decision makers from the temptation of following an interventionist policy.

Already, there are indications that during the ninth Malabar series of joint exercise USA and India are seeking to coordinate their strategy of sea-to-littoral manoeuvres off the Konkan coast, which will be followed by joint semi urban-counterterrorism exercise in Belgaum, Karnataka, by contingents of the US marines and the Sikh Light Infantry. US troops would be landed by USS Boxer. This is beside the usual joint naval exercises that includes ASW operations, maritime interdiction, weapon firing, dissimilar air combat, cross-deck flying etc.

Auxiliaries: Navy's capability to operate away from the bases depends upon its auxiliary vessels like replenishment tankers, supply vessels, repair ships, etc. India operates three large replenishment tankers-cum-supply vessels. Of them, Deepak will need replacement in the near future. Three replenishment vessels are inadequate if two Indian taskforces comprising of one aircraft carrier each and with even three surface vessels as escorts are to operate independently in different parts of the Indian Ocean over a length of time. India will have to induct at least three new vessels; one to replace INS Deepak in the near future and the remaining two to support India's task forces operating in the Indian Ocean Region in future. Thus, the strength of ocean-going large replenishment ships need to be raised from three in 2006 to at least five if not six by 2015.

Indian Navy also acquired two supply vessels (Nicobar and Andaman) from Poland between 1998-2000. These 19,200-ton vessels are capable of transporting 1,200 troops. Both ships are employed to transport stores and passengers to Andaman/Nicobar islands as a part of the ANC. They have large devits capable of operating LCVPs. To further strengthen the capacity for supplies, India also needs at least four roll-on roll-off ships of about 5,000 tons each that can operate even from intermediate ports. In peace time they can be operated on commercial basis on coastal routes or between the mainland and Andaman-Nicobar islands, with the proviso for their requisitioning during times of national emergency. This will not only strengthen India's force projection capability but also render important service during disasters by helping to off-load supplies quickly in the desired area.

India has a major programme dedicated to survey and research related to location and exploitation of its ocean-based resources as well as strengthening national maritime security. National Institute of Oceanography operates several survey ships like Sagar Kanya, Samudra Manthan, Sagar Sampada, Samudra Sarvekshak, Samudra Nidhi and Samudra Sandhari. Indian Navy also possesses eight modern survey vessels of the Sandhyak-class. These research vessels of about 2,000 tons each, were acquired between 1981-2002 from the dockyards at Goa and Garden Reach in Kolkata. These have a long range and can operate on survey duty for a long time. Beside crew members they also have provision for 30 scientists. Each vessel carries four survey launches on devits. These ships are equipped with laboratories as also with modern echo sounders. One of these vessels, INS Sandhyak, was employed, on request from Bangladesh in August 2001, to recover arms that were dumped in the waters about 110 n.miles from Chittagong. About 250 boxes were recovered. Some of these vessels have also been used as troops and transport vessels and as casualty landing ships while on disaster management duty. Sagardhawani of the Indian Navy, a vessel of 2,050 tons, is a marine acoustic research vessel and is employed for geological survey (underwater) as also for noise reduction experiments. Indian Navy also operates two SDBs of about 210 tons each that have been converted as survey vessels for operation in coastal waters.

Kadamba Naval Base: Indian Navy needed a new and exclusive base that would be large and safe as also strategically located so as to satisfy Navy's requirements for decades to come. The area around Karwar was finally approved and Rajiv Gandhi formally laid the foundation stone of the project in October 1986. Project Seabird languished for years for want of funds as also political will. Things began to move during the tenure of George Fernandes and continued afterwards. Pranab Mukherjee commissioned INS Kadamba on May 31, 2005. Shrimati Sonia Gandhi, Chairperson of the National Advisory Council, unveiled the plaque. The naval base is named after a dynasty that had ruled over the region during the fourth century AD.

The first phase of the project is estimated to cost Rs. 2,500 crore. The total cost is likely to be Rs. 35,000 crore spread over several years. When completed, it will also have a complete naval-air station. INS Kadamba will be the third operational naval base besides Mumbai and Visakhapatnam. A new base is proposed to be built between Rambili and Elamanchili about 50 km south of Visakhapatnam. The base at Port Blair in the Andaman is an experiment in joint command that involves active cooperation of all the three services; Army, Navy and the Air Force, and the Coast Guard.

Project Seabird covers a large area of 4,480 hectors and is spread over a long stretch of 26 km. Off-shore islands and hills as also forest along the shore give a natural protection to the base. The water depth was adequate and did not need extensive dredging. Main channels have been dredged to give a depth of 12 meters that is more than enough for all fighting ships including aircraft carriers. Steps have already been initiated for phase II of the project.

The Bingy Bay (Binaga) that will house the core sector of the base has ample protection due to the promontory in the north and River Tardi to the South. Three breakwaters have been constructed; 3.1 km long that links Round Island and Arge Island, 1.7 km long that spans the Binaga Point and the Anjadip Island, and 0.34 km long spur breakwater extending from Anjadip Island so as to provide stability to the harbour waters.

Naval ship repair yard at the new base when completed will have a unique 'sea lift' technique that will raise a platform on the seabed, with ship resting on it, to the level of the docking platform and then pulled further on a dry platform. This platform can also be moved laterally to make room for other ships. This mechanism will be adequate for ships up to 10,000 tons. Thus, all fighting vessels except aircraft carriers can be repaired in this new facility. This will not only reduce the burden of repair at the existing dockyards in Mumbai, Goa, Visakhapatnam and Garden Reach in

Kolkata, but will also ensure that ships of India's maritime security forces get prompt attention at this exclusive naval base when facilities are ready.

It will not be wrong to suggest that in the coming years India's other naval base structures will also be revamped. With the development of Karwar naval base, the main naval base at Mumbai will be reconstituted as a front line but not the most important naval base in the Arabian Sea. Its location is strategically very important in the context of forward defence not only of northern part of the Arabian Sea zone but also of Mumbai and the major energy-related infra-structure in that part of India's continental-shelf. It is possible that Kochi and Chennai will emerge as valuable mutually supporting bases for the security of Indian maritime interests in Central Indian Ocean Region.

India's newfound maritime frontiers stretching from the Bay of Bengal to South China Sea and the possible entry of Chinese Navy in the Indian Ocean would mean that the Eastern Naval Command at Visakhapatnam will be further strengthened. It will also act as a backup for ANC which is likely to emerge as an active frontline outpost and a sentinal guarding India's waters in the Andaman Sea and beyond.

The increasing importance of Visakhapatnam was illustrated by the holding of the Presidential Fleet Review on February 12, 2006, in which 58 vessels, two submarines and 37 aircraft participated, as also the presentation of colour to the Eastern Naval Command on February 13, 2006. A new naval base, proposed for the Eastern Naval Command, is reportedly to be built about 50 km south of Visakhapatnam between Rambilli and Elamanchili mandals. The new site has a deep and natural channel and an easy access to the sea. By contrast, the present naval base at Visakhapatnam is not only crowded but has a narrow and relatively shallow channel. The new base will require 5,000 acres. The Andhra Pradesh Government has reportedly allocated 500 acres and will allocate more land in the near future. [55] The new base will underline the Look East policy as also the growing concern about China's likely policy vis-à-vis the Indian Ocean.

No fleet can be maintained without adequate facility for repairs and refits. Also, not all the ships can be purchased from abroad. Hence, India will need adequate dockyards not only for building new ships but also for maintenance and repair of its fleet. As noted, repair facilities at INS Kadamba are being developed. That will reduce the heavy load from other dockyards.

There were recurring criticisms that naval dockyards face several constraints that erode their performance. The *Defence News* of September 8, 2003 said that three of them deserve to be noted. The first is the fear that the spares available for the ex-Soviet ships are being used up and their additional procurement was posing problem following the disintegration of the USSR. That will pose serious challenges because Indian Navy continues to operate many old vessels obtained from USSR or built in India with Soviet components. The second is the complaint that the machinery has not been updated. The third criticism is that facilities established were inadequate to meet the growing requirements of India's maritime defence forces. [56]

Facilities being developed at INS Kadamba will help to reduce the work load of the other dockyards. Also, the question of supply of spares was taken up when a Russian delegation visited Delhi in September 2005 to discuss that issue. It is said that the newly established Rosoboron Service India Limited (RIL) would be responsible for the supply of spares. The new company was established on April 28, 2005 as an Indian company under a special Russian governmental decree. Not only will RIL coordinate the supply of spares among several Russian firms but will also keep a warehouse in Mumbai stocked with spare parts. It would also have specialists available for the needed work, including repair and maintenance work. Though RIL would cater to the needs of all the three services it will focus first on the needs of the Navy. [57] It is a welcome step since Indian Navy will be a major customer of RIL.

Interestingly the *Defence News* of October 6, 2003, had quoted Ravinder Mohan Bhatia, the Chairman and Managing Director of Mazagon Dock Yard Limited (MDYL), as saying that

MDYL wanted to tap into export market for frigate, corvette, missile boat, supply vessel, off-shore patrol vessel, etc. He also said that MDYL would create a warship marketing organisation in collaboration with Goa Shipyard Limited and the Garden Reach Shipping and Engineering Limited. [58] One wonders how MDYL could be transformed from an overburdened and outmoded organization to one that could not only fulfil its obligations to the Indian Navy but also undertake export commitments.

In this context, it is important to look at the question of ship-building, maintenance, repair and refit afresh. During the previous decades, Indian capacity in the private sector in these fields was limited. That has improved and it can be further modernized and advanced if some of these tasks can be entrusted to the private sector. India's requirements for different types of fishery vessels, supply vessels for offshore installations as well as medium and small patrol boats for homeland maritime security provide an opportunity for greater synergy between civilian and government agencies in the entire spectrum ranging from ship building to repair and service facilities. India has several small and medium dockyards spread all over the coast whose service can be fitted into the larger framework of maritime security.

Maritime security will depend upon the financial resources that can be allocated for it. Today, only the Navy and the Coast Guard share that responsibility, and are funded by the central government. Navy's budget is linked to its percentage share in the overall defence budget. Of late it has oscillated between 17-18 per cent of the total defence budget. Navy's share in 2006-2007 defence budget is estimated at about 18.14 per cent. India's defence budget is approximately three per cent of national GDP. Thus, Navy's share in national GDP will be between 0.45 to 0.50 per cent. Add a bit more for the share of the Coast Guard. Thus, the share for the national maritime security of India at the GDP level is just about half per cent of national GDP.

Even that is not always fully utilized since the deals negotiated by the naval experts are often delayed and the funds allocated for them lapse year after year. The suggestion to create a non-lapsable defence modernisation fund so that unused allocation could be rolled over for utilization in the subsequent year has not been approved so far. The result is that large sums of fund ear-marked for modernization lapses year after year. In financial year 2004-2005 Defence Ministry could not utilize Rs. 1,145 crore. The amount was Rs. 2,500 crore in the financial year 2005-2006. Often the reason is delay in approval by the Cabinet Committee on Security. [59]

Since Navy's share in the national defence budget cannot be altered greatly, it is necessary to find additional ways and means to enhance nation's commitment towards maritime security. The question that needs to be answered is: can the Navy and the Coast Guard by themselves, with only a half-per cent share of national GDP, be held responsible for national maritime security? Sector that benefit from development in the field of maritime affairs also need to contribute towards it in some way or the other. Hence, port authorities, those who operate offshore platforms, fishery department and coastal states, whose security is threatened by the activities of the non-state actors also need to contribute towards strengthening national maritime security.

Table 4.1: Maritime Security Forces of India

Type of vessel and total strength	In active service	Ordered	Age of the vessels				Likely strength	
			Less than 10 years	10-15 years	15-25 years	25 years and more	2010	2015
1	2	3	4	5	6	7	8	9
Submarines								
Nuclear (ATV)	-	-	-	-	-	-	-	(1)
Conventional (Total)	16	6	-	-	-	-	14	14(+2)
F-class	2	-	-	-	-	2	(2)	-
Shishumar-Class	4	-	-	2	2	-	4	4
Kilo-class	10	-	2	2	6	-	10	10
Scorpene-class	-	6	-	-	-	-	-	(2)
Aircraft Carriers – Total	1	2	-	-	-	-	1(+1)	2
INS Virat	1	-	-	-	-	1	1	-
INS Vikramaditya	-	1	-	-	-	-	1	1
INS Vikrant	-	1	-	-	-	-	-	1

Contd...

1	2	3	4	5	6	7	8	9
Destroyers - Total	8	3	-	-	-	-	8(+1)	7(+4)
R-class	5	-	-	-	4	1	5	2(+3)
Delhi-class	3	-	3	-	-	-	3	3
Kolkata-class	-	3	-	-	-	-	(1)	2(+1)
Frigates – Total	13	6+	-	-	-	-	14(5)	14(3+)
Nilgiri – class	4	-	-	-	-	4	2(+2)	2
Godavari – class	3	-	-	-	3	-	3	(3)
Brahmaputra - class	3	-	3	-	-	-	3	3
Talwar – class	3	3	3	-	-	-	5(+1)	6
Shivalik – class	-	3+	-	-	-	-	1(+2)	3+
Corvettes Large								
Strike – Total	8	-	-	-	-	-	-	-
Khukri – class	4	-	-	-	4	-	4	4
Kora – class	4	-	4	-	-	-	4	4
Corvettes - Small								
Strike – Total	13	-	-	-	-	-	13	13
Veer – class	13	-	3	10	-	-	13	13

Contd…

1	2	3	4	5	6	7	8	9
Corvettes (ASW) – Total	4	6	-	-	-	-	6(+4)	4(+6)
Abhay – class	4	-	-	-	4	-	4	(4)
Project 28	-	6	-	-	-	-	2(+4)	4(+2)
Patrol Force Large								
Navy and Coast Guard – Total	19	4	-	-	-	-	22	20(+3)
Vikram - class	9	-	-	2	7	-	9	7(+2)
Sukanya – class	5	-	-	5	-	-	5	5
Samar – class	4	1(+1)	4	-	-	-	5	5(+1)
Environment protection vessel	-	3	-	-	-	-	3	3
Patrol Force Medium								
Navy and Coast Guard Total	19	5	-	-	-	-	13+	13+
SDB – 3	2	-	-	-	2	-	-	-
SDB - 5 Trinket-class	5	-	5	-	-	-	5	5
Bangaran - class	1	1+	-	-	-	-	1+	1+

Contd…

1	2	3	4	5	6	7	8	9
Sarojini - Naidu – Class	2	5	2	-	-	-	7	7
Jijabai – class	7	-	-	-	7	-	-	-
Raj – class	2	-	-	-	2	-	-	-
Patrol Boat, Small								
Navy and Coast Guard Total	16	Na	-	-	-	-	16+	16+
Super Dvora	5	Na	5	-	-	-	5+	5+
Interceptor boats	11	Na	5	6	-	-	11+	11+
Mine Countermeasure								
Ships large - Total	12	6	-	-	12	-	12	6(+6)
Inshore "	2	Na	-	-	-	-	Na	Na
Amphibious Warfare								
LPD	-	1	-	-	-	1	1	(1)
LST/LPD	2	3	-	1	1	-	3	5
LCT	5	-	-	5	-	-	(5)	-
LCU	6	-	-	6	-	-	6	6
Flect replenishment ships	3	1	1	1	-	1	3	3(+1)

Notes

1. Farrar, Mark, "From Strength to Strength: Indian Submarine Force", *Asia-Pacific Defence Reporter*, 31(6), July-August, 2005, pp. 30-1.

2. Mohanty, Deba R., "India and France Ink Scorpene Deal", *Military Technology*, 30(2), 2006, p.34.

3. *Military Balance, 2002-2003*. I.I.S.S., London, 2003, p. 125.

4. *Strategic Digest*, 32(10), October 2002, p. 1432.

5. Ibid., 35(8), August 2005, p. 1025.

6. Mohanty, Deba R., *Military Technology*, 30(2), 2006, p. 34.

7. Sengupta, Parun K., "Scorpene Once More", *Force,* 3(1), September 2005, pp. 25-6.

8. *Strategic Digest*, 35(12), December 2005, p. 1640.

9. Ibid., 35(10), October 2005, p. 1366.

10. *The Hindu*, October 6, 2005.

11. Ibid., March 2, 2006.

12. Singh, Admiral Madhvendra, *Indian Defence Review*, 20(3), October-December 2005, pp. 53-4.

13. Nadkarni, Admiral J.G. (Retd.), Interview, *Indian Defence Review*, 9(3), July 1994, p. 24.

14. Bedi, Rahul, "Nuclear Submarine is Being Built in India", *Jane's Defence Weekly*, 22(24) December 17, p. 1994, p. 3.

15. *Strategic Digest*, 32(3), March 2002, pp. 434-35.

16. Quoted in *Journal of Indian Ocean Studies*, 10(1), April 2002, p. 154.

17. *Strategic Digest*, 34(5) May 2004, p. 736.

18. *The Hindu*, November 17, 2005.

19. *The Hindu*, November 18, 2005, quoted in *Strategic Digest*, 35(12), December 2005, pp. 1649-50.

20. *The Hindu*, December 7, 2005, quoted in *Strategic Digest*, 36(1), January 2006, p. 65.

21. Ibid., November 5, 2005.

22. Farrer, Mark, *Asia-Pacific Defence Reporter*, 31(6), July-August 2005, p. 32.

23. *The Hindu*, June 2, 2001.

24. Suri, R.B., *Shape and Size of the Indian Navy*, United Service Institution, New Delhi, 1998, p. 37.

25. *The Hindu*, November 17, 2005, quoted in *Strategic Digest*, 35(12), December 2005, pp. 1678-79 and *The Hindu*, July 6, 2006.

26. "BrahMos-the JV Trendsetter", *Military Technology*, 30(2),

2006, p. 39 and *The Hindu*, November 21, 2005.

27. *The Hindu*, December 12, 2005.

28. Quoted in *Strategic Digest*, 35(11), November 2005, p. 1519.

29. *The Indian Express* (Kozhikode), November 16, 2005.

30. *Strategic Digest*, 35(2), February 2005, p. 199.

31. *New Indian Express*, January 19, 2006.

32. Singh, Admiral Madhvendra, *Indian Defence Review*, 20(3), October-December 2005, p. 55.

33. *Flight International*, 169(5017), January 3-9, 2006, p. 14.

34. *Strategic Digest*, 35(2), February 2005, p. 199.

35. MoD, *Annual Report, 2005-2006, New Delhi, 2006, p. 93, The Hindu*, July 9, 2006 and *Strategic Digest*, 36(7), July 2006, p. 902.

36. Bedi, Rahul, "UAV Receives Approval", *Jane's Defence Weekly*, 42(41), October 12, 2005, p. 15.

37. *The Hindu*, July 12, 2006.

38. Bedi, Rahul, "Indian Navy Expansion Advances", *Jane's Defences Weekly*, 43(5), February 1, 2005, p. 15.

39. Singh, Admiral Madhvendra, *Indian Defence Review*, 20(3), October-December 2005, p. 55.

40. Bedi, Rahul and Hunter, James, "India Consider Acquiring UK Sea Harriers", *Jane's Defence Weekly*, 43(7), February 15, 2006, p.6 and *New Indian Express* (Kozikode), October 14, 2006.

41. *Strategic Digest*, 33(3), March 2003, p. 247.

42. *Kommersant*, January 21, 2004 quoted in *Strategic Digest*, 34(2), February 2004, pp. 228-29.

43. Chopra, Vice-Admiral S.C. (Retd.), "Why Gorshkov?" *Defence Watch*, 1(5), January 2002, pp. 7-10 and Karnozov, Vladimir, "Major Reconstruction: Admiral Gorshkov in Becoming Indian Navy Ship Vikramaditya", *Asia-Pacific Defence Reporter*, 31(9), December 2005-January 2006, pp. 30-1.

44. Singh, Admiral Madhvendra, *Indian Defence Review*, 20(4), October-December 2005, p. 51.

45. MoD, *Annual Report, 2003-2004*, New Delhi, 2004, p. 40 and *Annual Report, 2005-2006*, New Delhi, 2006, p. 32.

46. Singh, Admiral Madhvendra, *Indian Defence Review*, 20(4), October-December 2005, p. 52.

47. *The Hindu*, June 8, 2006.

48. Singh, Admiral Madhvendra, *Indian Defence Review*, 20(4), October-December 2005, p. 55. Singh, Admiral Madhvendra, *Indian Defence Review*, 20(4), October-December 2005, p. 55.

49. *Jane's Defence Weekly*, 43(21), May 24, 2006, p. 14.

50. *Strategic Digest*, 34(9), September 2004, p. 1301.

51. Bedi, Rahul, "Indian Navy's Expansion Advances", *Jane's Defence Weekly*, 43(5), February 1, 2006, p. 15.

52. Singh, Admiral Madhvendra, *Indian Defence Review*, 20(4), October-December 2005, p. 54.

53. *Sainik Samachar*, 53(10), May 16, 2006, p. 4.

54. Mazumdar, Mrityunjou and Chattopadyay, Rupak, "Malabar 2005", *Indian Defence Review*, 20(4), October-December 2005, p.80.

55. *Defence and Technology*, 5(53), October 2006, pp. 12-3.

56. *Defence News*, October 6, 2003 quoted in *Strategic Digest*, 33(10), October 2003, pp. 1102-03.

57. *Strategic Digest*, 35(11), November 2005, pp. 1517-18.

58. Ibid, 33(11), November 2003, pp. 1235-37.

59. Dikshit, Sandip, "Defence Ministry Not Able to Spend Total Allocated Fund", *The Hindu*, June 16, 2006.

5

MARITIME SECURITY THROUGH COOPERATION: INDIA AND GREAT POWERS

OVERCOMING MARITIME ISOLATION

No single state can isolate itself so completely that it does not need outside cooperation in the context of maritime security. On the contrary, its isolation itself can become a cause for its insecurity. In the past, people of India had created a kind of 'sea wall' around themselves, and had virtually isolated themselves from the rest of the maritime world. Among other things, it contributed to the advent of Europeans at the end of the fifteenth century. If Indians had not insulated themselves from the rest of the world and if they had officially, at the level of the government, been represented in the courts of the Mediterranean states they would have noted the rapid advances not only in the construction, sailing technique and armament of the warships but also the overall impact upon trade and foreign relations. They would have been better prepared to meet the challenges coming from across the ocean. Economic prosperity of Calicut under Zamorin depended upon providing security and justice on land to foreign traders. The state should also have provided maritime security to that trade. If the state had possessed even six strong sea-going war galleys that were armed with heavy guns, even on the model of the Mamluk war galleys of that period, the Portuguese would have had a second thought about using force to obtain control over the trade and would have been reduced to the level of other contemporary maritime traders. India's maritime isolation was finally broken only after independence.

India's maritime diplomacy was the result of its conscious policy to develop cooperation with its extended neighbourhood that extended well beyond the narrow confines of so-called South Asia; a reflection of the sub-continental mindset and a geopolitical legacy of the colonial era. India's wider concept of neighbourhood was elaborated in the *Annual Report, 2000-2001*, of the Ministry of Defence. It stressed upon the need to strengthen the trends of cooperation, friendship and trust with countries of India's extended neighbourhood based on old civilizational and historical ties as well as strong contemporary relevance; countries of South-East Asia, the Gulf and the Indian Ocean Region who have a common stake with India in promoting peace, stability and development in this space. [1] Thus, maritime cooperation became a major aspect of India's regional diplomacy.

PORT VISITS

Not only India developed overseas merchant marine but ships of the Indian Navy also began to visit ports of the neighbouring states. Jawaharlal Nehru, with his sense of India's historical heritage as also his policy of fostering Afro-Asian solidarity, decided to travel to Indonesia on his first official visit in 1950 onboard the ship of the Indian Navy. He was also accompanied by his daughter Indira and her two sons. India and Indonesia also signed in Djakarta in December 1958 a five-year agreement for cooperation between the navies of the two countries. [2]

Ships of the Indian Navy also visited ports along the African coast, the Persian Gulf region and the islands of Western Indian Ocean. In 1957, warships of India visited Diego Suarez (in Madagascar), Mombasa and Dar as-Salam. [3] The next year, INS Shakti, a fleet tanker, visited Diego Garcia. Also, two frigates, INS Tir and INS Kistna, visited Diego Garcia, Seychelles, Addu Atoll and Male. INS Delhi also visited Addu Atoll in the Maldives. [4] These visits continued even afterwards. Vice-Admiral G.M. Hiranandani has given a table of such visits between 1965-1975. [5]

These visits were reciprocated by other navies. The Maritime Fleet Review, held in Mumbai during the third week of February 2001 can be called a major achievement of Indian Navy's diplomacy. Warships from 19 friendly countries from Indian Ocean Region and from outside as also delegates from 29 states participated. In all, 97 warships, 73 from the Indian Navy and 24 from other navies, participated in the review. [6] Prime Minister Atal Bihari Vajpayee, in his speech during the concluding ceremony, said that the Indian Navy had an important role in cooperating with the navies of the world to protect the sea lanes against acts of piracy, in curbing drug-trafficking, gun-running and protecting the depletion of ocean resources and preserving marine ecology. He said that only when we have established institutional arrangements for cooperation that we can truly say that we have built bridges of friendship across the ocean. [7]

JOINT NAVAL EXERCISES

The next step in fostering maritime cooperation is through hosting joint exercises, bilateral as also multilateral. Multilateral exercises symbolize cooperation on the basis of membership of an organisation or on the basis of regional cooperation. India used to participate in the Annual Commonwealth Joint Exercises held in the Bay of Bengal. These were organised by the Commander-in-Chief, East Indies Station, and included ships from Britain, India, Pakistan and Sri Lanka. These were held from late fifties till 1963 and were discontinued after Britain shifted its command from Trinomalee to Singapore.

There was a lull in such exercises partly due to Cold War perceptions and the so-called charge of India having hegemonic designs. Atmosphere was more conductive to maritime cooperation in the post-Cold War period, at least in the Bay of Bengal region. Indian initiative to conduct joint maritime exercises among the littoral states of that region, known as the Milan, has been widely accepted as a means to promote regional maritime cooperation as also as a viable confidence-building measure.

MARITIME COOPERATION

What are the broad parameters of maritime cooperation in the context of maritime security? India's Maritime Doctrine of 2004 lays down the need for collective security through multilateral cooperation. [8] Admiral Arun Prakash in an interview with *Indian Defence Review* said, "Our Navy's international maritime cooperation initiatives should be tailored to the needs of the individual country and its strategic alignments, as also the capability of its Navy". [9]

Cooperation is a very touchy area of international relations. It can neither be rushed into nor imposed upon others. It is also different from a formal alliance. In cooperation, commitments are based not only upon common concern but also upon willingness to respect each others susceptibilities. Moreover, cooperation is normally a peacetime commitment and hence use of force is limited by constraints of international law. This aspect needs to be underlined because of the new trend among some great powers to push their unilateralist, or even multilateralist, agenda in the name of regional cooperation, even upon those who have their own reservations. The PSI and MRSI are typical examples of such 'enforced' cooperation.

The best way to strengthen the basis of maritime security is to approach it gradually *via* bilateral cooperation among concerned states and then to seek to knit that into some form of regional cooperation among willing partners. The process can start with initiating confidence building measures, followed by defining the parameters of common maritime concerns and thus to agree on certain measures aimed at neutralizing well-defined illegal activities in respective maritime frontiers. That could also mean information sharing and reciprocal arrangements for overcoming legal constraints on actions to be followed subsequently, if agreed upon, for joint enforcement action or delegation of responsibility on an *ad hoc* basis or on a more permanent basis through creation of appropriate institutions or mechanism to strengthen regional maritime cooperation.

There are certain international obligations that *ipso faeto* presuppose maritime cooperation. Among other things, they include SLOC protection, eradication of piracy and fight against terrorism. While these are responsibilities of individual states in their territorial waters and even on the high seas, attempts are being made to use them as means to coerce some regional powers to 'cooperate' under diplomatic pressure. States cannot be coerced into cooperation. That can be achieved through a gradual process of persuasion and confidence building while respecting the susceptibilities of different states.

India's policy of strengthening maritime security has to follow a two-track approach. Both are complementary. The one obliges India to fulfil its commitments under traditional international law and the evolving practices legitimised through institutions like the UN and the IMO. That is its responsibility as a major regional maritime power. India cannot ignore its obligations just as the world cannot afford to ignore India's role in the context of establishing peace and stability in the Indian Ocean Region.

The other track is to build bridges with neighbours and with other maritime states so as to strengthen India's capability to perform its role more effectively. Thus, diplomacy and maritime cooperation can further buttress India's own efforts to safeguard its maritime security while simultaneously contributing to the strengthening of peace and stability in the surrounding waters. If India has to fulfil its obligations beyond the normal state responsibility the world needs to match obligations of India by extending to it adequate cooperation by regional as also extra-regional powers and other users of this ocean.

India, with its credible maritime capability, can be an asset. This was amply proved during the tsunami tragedy that devastated the coasts of Indonesia, India, Sri Lanka and the surrounding areas. Indian response was quick. It helped to stabilise the situation pending the large-scale relief that came subsequently. Within twelve hours of the tragedy i.e., by the evening of the day that the tsunami had hit the coast of Sri Lanka, Indian helicopters with relief material had reached the site of the tragedy. The next day, Indian Navy's INS Sharda and INS Sandhyak dropped anchor at Galle and Tricomalee respectively. INS Sutlaj reached Galle on December 28, 2003. INS Mysore reached Male in the early morning of December 28. Two other ships, INS Udaigiri and INS Aditya reached there the next day. Most of them had integrated helicopters that enabled the relief supplies to reach the point where they were most needed. INS Nirupak was converted into a hospital vessel and reached Aceh in Indonesia on December 30. Resources of the Indian Navy and the Air Force were also deployed for disaster relief in the long coastal belt of India. [10]

Some foreign media equated the Indian capability to extend help so quickly as a sign of India's 'power projection'. They also could not accept the fact that India had rejected all help by foreign NGOS and countries particularly in Andaman and Nicobar Islands. That partly reflected their envy as also their ignorance about India's growing maritime capability as also image of India as a friendly neighbour in the region.

India's capability to respond to humanitarian challenges was once again put to test during the Lebanese crisis in July 2006. There was an exodus from Lebanon of foreign nationals due to sustained large scale air offensive by Israel all over Lebanon. Large number of people from India were also affected. Three warships of the Indian Navy that were returning after a friendly cruise in the Mediterranean were ordered to proceed, while they are passing through the Suez Canal, to Beirut to help in their evacuation. INS Mumbai, with two of its escorts, reached Beirut on July 20, 2006. In three sorties, code named Operation Sakoon, these ships transported 2,280 persons from Beirut to Larnaca in Cyprus from where they were airlifted by Air India to India. Beside Indians, these ships also helped to evacuate 57 persons from Sri Lanka, 47 from Nepal, eight from Lebanon and two from USA.

MARITIME COOPERATION: GREAT POWERS

India's relations with great powers and immediate maritime neighbours were governed by two different sets of variables. India's relations with great powers were related to their historical role in Indian Ocean and their perception of India in that context. Hence, during the Cold War period India's relations with Western powers were rather strained except with UK which were influenced more by the Commonwealth ties than Cold War relations *per se*.

India's relations with the West that were cold during the Cold War period began to thaw after 1990-91. They were once again derailed following the Pokhran II of 1998. It took the events of 9/11 (September 11, 2001) to make the West realize that it could not really ignore India in their strategy in the Indian Ocean Region. Though the issue of nuclear non-proliferation continues to cloud the relations, as was evident during the negotiations for support to India's civilian nuclear programme, relations have become more cooperative. That gets reflected in the field of maritime strategy as well, especially joint exercises with major powers like USA, UK, France and Russia.

USA: Indo-US cooperation in maritime security developed haltingly. While USA took time to rid itself of the Cold War mindset, India too had to overcome the Enterprise syndrome because not only did USA have a much stronger military presence in Indian Ocean Region but it had also intervened militarily since 1988; during the last days of the Iraq-Iran war as also after the Kuwaiti crisis. By 1991-92, while USA had emerged as the dominant extra-regional power with proven interventionist capability, India two had grown as a major regional powers that could not be ignored in any future strategy concerning the Indian Ocean Region. Gradual realisation of these hard realities of international relations paved the path for mutual cooperation. The *Annual Report, 1991-1992*, of the Ministry of Defence noted that India's security considerations are determined by the events beyond its immediate neighbourhood as well as by those in our immediate neighbourhood. It added that India had pursued a policy of improving relations with the USA, based on a perception of our common strategic concern in this region. [11]

During the Cold War era, especially after 1971, visits of US warships were discouraged. The end of the Cold War and more so the Kuwaiti crisis of 1990-91 provided the opportunity for renewal of contacts. Reportedly, US ships on their way to the war zone were allowed refuelling stops. Indo-US naval steering committee was formed and its first meeting was held in New Delhi in March 1991. [12]

Further steps were taken but haltingly. They began with low level joint naval exercise off the coast of South West India–the Malabar. The exercise of May 1992 was at a low level. Malabar-2 of May 1995 was spread over two days. Malabar-3, held in 1996, was a three week long exercise and involved besides surface vessels two US SSNs as also P-3 Orion MR aircraft. India offered Indian Tu-142 LRMP aircraft and a conventional submarine. The Pokhran II of 1998 and the US policy of 'sanctions' halted that process for some time.

US response to Pokhran II was a knee jerk response and could not be the basis of long-term policy. Visit of President Clinton in March 2000 and Indian Prime Minister's visit to USA restarted the process of cooperation. *Annual Report, 2000-2001*, of the Ministry of Defence summed up the situation as follows, "India has a continuing interest in improving bilateral defence cooperation with USA based on mutual respect, mutual benefit, equality and understanding. Although there has been limited resumption of contacts between high level military officials and seminars since March 1998, the institutional framework for cooperation that had evolved over the years remains suspended by the USA". [13]

The change of government in Washington in January 2001 and the new presidency of George W. Bush gave a new momentum to the process of Indo-US cooperation. Not only did Indian Prime Minister visit USA on the invitation of President Bush but USA lifted some restrictions that were imposed in May 1998. That helped in the renewal of official contacts and in further strengthening of institutional contacts. [14] That paved the way for Malabar-4 that was held in September-October 2003. Since then the Malabar has become an annual feature. During the joint exercise held between September 25 and October 4, 2005, aircraft carriers of both the countries took part to develop aviation interoperability, as also to conduct anti-air and anti-submarine exercises. Earlier, between September 12-15, joint exercises were held off Kochi with emphasis on joint diving, salvage, underwater demolition etc.

Over the years the nature and content of these exercises have been changing. They have become more interactive. Both sides are prepared to 'expose' their sophisticated hardware. While USA has contributed large attack carriers armed with latest F-18 aircraft as also SSNs, India has contributed its latest destroyers as also conventional submarines built with German technology. Deployment of Indian conventional submarine gives USA a valuable lesson in ASW operations *vis-à-vis* small and sophisticated submarine operating in shallow and warm waters. This experience is very important for US Navy which has no comparable submarine or facility to operate such submarines in water conditions found in the Indian Ocean. There is no report of US Navy exercising with submarines of Pakistan. India, in turn, must have learnt the plus and minus points of large SSNs operating along its waters.

Though Indo-US joint exercises have been held for the past fourteen years they have been confined to waters around India's western coast south of Goa. Also, India and USA have cooperated in the Malacca Straits when Indian patrol vessel escorted high value US ships through the Malacca Straits in 2001-02 during Operation Enduring Freedom under the code name Operation Sagittarius. Thus, formally or informally, Indo-US maritime cooperation does not extend to areas that are of greater strategic importance to India–the Persian Gulf and the Gulf of Oman that constitute the northern half of the Arabian Sea.

That is sought to be explained in the context of institutional framework. India, under the US division of maritime zones, comes under the Pacific Command and not under the Central Command (CENTCOM) that, along with the Fifth Fleet, covers that region. Probably that is a good enough excuse to keep India off the waters in which Pakistan is a strategic partner of USA. But, can Pakistan, tucked away in the north-eastern part of the Arabian Sea, really provide the type and degree of maritime security to major SLOCs of that zone that India can provide? Lack of Indo-US maritime interaction in the northern part of the Arabian Sea also acts as a constrain on India developing bilateral and multilateral structures of cooperation for maritime security with most of the GCC states.

What are the expectations of USA and India from such bilateral cooperation? According to one scholar, US Navy had asked India to make Goa and Cochin 'permanent ports of call' for American warships operating in the Indian Ocean. [15] Given the reaction of certain political and religious groups in India, it is doubtful whether Indian government can risk such an overt invitation that would amount to giving *de facto* base rights to US Navy in India.

Some circles in India would like a more intimate contact between Indian forces and the CENTCOM. According to dispatch by Sandeep Dikshit in *The Hindu*, despite reservations expressed by Defence Minister Pranab Mukherjee, the Navy was discussing the posting of officers at two US global military commands. According to Navy officials, USA had in principle agreed to the posting of an officer at the Pacific Command that keeps an eye on India and other countries in the east. However, the Navy was keen to post an officer at the US CENTCOM that overseas the area west of India which also comprises of the bulk of geographical area of operation for the Indian Navy. [16] Beside the disagreement on the question of 'areas' of US naval command in the Indian Ocean Region, India had also made it clear that its participation in joint naval exercises, though they include visit, boarding, search and seizure of vessels, did not relate to PSI to which India was not a signatory; [17] a legal and diplomatic point but meaningless in content keeping in view the nature of its joint exercises with great powers.

There is no doubt that India and USA are entering into long-term agreement on bilateral defence cooperation. As a follow-up of the 10-year Indo-US Defence Cooperation Agreement of 1995-2005, Pranab Mukherjee and Donald Rumsfeld signed a new 10-Year Framework for Indo-US Defence Relations. [18] *Military*

Technology commenting upon the June 2005 agreement said, "India significantly agreed to take part in multilateral military operations with the US in the absence of UN mandate, thereby paving the way for gradual participation in US-led Proliferation Security Initiative (PSI)". [19]

Probably the fast pace of Indo-US bilateral cooperation in defence matters had raised some eyebrows. *The Hindu* reported that an internal advisory had advised senior Defence Ministry officials and the three service chiefs to limit their interaction with US officials. The reason given was that large number of such engagements with USA left little time for interaction with other countries. [20]

Defence cooperation between India and USA should not be viewed at bilateral level only. It needs to be analysed in the context of their regional and global strategic perceptions. For USA, relations with Pakistan is significant in the context of its 'war on terrorism', especially along the frontiers of Afghanistan. Indo-US cooperation on war on terrorism has a different connotation, and revolves more around maritime dimensions of terrorism especially SLOC protection in the context of WMD/PSI and RMSI.

Besides, USA sees India as a potential counter-weight to China in the Asia-Pacific Region. USA is well aware of India's policy of establishing a détente with China as also to further strengthen its relations with Russia. It is important to understand that multilateral patterns of interest partnership are emerging so as to permit a more balanced view of the emerging world order and its implications for India's strategy in the Indian Ocean Region needs to be noted.

UK: Though UK participates with USA in military operations in the Indian Ocean Region extending up to Afghanistan and even Pakistan, its reach did not in practice cover India. One reason could be that UK was limiting its participation to the area covered under the CENTCOM. Hence, one did not hear much about the British Navy extending its area of effective maritime cooperation with India as reflected in joint exercises. Though British warship did not conduct bilateral exercises with those of the Indian Navy yet there were reports that one British warship was included as a part of the French naval contingent while it was conducting bilateral exercises with ships of the Indian Navy.

Ice seems to have been broken when the warships of the two countries conducted the first major joint naval exercise Konkan-2000 in May 2006. In this exercise, British aircraft carrier Illustrious and its Indian counterpart Virat took part. Sea Harrier aircraft from both sides conducted cross-deck operations. Both sides had fielded, besides their aircraft carriers, large surface combatants. While Royal British Navy operated a nuclear powered submarine (SSN), India fielded the conventional submarine Shankush. The Royal Navy's task force also had one French frigate embedded within it.

Australia: Australia, a partner in this Anglosphere, was more vocal than even USA in criticising India's growing naval capability. It also has been a firm supporter of US interventionist policy in the Indian Ocean Region since 1990-91. After USA decided to restart the dialogue on maritime cooperation with India under the Bush presidency, Australia also initiated the process of coming closer to India. In June 2003, an Australian guided missile frigate paid a four-day visit to Chennai in what was called an 'exploratory visit' to further cooperation between the two navies. This was an attempt to renew contacts after about 20 years. Australians, who claim to have a special responsibility in South-East Asia and South Pacific region, have seen India as an 'intruder' in their zone of influence. They are, however, getting reconciled to India's role in Australia's neighbourhood not only because of India's success in countering the propaganda about its alleged hegemonic designs in that region but also because of growing recognition by Japan and South Korea of India's positive role in enhancing maritime security in the crucial SLOCs. In spite of the change in the perception of US and Japan, Australia has still to recast its version of India as was seen from its outright refusal to support India's policy of developing nuclear power for civilian use and going all out to help China in pursuing a similar policy despite the well documented evidence of China's contribution to clandestine proliferation of nuclear weapon and delivery systems. So be it. But, Australians can no longer afford to ignore India because of growing bilateral economic relations. That was reflected in the large Australian delegation that accompanied Prime Minister John Howard during his visit to India in April 2006. Australian's stance on selling uranium ore to India is also changing.

Japan: For India, the change in Japan's policy is more significant in the context of its maritime security because Japan rather than Australia will prove to be a more acceptable partner by ASEAN members in regional cooperation in India's 'Look East' policy. Japan's policy towards India had to be reoriented from its Cold War era perspective based upon three main variables. First, it tended to look at India solely in the context of South Asia in general and particularly as a part of Indo-Pakistani balance. Second, it evaluated India's nuclear policy from the perspective of one that had surrendered, if not totally renounced, its nuclear weapon option and thus was a more ardent proponent of nuclear non-proliferation than even the great powers that had acquired nuclear-weapon capability before the signing of the NPT. Lastly, Japan for a long time had been content to be a Pacific Ocean power in concert with its major ally USA. Even after the end of the Cold War that partnership survived in the context of China and North Korea.

Few of these factors could have become the basis of India-Japan maritime cooperation. Their relationship had to be based primarily upon new threats that were emerging in the post-Cold War period like piracy, threat from acts of terrorism, SLOC protection especially in the context of energy security etc. These were the areas in which India and Japan could hope to build bridges of bilateral and even multilateral cooperation in the field of maritime security.

This cooperation began step by step. The visit of a ship of the Indian Navy to Tokyo in 1995 could be said to be the beginning of this policy. That visit was followed by the visit of a training ship of the Japanese Maritime Self Defence Force to Mumbai in 1996. Visit of India's Chief of Navel staff, Admiral Vishnu Bhagwat, to Japan in June 1997 could be called the first major milestone in this relationship since it was followed by the visit of Admiral Yasumasa Yamamoto, Japanese Chief of Naval Staff, in February 1998. [21] Interestingly, unlike Indo-US joint naval exercise, the Malabar series, that halted after Pokhran II, India-Japan maritime cooperation continued and Japanese Coast Guard vessels visited India in 1999 for exercise with ships of Indian Coast Guard. These visits have continued since then. Large multi-role Japanese Coast Guard vessel Yashima paid a four-day visit to Chennai and despite poor weather conditions conducted joint exercises with the ships of the Indian counterpart. India's role in anti-piracy operations had been recognised since it had intercepted the Japanese ship Alondra Rainbow off the Indian waters on 14 November 1994. It had been pirated off the Indonesian coast.

Second major step was taken by Japan following Operation Enduring Freedom and US-led 'war on terrorism' in 2001. For the first time ships of the Japanese Maritime Self Defence Force operated in the Indian Ocean Region in support of US-led operations. According to newspaper reports, India was assisting these vessels. [22] Japan's entry into the Indian Ocean in 2001 signified that Japan's maritime policy towards Indian Ocean was reaching beyond its support to US-led war on terrorism to 'war on terrorism' itself. This was, therefore, a change in strategic perception of Japan. Visit of Japan's Foreign Minister Yoriko Kawaguchi to India in January 2003 needs to be seen from that perspective. That visit was followed by the visit of Brijesh Misra, India's National Security Advisor, to Japan in April 2003. A foundation for dialogue on strategic level was thus laid.

The spillover of close cooperation between India and Japan was that South Korea too showed its willingness for maritime cooperation especially at the level of its Coast Guard. A MoU was signed between Indian and South-Korean Coast Guard on March 13, 2006 for mutual cooperation. A large, 4,000 ton South Korean

Coast Guard vessel, Taepyuagyang No. 6, conducted joint exercise with vessels of the Indian Coast Guard off Chennai. The exercise included SAR, pollution control, checking transnational crimes and exchange of information with references to 'rogue' vessels. [23]

Visit of Japan's Prime Minister, Juhichiro Koizumi, to India in April 2005 further cemented this bilateral cooperation. The joint statement of April 29, 2005 mentioned common interest and complementary responsibility for promoting security, stability and prosperity of Asia as well as in advancing international peace and equitable development. It listed three layers of cooperation; bilateral, regional and global. In their regional cooperation, the two countries agreed to develop closer dialogue and collaboration to secure peace, stability and prosperity in Asia, promote democracy and development, and explore a new architecture for closer regional cooperation in Asia. Enhanced security dialogue and cooperation was listed among the eight-fold initiatives for strengthening India-Japan global partnership. Under it, the Coast Guards of both countries were urged to work together on a sustained basis, including annual exercise. It also instructed the Indian Navy and the Japanese Maritime Self Defence Force to enhance their cooperation. Prabhakaran Paleri, who was the Director-General of Indian Coast Guard, underlined the need for Indo-Japanese maritime convergence with focus on the Malacca Straits. [24]

Japan initiated the third step when it sought to co-opt India in a trilateral security-related cooperation *vis-à-vis* China. According to Siddharth Varadarajan, the move was to be made during the visit to India of the Chief of Japan's Maritime Self-Defence Force, Admiral Takashi Saito. That was to be followed by the visit of Chief of the Army and the Air Force. Japan also wanted USA to be invited to their bilateral annual security related dialogue with India to be followed by a discussion at the level of foreign ministers. [25]

This quantum jump to new level of cooperation had to wait since it implied a major change in India's foreign policy. It not only meant that India would join USA and Japan in 'containing' China but also that it would venture beyond the Indian Ocean deep into the Pacific and into waters of strategic significance to China as also Russia. Such a policy would have amounted to virtual alliance against China (and possibly Russia) and would have closed the option for developing close bilateral ties with these states. It was premature to expect Indian Government to favour such a reversal of its policy at this stage when India's relation with China and Russia were being further cemented. These moves, however, have not been totally rejected. There are reports that some elements in India are not totally averse to a more intimate security related dialogue with Japan, USA and Australia.

There is no reason why India should join USA in its policy of containing China in the Pacific. Pentagon's Quadrennial Defence Review of February 6, 2006, said that USA would be the dominant power in Asia-Pacific. It said that strategic decisions made by India, Russia and China would be key factors in determining the international security environment of the 21st century. It added that China has the greatest potential to compete with US and field 'disruptive military technology that could eventually offset traditional US advantage about US countermeasures. [26] It is also curious that while India is being encouraged to contain or balance China, USA is opening up its doors to China for greater economic cooperation.

France: France has historical links with the Indian Ocean Region. It had a colonial empire and even now some of the islands like Reunion are considered as part of the Metropolitan France. Though small in size these islands give France control over vast EEZ and continental-shelf in the Indian Ocean and the adjoining Antarctic Ocean. Besides, French maritime strategy is conditioned by geostrategic considerations like protection of its SLOC *via* Bab al-Mandeb to the Mediterranean and *via* the Cape of Good Hope to Europe.

France had always kept a modest taskforce (LAINDEIN) that included a replenishment tanker-cum-command ship, two or three large surface combatants, some light force and small amphibious ships in support of operations in the islands. France had also maintained a military presence in Djibouti since late sixties. Though a part of the NATO alliance, French deployment in the Indian Ocean Region need not be seen as a part of the US-led coalition. Though France had participated in military operations against Iraq in 1991 and had also kept a small air component in the GCC states it had virtually disassociated itself from the Anglo-American policy towards Iraq since 2000. It not only did not participate in US-led operation against Iraq in 2003 but had even opposed it in the UN. France, however, took active part in Operation Enduring Freedom and continues to support NATO-led peace-enforcement operations in Afghanistan. Thus, France has been playing an autonomous role that dove-tails with that of India.

Joint naval exercises between India and France (Varun) began since 2001. Rear-Admiral Shankar claimed that they started in 1998. [27] These exercises give India an opportunity to interact with modern warships like nuclear-powered aircraft carrier Charles de Gaulle and the state of the art Rafael aircraft, French SSN, frigates and destroyers as also French maritime reconnaissance and ASW aircraft. Indian Navy also fielded the Virat with its Sea Harriers, modern destroyers and frigates, conventional submarines of German design, shore-based Jaguars armed with Sea Eagle anti-ship missiles etc. Indo-French joint naval exercise Varun 04/1 held between April 6-15, 2004 off Goa was a major affair. It involved six French warships that included one aircraft carrier as also one nuclear-powered attack submarine (SSN) and seven aircraft. Indian Navy fielded six surface combat vessels, one submarine and five aircraft. Varun 05/1 was held off Kochi between February 28 and March 7, 2005 while Varun 05/2 was held in November 2005 in the Red Sea. In February 2005, the French brought two of their mine counter-measure ships (MCMS) along with a mine warfare command ship. Indian Navy also fielded three minesweepers. The exercise was held near Kochi. [28] If anything, this was a sales promotion exercise. Indian Navy needs new MCMS to replace ex-Soviet vessels, and France probably wants to sell some to India. France had already sold three such ships to Pakistan.

Normally Indo-French naval exercises are held off Goa but the venue of the seventh series of the joint naval exercise Varun, was held off the Gulf of Aden. It was a large-scale naval exercise involving Indian and French aircraft carriers, large surface combatants, SSN, and Atlantic MR aircraft as also Djibouti-based French Mirage 2000 aircraft. The thrust was on dissimilar air combat exercise involving Indian Sea Harriers and French Mirage 2000, advanced anti-submarine warfare, maritime interdiction operations as also boarding operations, and interaction between India's naval marine commandos and Army troops with French Special Forces. One platoon of Army personnel and four IAF pilots were on board Indian ships for interaction with their French counterparts. [29]

As noted earlier, France has a military presence there since some decades past. Of late, some warships belonging to USA, Spain, Germany, etc. also maintain their presence in that region in the context of war on terrorism. For India, that is an important SLOC to Europe *via* the Red Sea. Indian ships were also involved in support of UN-sponsored operation in Somalia. That area is also subject to piracy and some Indian ships were attacked in these waters. Thus, in the light of US reluctance to operate with India in this zone, the role of France as also of Oman become crucial in the context of India's maritime security in the northern half of the Arabian Sea and the Horn to Africa.

Russia: USSR was a major naval power in the Indian Ocean Region during the Cold War era. Its Navy was withdrawn following the disintegration of USSR. It took some time for the new regime in Moscow to recreate a Navy. Navy of the Russian Federation was fully operational by 2000-2001. Once again, Moscow became aware of the need to make its presence felt in the Indian Ocean. It must not be forgotten that though the old Zarist Empire and its successor, the USSR, has lost a part of its territory, Indian Ocean still remains a major lifeline connecting the 'European' half of Russia with the Pacific coast. The Pacific coast is becoming increasingly important for Russia. The Indian Ocean will acquire even greater geo-strategic significance for Russia once the North-South corridor connecting Russia-Caspian Sea-Iran becomes fully operational. This will provide a valuable route that will not only be shorter but also free of the political constraints of pro-NATO Ukraine, Turkey, the VI Fleet in the Mediterranean and the choke points of the Turkish Straits, Suez Canal and Bab al-Mandeb.

Russian Navy began its new debut in the Indian Ocean in 2003. It sent two task forces; one from the Black Sea Fleet and the other from the Pacific Fleet. Both exercised with the ships of the Indian Navy in May 2003. Ships from the Black Sea Fleet held joint naval exercise with ships of India's Western Fleet in the Arabian Sea while those of Pacific Fleet held joint exercises with ships of India's Eastern Fleet in the Bay of Bengal. The Black Sea task force comprised of Moskva, a large missile cruiser, that also served as the command ship, two minor surface combatants, a large tank landing ship and auxiliary ships. The taskforce from the Pacific Fleet comprised of two large anti-submarine destroyers and a tanker. Whether this taskforce also included SSNs is not confirmed. Both the taskforces, having completed their exercises, returned to their respective bases. Though these visits had coincided with US-led war or Iraq yet Russians had made it clear that their deployment had nothing to do with the US-led war.

The second Indo-Russian joint naval exercise was conducted in the Bay of Bengal in October 2005. It was named INDRA-05. Though both sides sought to explain the joint exercise in the context of combating threat to maritime security posed by piracy and terrorism, highly sophisticated missile armed large surface combatant fielded by both parties during that exercise fail to fit into that role. It was more in the nature of testing the waters of this important SLOC for future operations.

Russia's entry into the Indian Ocean also assumes significance in the context of growing strategic cooperation between Russia and China in Central Asia under the framework of Shanghai-5 as also their joint military exercises along the Pacific coast. Hence,

India can well be confronted with the difficult task of charting its maritime course in the troubled waters of US-led coalition seeking to confront the newly emerging Sino-Russian axis on the Asian mainland and its logical fallout in the Indian Ocean Region. According to Vice-Admiral G.M. Hiranandani, India and Russia had signed in October 2000 a Strategic Partnership Declaration and pledged that the two nations would not join any political or military bloc and avoid treaties that would infringe on each other's national security interests. [30]

China: China has not as yet shown any sign that it is seeking to play the role of a great power in the Indian Ocean Region. Yet, it has high stakes because of the energy security as also security of SLOC connecting China not only with the Gulf but also with Europe. Moreover, China has over the years cultivated several littoral states and has generated a fund of good will that can be useful when it does seek to make a formal entry into the Indian Ocean. China can also act as a buffer against USA for countries like Iran.

Unlike other countries, China uses ambiguity as a tool of diplomacy. While all experts acknowledge that China has vital stakes in Indian Ocean Region and has been cultivating some of the littoral states, yet China has not shown its cards as to how it approaches the question of its maritime security in the Indian Ocean Region. While listing all the relevant facts about China's interests in the region, Admiral Arun Prakash could only comment, "and it now remains to be seen what direction this relationship will take". [31]

Unlike some Indian as also Western experts who have been commenting on possible anti-India role in China's Indian Ocean strategy, Chinese have as yet not given a clear hint that they are pursuing a policy that is hostile to India's national interests. Rather, they are taking small steps towards enhancing bilateral cooperation. The trend is clear since the end of the Cold War especially after the visit of Indian Defence Minister Shared Pawar to Beijing in July 1992. Chinese reciprocated. Chinese Minister for National Defence, General Chi Haotian, visited New Delhi in

November 1994.

Naval cooperation between India and China in the post-Cold War period can be traced to the Bombay (Mumbai) visit of Chinese training ship Zheng He in November 1993. Admiral V.S. Shekhawat visited China in March 1996. INS Delhi and a frigate of the Indian Navy made port calls at Shanghai in September 2000. Earlier, during the days of Hindi-Chini Bhai Bhai', cruiser INS Mysore had made a port call at Shanghai in 1958. In May 2001, two training ships of the Chinese Navy made port call at Mumbai. [32]

Bilateral naval interactions began with warships of India and China conducting naval drills near Shanghai. Two surface combatants and one fleet replenishment tanker participated in that exercise. In November 2005, a Luhai-class missile destroyer and a fleet replenishment tanker paid a four-day visit to Kochi. To say the least, they were warmly welcomed. [33]

The developing detente between India and China in the field of maritime affairs is reflected in the interview given by Rear-Admiral Yang Yi, Director of the PLA Institute of Strategic Studies at China's National Defence University, to P.S. Suryanarayan of *The Hindu* at Singapore. He told him that Chinese Navy was happy to see Indian Navy develop. He added that China can cooperate with Indian Navy in dealing with the traditional and non-traditional security threats. He added, "If you are stronger, play important, active and positive role in the region". All these are value-loaded terms. He emphasised that India and China are two major powers in the region. He said, "We need further cooperation in the future, even further joint military exercises." Major-General Chenghu, Commandant of the College of Defence Studies in PLA's National Defence University, expressed similar views. He said that India and China can contribute to maintenance of peace and stability and promote prosperity in the region. He added that both are working in that direction. [34] It remains to be seen if these are feelers and if so, how would India factor India-China cooperation with its active policy of cooperation with US-led coalition. Can India have multiple interest partners? Will it be allowed to pursue such a policy?

The political will to sustain the ongoing process of détente was demonstrated when Indian Defence Minister Pranab Mukherjee and his Chinese counterpart General Cao Gangchuan signed the first ever memorandum of understanding (MoU) in May 2006. Among other things, the MoU said, "The two sides reiterate that strengthening effective contacts in the field of defence is of vital importance to enhancing mutual trust and understanding between the armed forces and ensuring a peaceful environment in which they can purse their respective national developmental objectives. [35] Upon his return, Pranab Mukherjee, in a press conference, said, "Neither do we consider them a threat to us nor do they consider us as a threat for them. There is enough space for both to grow in their own areas. [36] Sino-Indian détente also dovetails with the US policy of improving military ties with China. US Defence Secretary Donald H. Rumsfeld during his China visit in October 2005 had signed with the Chinese an agreement to strengthen military ties even though Rumsfeld said that China needed to clarify its regional military goals. [37] USA is more interested in China's Pacific Ocean policy than Indian Ocean policy.

Madhu Bhalla, commenting upon improving Sino-Indian ties said that at the strategic level, Chinese domestic concerns have changed its policy towards India in significant ways. For India, the pay off of China's current concern with its ethnic problem in Xinjiang is that there is more sympathy for India's position on cross-border terrorism and a marked coolness towards position on the Kashmir dispute. "It is to be noted that China has not used the phrase 'all weather friend' to categorise its relationship with Pakistan since 11 September 2001." Thus, an understanding of the hazards of Islamic fundamentalism in destabilizing domestic politics has brought it into partnership with India on terrorism and a willingness to view security in cooperative terms. According to her, both countries share concern over many security issues like maritime crime, implications of unilateral use of power, geopolitics of energy in West Asia and Central Asia and terrorism and trafficking in arms which could conceivably be tied into an ongoing dialogue process. [38]

It is true that China has not shown all its cards. May be it is not yet ready in terms of naval force projection capability, as opposed to flag showing capability, to play a decisive role in the Indian Ocean Region. Its primary zone of interest still remains the Pacific and South China Sea and is likely to be so for at least some years to come. India will, however, have to anticipate the possible moves of the Chinese and take appropriate measures.

One wonders how China will benefit by overtly antagonizing India. India dominates major SLOCs connecting China with the Gulf and Europe. Also, will China by its anti-India policy prefer to push India firmly into US-led coalition with Japan and South Korea as other partners. Will China and Russia, that are seeking to build closer strategic understanding, prefer India as a member of US-led coalition? How will that affect Russia-China-India dialogue that is also proceeding rapidly under the Shanghai-5 cooperation network. Will China and India not benefit by pursuing a policy of mutual cooperation that will not only help to stabilize the Indian Ocean Region but also have a positive impact upon both the flanks of India; in South-East Asia as also in South-West Asia?

It is easy to project China as the new threat so as to justify the expansion of the Indian Navy in the years to come. It should not be forgotten that generating a maximum threat scenario (on the basis of 1962 syndrome?) to justify India's militarization, that cannot be limited only to the Navy but will also extend to the Army and the Air Force, as well as in refashioning India's foreign policy itself, can turn out to be a self-fulfilling prophecy. Hence, such exercises in projecting threats need utmost care and far sight lest they adversely affect for decades to come chances of developing cooperative linkages with a major next door neighbour of India.

In pursuance of its Look East policy, India is seeking to register its naval presence in the Asia-Pacific. Though ships of the

Indian Navy have been making regular port calls they had not conducted joint naval exercises with the navies of major regional powers in the Pacific. It is reported that an Indian task force will be sailing in mid-2007 for the Pacific. It will conduct exercises with naval vessels of USA and Russia and visit ports of Japan and South Korea. This has given a new meaning to 'bilateral' naval exercise. Not only will India conduct such exercises with non-regional navies in the Indian Ocean Region but will also conduct them in the maritime zones of these foreign powers.

There is no doubt that since the end of the Cold War, India has been able to develop cooperative linkages at bilateral level with almost all great powers without being a part of any coalition. Such a policy not only corresponds with India's traditional policy of non-alignment but also with the newly emerging strategic environment that promotes interest partnerships rather than alliances. While this offers India a larger space to structure its maritime strategy in the newly emerging international and regional environment, it also means that India needs to be careful that its interest partnerships do not turn into overt or covert alliances since that will negate all the advantages that the newly emerging international orders offers for fashioning a multi-faceted maritime security strategy for India for the years to come.

Notes

1. Ministry of Defence, *Annual Report, 2000-2001*, New Delhi, p. ii.
2. Ministry of Defence, *Annual Report, 1958-59*, New Delhi, 1959, p. 17.
3. Katari, Admiral R.D., *A Sailor Remembers,* New Delhi, 1982, pp. 84-5.
4. Ministry of Defence, *Annual Report, 1958-59,* New Delhi, 1059, pp. 12-13. Ministry of Defence, *Annual Report, 1958-59,* New Delhi, 1059, pp. 12-13.
5. Hiranandani, Vice-Admiral G.M. (Retd.), *Transition to Triumph : History of Indian Navy, 1965-1975*, Lancer Publishers, New Delhi, 2000, pp. 375-79.
6. Banger, Commodore N.K. (IN), "International Fleet Review 2001 at Mumbai", *Naval Review*, 91(2), May 2003, p. 140.
7. Singh, Anil Kumar, *India's Security Concerns in the Indian*

Ocean Region, Har Anand Pub. Pvt. Ltd., New Delhi, 2003, pp. 147-48.

8. *Indian Maritime Doctrine*, Integrated Head Quarter, MOD (Navy), April 29, 2004, p. 51.

9. *Indian Defence Review*, 19(3), July-September 2004, p. 15, (Interview by Bharat Verma, editor of the Journal.

10. Udai Bhaskar, C. "Tsunami Tragedy. India's Responses and Anomalous Apathy", *Strategic Analysis*, 28(4), October-December 2004, p. 590.

11. MoD, *Annual Report, 1991-1992*, New Delhi, 1992, p. 3.

12. Singh, Anil Kumar, *Indian Security Concerns in the Indian Ocean Region*, Har Anand, New Delhi, 2003, p. 128, and Roy-Chaudhuri, Rahul, "US Naval Policy in the Indian Ocean", *Strategic Analysis*, 22(9), December 1998, p. 1325.

13. Ministry of Defence, *Annual Report, 2000-2001*, New Delhi, 2001, p. 9.

14. Ministry of Defence, *Annual Reports 2001-2002*, New Delhi, 2002, p. 11.

15. Scott, A. Cuono, "US and Indian Navies Close Again", *US Naval Institute Proceedings*, 128(2), February 2002, pp. 42-3.

16. Dikshit, Sandeep, "Navy for Posting Officers at the Central Command", *The Hindu*, November 17, 2005.

17. *The Hindu*, September 25, 2005.

18. Mazumdar, Mrityunjoy and Chattopadhyay, Rupak, "Malabar 2005", *Indian Defences Review*, 20(4), October-December 2005, p. 75.

19. "India: Naval Posture: An Assessment", *Military Technology*, 30(2), 2006, p. 33.

20. *The Hindu*, July 29, 2006.

21. Basu, Baidya Bikash, "Indo-Japan Naval Cooperation", *Strategic Analysis*, 22(3), May 1998, 321-22.

22. *The Hindu*, January 2, 2003, quoted in *Strategic Digest*, 33(2), February 2003, pp. 200-201.

23. *Indian Express*, August 2005, quoted in *Strategic Digest* 35(9), September 2005, p. 1193, and *The Hindu*, July 7, 2006.

24. For the text, see *Strategic Digest*, 35(5), May 2005, pp. 538-42, and Paleri, Prabhakaran, "Maritime Activities in the Choke Points of Indian Ocean", Journal of Indian Ocean Studies, 14(2), August 2006, p. 224..

25. Varadarajan, Siddharth, "Perils of Three-Way Security Cooperation", *The Hindu*, February 140, 2006.

26. "US Reveals Long-War strategy", *Asia-Pacific Defence*

Reporter, 32(1), February 2006, p. 7.

27. *The Hindu*, April 10, 2004.

28. *Indian Defence Review*, 20(4), October-December 2005, p. 73.

29. *Strategic Digest*, 35(12), December 2005, p. 1688.

30. Hiranandani, Vice-Admiral, G.M.,*Transition to Eminance: The Indian Navy, 1976*-1990, Lancer, New Delhi, 2003, p. 120.

31. Admiral Arun Prakash, "Indian Maritime Doctrine", in Nambier, E.K.G. and Suryanarayan, V, eds, *Lectures in Maritime Studies*, Publications Division, University of Calicut, 2005, p. 30.

32. MoD, *Annual Report, 2001-2002,* New Delhi, 2002, p. 35.

33. *The Hindu*, November 29, 2005.

34. Ibid, January 6, 2006 and August 27, 2006.

35. *Strategic Digest*, 36(6), June 2006, pp. 804-805.

36. *The Hindu*, June 14, 2006.

37. *Strategic Digest*, 35(11), November 2005, p. 1590.

38. Bhalla, Madhu, "Domestic Roots of China's Foreign and Security Policy", *International Studies*, 42(3-4), July-December 2005, p. 221.

6

INDIA AND REGIONAL POWERS

India's relations with immediate neighbours were influenced primarily by India's nationalist movement as also the fragmentation of the British Indian Empire. While the role of the Indian National Congress during the independence movement drew India closer to the countries of West Asia and South-East Asia the fragmentation of the British Indian Empire, ending in the partition of 1947, led to an environment of hostility between India and Pakistan that was carried on by some in Bangladesh even after 1971. Other neighbours like Ceylon (Sri Lanka) suffered from a self-generated fear of Indian hegemony. Thus, India-Sri Lanka relations oscillated between deep distrust of India and the need for India's involvement in preserving Sri Lanka's domestic peace and security as also territorial unity whether during the Janatha Vimukhti Peramuna (JVP) uprising in 1971 or the Tamil militancy after 1983. This love-hate relationship continues even now except that India has been able to reduce the quantum of distrust over the years.

India's relations with its maritime neighbours also demonstrates this characteristic while delimiting maritime boundaries. It was relatively easy to delimit maritime boundaries with Sri Lanka in 1974 and 1976, the Maldives, 1976, Indonesia, 1974, Thailand, 1977 and even Myanmar in 1982. Efforts to agree on the formula for delimiting maritime boundary between India and Pakistan and India and Bangladesh have proved futile so far. Part of the season was the expectation in Pakistan and Bangladesh that the area near their maritime boundary with India was rich in oil and gas. Efforts to find them over the years have proved futile. May be that factor will facilitate a framework for delimitation of their maritime boundaries in the near future.

There can be no uniform formula for determining India's

maritime cooperation policy *vis-à-vis* the littoral and island states of the Indian Ocean Region. Since the geographical and strategic environment is different in each of the neighbouring zones, it will be useful to analyse India's maritime cooperation policy with its neighbours in the context of the following four zones as seen from the Indian perspective. They are Central Indian Ocean, Bay of Bengal and its natural extension, North Arabian Sea and its natural extension and South-West Indian Ocean that will include the African littoral south of the Horn of Africa and various island republics in that zone.

CENTRAL INDIAN OCEAN ZONE

For India, Central Indian Ocean zone has great strategic significance for three main reasons. It connects India's Arabian Sea littoral with that in the Bay of Bengal. Proximity of Sri Lanka and the Maldives to India's coast, especially of Tamil Nadu and Kerala has its impact upon domestic policy of India. Lastly, this part of the ocean dominates major SLOC of the Indian Ocean. Thus, India has to reconcile its domestic compulsions, its regional responsibilities as also its international obligations to chalk out a policy that would ensure maximum maritime security while simultaneously keeping in mind the possibility that India is not accused of having hegemonic designs over this zone. As events have unfolded over the decades, this was no easy task.

Sri Lanka: Boundary agreements between India and Sri Lanka, that also helped to fix the trijunction between India, Sri Lanka and the Maldives, was a triumph of diplomacy. While India conceded to Sri Lanka the right over Kachchativu island, Sri Lanka conceded to India the right of Indian fishermen to visit the island to dry their nets as well as to visit the shrine on that island. Sri Lanka also did not insist upon using that island as a base to delimit its territorial sea boundary. The maritime boundary between the two states by and large followed the median line principle and skirted the island of Kachchativu by about half a mile. This agreement of 1974 paved the way for the second agreement of 1976 that extended the lines further into the sea up to the limit of EEZ. This triumph of diplomacy and a major step towards confidence building between India and Sri Lanka subsequently became an issue of domestic politics in Tamil Nadu and several politicians as also scholars even accused the Central Government of surrendering the interests of the people of Tamil Nadu.

Two developments since 1974 were responsible for this perçeption. The one was the ever increasing number of medium size mechanised fishing craft or trawlers that were being encouraged to operate in the narrow Palk Straits and the adjoining Gulf of Manar. They gradually replaced the small indigenous fishing boats and kattumaran that had been traditionally used for fishing in that area. That led to over exploitation of limited fishery resources in the Indian waters thereby tempting Indian fishermen to intrude into Sri Lankan waters for a better catch.

Sri Lanka Navy would otherwise also have challenged that action but the question of poaching by Indian fishermen got mixed up with cross-border illicit trade as also activities of Sri Lankan Tamil militants and operations by Sri Lanka Navy to curb those activities. In that process Sri Lanka's naval personnel would intercept and detain Tamil Nadu fishermen found fishing in Sri Lankan waters and some times even open fire believing them to be Sea Tigers.

Public opinion in Tamil Nadu was often incited by interested parties and some responsible Tamil Nadu politicians even demanded that India should acquire the island of Kachchativu on perpetual lease. Even if Sri Lanka agrees to that demand it will not solve the problem unless Indians are also allowed to fish in Sri Lanka's territorial waters beyond that island. Given the presence of the LTTE and the Sea Tigers in these waters such a demand is not even feasible. Even if Sri Lanka concedes that demand one doubts if the LTTE will approve of it. Will Indian Navy and the Coast Guard be sent into Sri Lanka's territorial waters to protect Indian fishermen there?

If India now backs out of a negotiated bi-lateral agreement it will not only lose face but also make the process of negotiating maritime boundary agreements with Pakistan and Bangladesh more difficult. India has still to negotiate continental-shelf boundaries with several states. Refutation of UNCLOS-III based agreement will cost India dear.

The real solution lies in gradually reducing the number of small and medium mechanised fishing boats, encouraging deep-sea fishing and to restore the ecological balance in these waters that has been distributed by over fishing for at least two decades. No government in Tamil Nadu can be expected to take such allegedly 'anti-people' steps. It is easier to blame the centre than to find a solution to the basic problem that is the result of unrestrained proliferation of small and medium mechanized fishing craft in these waters since mid-seventies. This backdrop is necessary to understand the constraints under which Indian maritime forces like the Navy, the Coast Guard, Tamil Nadu Police etc. have to work and coordinate their activities with the maritime forces of Sri Lanka.

It look some time for India and Sri Lanka to move away from their perceptions based upon mutual suspicion to one based upon shared understanding on the need for maritime cooperation in the light of challenges that Tamil militancy in Sri Lanka posed to territorial integrity and domestic stability of both the states. Once that was achieved steps were taken to move forward from an informal basis of cooperation to a formal agreement.

India-Sri Lanka Accord of July 29, 1987 among other things bound India to support Sri Lanka even militarily. Under Article 2.16 (b), Indian Navy and Coast Guard were obliged to support Sri Lanka Navy in preventing Tamil militant activities from affecting Sri Lanka. Article 2.16(c) stipulated that in the event the Government of Sri Lanka requested the Government of India for military assistance to implement these proposals (in the Accord) Government of India will cooperate by giving to the Government of Sri Lanka such military assistance as and when required. [1] That article was invoked by President Jayavardane with the result that the Indian Peace Keeping Force (IPKF) that was sent to Sri Lanka for peace keeping role was turned into a 'peace enforcement' force with disastrous consequences for all. Indian forces continued to battle those of the LTTE till the IPKF was finally withdrawn from Sri Lanka under domestic pressure in India in March 1990. The assassination of Rajiv Gandhi in May 21, 1991, introduced a new domestic angle to the entire issue. LTTE was declared by India as a terrorist organisation.

There is no report that either side has formally renounced the 1987 Accord, though no one refers to it after the withdrawal of the IPKF from Sri Lanka. There were reports that both countries were negotiating a new agreement on maritime cooperation. But none has been formally signed so far though there could be mutual understanding about the nature of this cooperation. Hence, until it is formally abrogated, the 1987 Accord, especially article 2.16 b and c, continue to be part of a legally binding bilateral agreement between the two countries; likely to be invoked by Sri Lanka in future.

That Accord also committed India to deport all Sri Lanka citizen who are found to be engaging in terrorist activities or advocating separation or secessionism. This can be treated as a *de facto* extradition treaty with no scope for India to provide political asylum even to moderate Tamil political activists. Such activists including those belonging to LTTE were, however, provided political asylum by several European states and allowed to operate against Sri Lanka from their soil. Some of these European states are even acting as mediators in the so-called peace process between the LTTE and the Government of Sri Lanka. Ever escalating violence by the LTTE has, however, prompted the European Union to declare LTTE as a banned organisation. It will have serious impact on the peace process as supported by European states and Japan.

Legalistic interpretation of India-Sri Lanka Accord of 1987 would term it as a bilateral defence cooperation treaty with political overtones. Under such an interpretation India is no longer a neutral party in what is basically an intra-Sri Lanka dispute. India's coercive action against Sri Lankan Tamil militants, therefore, needs to be analysed in that context. A legalistic view of the Accord could also mean that India and Sri Lanka have accorded a *de facto* status of belligerency to the Tamil militants of Sri Lanka, especially the LTTE; an issue of debate since May 2006.

The LTTE, because of its firm and effective control over a part of Sri Lanka, is claiming right of a belligerent and consequently seeking recognition of its so-called sovereignty not only over the land but also over the adjoining sea, and air space above it. No one has endorsed that status. LTTE is now termed as a non-state actor and, therefore, not entitled to the privileges of a state actor, including the right of belligerency. But, in the past under traditional international law even rebels, if they had established *de facto* control over a given territory, were accorded the status of belligerent.

Those who do not want to accord the status of belligerency to the LTTE have threatened to declare it as a terrorist organization. Will that mean an end to a 'negotiated' peace? Will it mean that negotiators will search for others amongst the Tamils who can claim to represent Sri Lanka's Tamil community? Will such a policy not lead to a new round of intra-Tamil civil war? European and Japanese can wash their hands off the affair. Can India do so, especially in the context of its endemic coalition polities in the centre as also in Tamil Nadu.

As seen in the context of 1987 Accord, Indian action *vis-à-vis* M.V. Ahat (or M.V. Ahata) takes a different shape. It was a small 400-ton merchant vessel registered in San Lorenso. It was reportedly carrying a shipment of arms and ammunition as also other provisions for the LTTE when it was sighted by Indian Coast Guard vessel Vivek on January 15, 1993. Its frequent change of course reportedly led the Coast Guard to keep an eye on it. It was also reported that Indians were tipped about that vessel. According to the *Asian Recorder*, February 5-11, 1993, the LTTE suspected the Tamil Ealam Liberation Front of informing Indians about it. LTTE reportedly massacred more than 200 of its cadre including its leader Sri Subaratnam. According to another source, a top LTTE leader Gopalaswamy Mahendarajah, *alias* Mahattaya, was suspected of it and was reportedly executed by the LTTE. [2]

It is not clear where the vessel was first sighted though the term 'Indian waters' is used. Vice-Admiral K.K. Kohli, the then Director-General of Coast Guard, is reported to have said that the Coast Guard vessel had sighted it off Point Calimore. As per newspaper reports, Coast Guard vessel Vivek sighted it on January 15 and probably kept an eye on it. INS Kirpan of the Indian Navy joined it on January 16. M.V. Ahat was asked to surrender. Satasivan Krishnakumar, *alias* Kittu, who was on board the vessel, refused. Reportedly, instead of surrendering, he managed to set fire to the vessel. While the crew jumped into the sea and were rescued, Kittu with other LTTE members on board went down with the ship.

The incident raised some controversy. Was the vessel in Indian waters or on the high seas? Did India have the right to intercept it or did the vessel have the right of innocent passage? These arguments become meaningless in the light of Article 2.16(b) of India-Sri Lanka Accord under which India was duty bound to prevent that ship from reaching Sri Lankan waters. Kittu and other LTTE members were given the option to surrender which they refused. According to Rohana Gunaratna, Kittu, who was the then head of the London-based LTTE International Secretariat, when challenged reportedly informed the Indian Navy that he was on a peace mission and requested that the Amnesty International or LTTE's Indian supporter Pazha Nedumaran be sought for mediation. According to Gunaratne, after the Indian Navy had towed the vessel from international waters to Indian territorial waters, Kittu told the Indian Navy not to board the vessel. When Indian Navy tried to board it he ordered the crew to jump and then destroyed the ship killing himself and LTTE crew members. [3] None of these details mean that India could not take action under the terms of the 1987 Accord. If Kittu was indeed on 'peace mission' he should have had no objection to surrendering to India because he had been earlier entrusted with an abortive peace mission in 1988.

Indian security forces, including the Navy and the Coast

Guard, became deeply involved in internal affairs of Sri Lanka after the signing of the India-Sri Lanka Accord to 1987. The Navy initiated Operation Pawan in support of IPKF. The IPKF was inducted on July 30, 1987. The deinduction process began in August 1989 and bulk of the forces were out of Sri Lanka by October 1989. [4] As long as the IPKF was stationed in Sri Lanka Indian Navy and the Coast Guard could operate even along the Sri Lanka coast. But that was not possible after the deinduction of the IPKF that was complete by March 24, 1990.

The truce between LTTE and Sri Lanka also broke down on June 11, 1990 leading to an influx of about two lakh refugees from Sri Lanka into India. With the deinduction of the IPKF the joint patrolling by the maritime forces of the international boundary also suffered a setback thereby encouraging incidents of smuggling and illegal entry of Sri Lankan nationals into India. Indian Navy and the Coast Guard resorted to intensified patrolling of the Palk Straits and along the coast line of India. Operation Tasha that began in April 1990 continue till today. Naval detachments were also setup at Rameshwarm and Nagapatnam to curb these illegal activities. [5]

It was necessary to restart the process of cooperation between the two sides to ensure greater maritime security. Two agreements were reportedly signed on March 1, 1993 during the Colombo visit of Indian External Affairs Minister Dinesh Singh. They provided for 'coordinated' naval patrolling in the Palk Straits to prevent smuggling or illegal arms trade as well as to prevent fishermen from straying into each other's territorial waters. [6] Rajesh Pilot, the then Minister of State for Internal Security, also said in Madras (Chennai) on February 1, 1994 that bilateral cooperation between security agencies of India (Tamil Nadu) and Sri Lanka was going on. It involved weekly security-related stocktaking meeting at the district level and a monthly meeting at federal and state level of intelligence, law enforcement and administrative departments. [7]

The events of April-May 2000 in northern part of Sri Lanka once again brought fresh anxiety to decision makers in India. The

LTTE in its steady advances towards the Jaffna Peninsula had succeeded, by inducting troops from the sea, in cutting off links between Sri Lanka's troops guarding the Elephant Pass and their bases further north thereby forcing them to evacuate the strategic area from where the LTTE could threaten Jaffna *via* land as also *via* the Jaffna lagoon. The situation was desperate. The fear of possible LTTE success caused exodus of Tamil refugees from Jaffna to India. Indian armed forces also discussed the eventuality of helping Sri Lanka in evacuating the trapped troops, if it became necessary, by air as also by sea. Reportedly the Navy was on 72-hour alert and two tank-landing ships (LST), a Kashin-class destroyer and a Khukri-class corvette were based in Chennai for deployment if needed.

The official response of the NDA government was more cautious. Shri L.K. Advani, the then Home Minister, ruled out the IPKF route. Jaswant Singh, the then Foreign Minister, said that India would provide humanitarian assistance if asked for. Indian role was also conditional upon ceasefire being agreed upon by the two parties. The military option was further constrained by a remark attributed to the then Tamil Nadu Chief Minister Karunanidhi in which he had suggested a Czechoslovakia-type solution for Sri Lanka. Prime Minister Atal Bihari Vajpayee rejected any such proposal. He said that Shree Karunanidhi might have made that comment in his personal capacity or was expressing the views of his party. Those were not the views of the Indian Government. [8]

The refusal of hardline leaders of Sri Lanka including important Buddhist clerics to concede regional autonomy demands of the Tamils kept the island in a state of high alert. Victory of Mahanida Rajapakse as the President of Sri Lanka in December 2005 and the appointment of Ratnagiri Wikramanayke as the new Prime Minister gave the impression that the rejectionist mindset among many of the Sinhala leaders had not changed. The JVP, an ally of the ruling group, also pursues a hardline policy *vis-à-vis* Tamils. To compound the matter further, internal divisions within LTTE were coming out into open. The so-called Karuna group broke off from the LTTE in 2004. The split led to further blood bath among the Tamils of Sri Lanka.

May 2006 witnessed three crucial interrelated developments. The one was the rapid escalation in violent confrontation between the LTTE and the Sri Lankan forces. Second was the demand that LTTE should be accorded the status of a belligerent and be allowed to exercise sovereign rights over the sea and its airspace near the coastal belt under its control. That was refused. Finally, LTTE directly challenged the Sri Lanka Monitoring Mission (SLMM), a body of Nordic Truce monitors that had been monitoring ceasefire since February 2002. LTTE boats attacked a Sri Lankan ship that was transporting troops and which had a SLMM monitor on board.

Consequently, LTTE began to face increasing pressure from its international supporters like the quartel of international donors, backing Sri Lanka peace process, comprising of USA, Europe, Japan and Norway. LTTE was warned of deeper isolation unless it ended violence and entered into negotiations. Increasingly, these acts of violence were being equated with acts of terrorism. Finally, Europe listed LTTE as a 'banned' organization (not a terrorist organisation). Thus, it was put under economic sanctions in Europe as also in USA. Also, its office in Paris that was used for political activities, would have to be closed. The breakaway faction of Karuna was also similarly warned.

Sri Lankan government also took steps to evolve a political package based upon national consensus. Main political parties agreed to discuss and give shape to a new power sharing offer to the LTTE. The first meeting of the multi-ethnic expert group on devolution of power and associated draft of a new constitution held its first meeting on June, 11, 2006. The only condition put forward by President Rajapakse was that sovereignty, unity and territorial integrity of Sri Lanka were not negotiable. The first reaction of the LTTE to the proposal was that the solution to the conflict should be based on the right of self-determination, thereby virtually rejecting the federal model. [9] Even if the diverse Sinhala parties and Tamil groups come to some consensus, LTTE's present stance does not promise peace for a long time to come.

Tamil-linked issues in Sri Lanka were and will continue to be influenced by domestic politics in India, particularly in Tamil Nadu. The Central Government in New Delhi is bound to come under increased pressure when ethnic conflict in Sri Lanka is forcefully projected in India. Sri Lanka's Tamil leaders and their Indian supporters are already active. Already V. Anandasangaree, President of Sri Lanka's Tamil United Liberation Front (TULF) has sought the intervention of Shree Karunanidhi in the resolution of the conflict and has requested him to visit Sri Lanka at the earliest. In a letter dated May 21, 2006, he is reported to have written, "As a matter of right, I seek your participation in solving our problem." [10] Shri Vaiko, (V. Gopalasamy) the General Secretary of the Marumalarchi Dravida Munnatra Kazhagam (MDMK), has urged the Central Government not to provide any military assistance to Sri Lanka, including sale of arms. He specifically mentioned the sale of radars to Sri Lankan Air Force. He also said that Sri Lankan Tamil refugees fleeing to India be provided all succour and solace. He also requested the Indian Prime Minister to give an opportunity to the Tamil MPs elected by the Tamil population to meet him so that they could explain the real situation. Their visit to Delhi was subsequently arranged in September 2006.

Fresh wave of fighting in Sri Lanka and the influx of Tamil refugees in Tamil Nadu has once again increased the pressure upon the government of Tamil Nadu as also upon the Central Government. On August 20, 2006, in an effort to reduce the tension India offered a devolution formula based upon Sarkaria Commission recommendation and federal principles. That evoked sharp adverse reaction from pro-LTTE groups in Tamil Nadu. On August 22, Vaiko reportedly warned that India should not entertain the idea of devolution of power on a federal basis. He said that India had no right to interfere in the internal affairs of Sri Lanka. He even warned of a 'Kashmir in South'. [11]

As noted, negotiations between India and Sri Lanka for

arriving at an acceptable formula for managing the growing challenges to maritime security in this sensitive zone have been dragging on since 2003. Even though termed as defence pact by the media this is in essence an exercise in defining the terms of reference that would not give an impression that Sri Lanka is succumbing to the demands of the big brother. As per Sri Lanka's Defence Secretary, Cyril Herath, the high level official teams from both sides had agreed on a common draft for defence cooperation that would include subjects like exchange of information and sharing of experience as well as enhanced training. The two countries would also work together in the field of marine surveillance to prevent illegal activities from disrupting bilateral ties. [12] The signing of the agreement was postponed till the final outcome of elections in both countries. There is no report that the 'draft' on cooperation has been finally converted into a formal treaty.

Security forces on both sides have been observing *de facto* cooperation in which their activities are restricted to their respective territorial waters. According to Vice-Admiral Suresh Mehta, the then Flag Officer Commanding-in-Chief of the Eastern Naval Command in Visakhapatnam (and the current Chief of the Naval Staff), both sides exchange information on the location of their vessels and share details of any suspicious activity in the region. The aim is to ensure that there is no instance of firing at genuine fishermen and also that criminals do not travel freely between the two countries. He also added that there was no proposal to upgrade the present arrangement of coordinated patrolling to joint patrolling. [13] As per press reports, officers of both navies met in Chennai in February 2006 to work out modalities for 'coordinated patrolling' along their international maritime boundary. The two navies had already commenced such exercises about six months ago. [14]

To meet the threat from the LTTE, Sri Lanka Navy has been acquiring warships from divergent sources ranging from China to France and Israel. Most of these ships are small and medium size fast attack craft with limited endurance and firepower. It acquired only one Sukanya-class large patrol vessel along with a light helicopter from India. It had the option for another such vessel but it did not exercise it. Instead, it acquired two Saar-class missile armed small corvette size ships from Israel. Thus, ships of Sri Lanka's Navy have high agility but inadequate firepower or long-range endurance to confront the Sea Tigers in their 'home' waters.

Though Sri Lanka and India are next door neighbours and participate in multilateral naval meet like the Milan they had not conducted joint naval exercise till recently. Only in 2004 did Sri Lanka Navy and the Indian Coast Guard conduct a joint exercise-Operation Sirius - in the southern coast of Sri Lanka. The navies of the two states conducted their first three-day joint naval exercise off Colombo in mid-December 2005. INS Sukanya and INS Kirpan exercised with three ships of Sri Lanka Navy in the first SLINEX (Sri Lanka, India Naval Exercise). [15] In this exercise named Operation Eksath ships of both the states participated in SAR, anti-piracy and pollution control exercises. Thus, emphasis was on SLOC protection rather than bilateral issue of combating cross border terrorism.

It is very important that India and Sri Lanka reach an agreement on monitoring and if necessary acting decisively in maintaining maritime security in the waters around Sri Lanka, the Maldives and South India for two other reasons. This SLOC would become increasingly important once the Sethu Samudram project is completed. The other is the role that the Maldives, due to its strategic location in North Central Indian Ocean, is destined to play in the overall maritime security of the region.

The Maldives: India has long and intimate contacts with the Maldives. Operation Cactus was launched during the first week of November 1988, when Indian Government airlifted troops to Male to thwart the coup attempt by about 300 Tamil mercenaries belonging to the PLOTE of Sri Lanka who had reached Male in fishing boats in the early hours of November 3, 1988. India also dispatched naval vessels, INS Betwa and INS Godavari, and MR aircraft to track and intercept merchant vessel MV Progress Light that had been hijacked by mercenaries. That ship was intercepted about 150 km off Sri Lanka's coast and hostages were rescued though the ship could not be saved.

India's quick response within twenty-four hours of the call for support by President Mamoon Abdel Gayoom symbolized that relationship as also concern. The fact that great powers that had been criticising India for having hegemonic designs in the region had no objection to India's response also proved that they had come to realize the benign role that India's maritime capability and limited power projection can play in maintaining peace and stability in this strategically sensitive zone.

India and the Maldives have reached a deep understanding on the need for cooperation and though no formal agreement has been signed security forces of both countries interact regularly to strengthen their bonds of mutual cooperation. Their annual maritime joint exercise *Dosti* that has been held since mid-nineties is a symbol of that cooperation. The Coast Guard of the Maldives also maintains close contacts with Indian Coast Guard and the Indian Navy.

Islands of the Maldives have emerged as of great strategic significance for India since they overlook major East-West SLOC in the Central Indian Ocean Region. The *Defence News*, April 24, 2006, quoted a source in the Ministry of Defence that India and the Maldives have decided to develop a 'privileged partnership'. One possible reason could be the growing Chinese presence there. In 1999, Maldives had leased the island of Marao to China for maritime traffic management. The facility is also reportedly used by the Chinese to monitor movement of Indian and American warships in the Indian Ocean. Though India has built strong security- related relationship with the Republic of Maldives, the Defence Ministry source said that there was no plan to establish a base there. [16]

India, on the request of the Government of the Maldives, gifted to it a fast attack craft. INS Tillanchang was built by the Goa Shipyard Ltd. for the Indian Navy and was operating in the Andaman-Nicobar area for the past five years. It is a very sophisticated vessel for surveillance and interception. Reverse osmosis process provides for drinking water on board the vessel. Also, adequate food and fuel capacity ensures a long range operation of about 3,600 km or a long loiter time. The vessel also has two high speed boats on board and can induct and deinduct 35 personnel who can operate as Special Force. Indian Navy has agreed to maintain the ship in its lifetime. The vessel can foil attempts at illegal fishing in EEZ, as also curb acts of terrorism. Its capacity to project force, though in small number, also enables it to be used to 'control' far-off places in the long chain of islands that constitutes the Republic of Maldives.

This gesture of good will has generated certain uneasiness especially among the 'opposition' groups in that country. The Maldives is already under pressure from the Commonwealth for ensuring more transparent democracy. Presidential elections are due in 2008 and there are demands for electoral reforms. Ibrahim Hussain Zaki, Vice-President of Maldive's Democratic Party, in an interview to *The Hindu* on the eve of the handing over of Indian ship INS Tillanchang, asked India to play a more active role in ushering in democracy rather than strengthening the hands of a 'dictator'. He was also critical of India's defence-related support to the regime of President Gayoom. He said that the Indian fast attack craft was employed to arrest opponents in the south who were brought to Male and imprisoned. [17]

It was also hinted that the present regime was trying to play the China card and was warming up to the Chinese so as to replace Indians. In that case it could also linkup with Pakistan thereby providing a much needed strategic link up between China and Pakistan in the Indian Ocean. India ought to learn from USA's experience. Gifted arms are often used to strengthen the ruler against the opposition with the result that people begin to equate the foreign supporter with the regime; something that India needs to avoid in its maritime diplomacy in island republics.

The Bay of Bengal Zone: India's maritime neighbourhood in its eastern zone stretches from the Bay of Bengal to South China Sea and even beyond and includes the Andaman Sea and the Malacca Straits. India's policy of promoting maritime cooperation in this zone can be analysed at bilateral as also multilateral or regional level. India's extent of bilateral cooperation varies from country to country depending upon the past experience as also their individual approach to the broader question of maritime cooperation *per se*.

INDIA'S LAND-SEA PARTNERS

Bangladesh: India's efforts at cooperation with Bangladesh is constrained by long term negative political relations at bilateral level, failure to resolve the maritime boundary dispute as also Bangladesh's heavy dependence upon China for its military equipment, particularly for its Navy. Bangladesh claimed in 1974 that its baseline for delimiting maritime boundary be based at ten fathom depth as against the low water mark as proposed under the terms of UNCLOS-III. Bangladesh also laid claims to the New Moore Island which emerged in early 1970s on a previously charted sand bank in the estuary of Haribhanga, Jamuna and Raimangal that divides India and Bangladesh. The island lies about five kilometres from the Indian shore and about seven kilometres from that of Bangladesh. Deep water channel separates it from the Bangladesh. Tension escalated in 1981-82. India stationed BSF personnel there under Operation Starling. Indian Navy also deployed its forces to neutralize any possible misadventure on the part of Bangladesh. Tension has diffused over the years though the maritime boundary dispute still remains unresolved.

India-Bangladesh relations are showing a positive sign now. Bangladesh has begun participating in the Milan naval meet in Port Blair. Also, Bangladesh had no hesitation in seeking Indian expertise in 2001 in locating about 250 boxes of arms and ammunition that were dumped in its waters near Chitagong by smugglers. INS Sandhyak helped to locate them. [18]

Myanmar: Regional powers as well as the West had for long ignored the regime of Myanmar because of its human rights violations. That isolation was broken by China in 1985. China saw Myanmar as a land route connecting South-West China to the

Bay of Bengal as well as a potential partner if it decided to operate in the Indian Ocean Region. China's dependence upon oil import at that time was insignificant. It grew only after 2000. However, by 1992 the two countries had come close. According to William Ashton, China had supplied to Myanmar about US$ 1.4 billion worth of arms and military equipment. That included jet fighters, transport aircraft, patrol boats, armour, trucks, small arms and ammunition as well as radars and communication equipment. Thus, China strengthened the regime *vis-à-vis* the armed opposition groups.

Chinese were also reported to be helping Myanmar modernize and expand ports and naval base facilities at Mergui near the Thai horder, Moulmein near Rangoon, and Kyankpyu and Akyab in the Arakan Coast. There were reports of China building a jetty at the Coco Island and a 50 meter antennae tower reportedly to monitor missile testing by India as also to monitor various electronic signals in the zone. Myanmar's Intelligence Chief, Major-General Khin Nyunt, during his visit to India in October 1994, denied that allegation. There were also unconfirmed reports that China would build a deep water port on Hainggui Island at the mouth of the Bassein River. Experts, however, warn that the site is not suitable for a deep water port. [19] One is not sure how much the Chinese have succeeded in turning these facilities into their potential bases but these radars, naval bases and ports have greatly helped Myanmar in dominating its EEZ and continental-shelf and reduced illegal fishing in those waters.

For a long time India has shunned contacts with Myanmar; a next-door land and maritime neighbour. That was in response to international environment that was adversely responding to the denial of democracy and human rights by the military-led ruling elite in Myanmar. Three factors helped India in altering its stance. The one was the gradual change in the ASEAN states' perception of Myanmar. Myanmar came closer to the ASEAN. It was accepted as a member of regional bodies like the ASEAN, BIMST-EC and Mekong-Ganga Cooperation. The other was the desire to balance China's growing influence in Myanmar that was facilitated by international isolation imposed upon Myanmar. Chinese presence was seen as posing a long-term threat to India. Finally, Indo-Myanmar cooperation was seen as crucial in the context of resolving the threat posed by militancy in the North-East. Hence, series of steps were taken after 1992-93 that paved the way for growing cooperation between India and Myanmar. The delimination of the bilateral maritime boundary in 1987 and the finalization of the trijunction between India, Myanmar and Thailand in October 1993 settled a long-drawn dispute.

Chinese policy of developing a North-South corridor connecting China to the Bay of Bengal *via* Myanmar as also Chinese help in modernising and building three ports/bases as also radar sites rang alarm bells in India. These moves coincided with large-scale arms transfer to Myanmar that included sixteen large offshore patrol craft. An impression was created that China was investing in these facilities with a view to using them when its Navy would project its power in the Indian Ocean Region. If China did have that use in mind it would have concentrated upon building one large base/port, like the one being built in Gwader in the Makaran coast of Pakistan, rather than three relatively disjointed, from the Chinese point of view, ports or bases that serve the interests of Myanmar more effectively.

The radar base at the Coco Island near the Andamans was termed as a post from where Chinese would monitor missile tests of India. It is difficult to verify or negate these claims because those who make them provide no real evidence about the capability of the Chinese instruments that are reportedly installed there or the presence of Chinese experts manning them.

One can explain these radars and their location in the context of Myanmar's policy to keep its vast EEZ and continental-shelf under surveillance. Myanmar has been complaining since long that outsiders have been poaching in its EEZ. Myanmar is also keen to halt the transfer of men and material including weapons to its own insurgents. In the absence of maritime reconnaissance aircraft carefully sited radars provide that much needed surveillance facility.

That policy also explains the type of ships it acquired from China. China sold Myanmar six Houxin-class and ten Hainen-class large patrol craft of about 400 tons each. While the Hainen-class ships are armed with four 57 mm guns each, the Hauxin-class ships carry, beside four 37 mm guns, four short range (40 km) YJ-1 (C-801) anti-ship missiles. These ships would not only have supplemented or even replaced many of its WW II vintage patrol vessels but would also have proved useful in monitoring its EEZ. The only point of incongruity is the arming of the Hauxin-class patrol boats with short-range anti-ships missiles. Sri Lanka's two Saar-class boats acquired from Israel are also armed with such short-range anti-ship missiles. Since one does not threaten fishing boats with missiles, the only rational for their presence is the possibility of an encounter with an armed boat used by insurgents. Sri Lanka's Saar-class boats too could be so used though there is no report of their use so far. These missiles pose practically no real threat to India. Bangladesh Navy and Pakistan Navy have more sophisticated long-range missiles.

Because of the combination of factors discussed above India initiated the move in 1992-93 to develop cooperative relationship with Myanmar on bilateral level. [20] Official level talks in Delhi and Rangoon in the nineties paved the way for formal bilateral exchanges after 2000. They began with the visit of General Maung Aye in November 2000. It was followed by the visit of Shri Jashwant Singh to Myanmar in February 2001 to inaugurate Tamu-Kalemyo-Kalewa road as also the Remote Sensing Data Processing Centre. The upgradation of that 160-km long road by India's Border Road Organization had started in 1997. There are also proposals to connect India and Myanmar by road *via* Mizoram.

There was also a conscious attempt to open up the North-Eastern part of India to the Bay of Bengal *via* Myanmar. Thus, India too was utilizing the geographical advantages of Myanmar to link its isolated land frontier in the North-East to the sea. India agreed in 2001 to carry out the first phase of the project consisting of upgrading of the port of Sittwe, improving the navigability of

River Kaladan up to Kaletwa and to develop a modern highway from Kaletwa to Indo-Myanmar border up to the state of Mizoram. Progress on these projects has been slow. Hopefully, visit of President Abdul Kalam in March 2006 will help to expedite that.

Another Indian delegation visited Myanmar in July 2001 for site-assessment for the development of a deep sea port at Kyaukphu. [21] These attempts by India to reach the Bay of Bengal *via* Myanmar laid the foundation for long term interaction between the two countries. These were further cemented by the acquisition by ONGC-Videsh Nigan and GAIL of 20 per cent and 10 per cent shares respectively in A-1 Block off the Rakhine coast. India also proposes to build a pipeline to acquire natural gas from Myanmar.

Thailand is emerging as a third partner in this regional cooperation. A meeting held in 2002 under the Mekong-Ganga Cooperation proposed the construction of a highway that would connect Morch in India to Mae Sol in Thailand *via* Began in Myanmar, as well as a highway from Kanchanbauri in Thailand to the Dawei Port in Myanmar as also shipping links from there to Indian ports. [22]

MALACCA STRAITS PARTNERS

Though India has been able to develop bilateral cooperation with states bordering the Malacca Straits these relations are not uniform in nature. India's maritime security cooperation with Singapore is more intimate as compared to that with Indonesia, Thailand or Malaysia.

Singapore: India - Singapore maritime security cooperation needs to be understood in the context of following interrelated variables. Singapore is a small but trade and commerce dependent state. It is strategically located at the southern (and narrower) end of the Malacca Straits and, thus, controls it in conjunction with Indonesia on the other side. It is very sensitive to threats from piracy and armed robbery. That fear has been further compounded by the possible threat from radical Islamic groups that are active in South-East Asia from the Philippines to Indonesia.

Singapore was always close to the West. Its significance has increased greatly in the post- Cold War period. Singapore has become a *de facto* ally and a port of call for American warships that operate between the Pacific Ocean and the Indian Ocean. This relationship has been further strengthened after its Changi dockyard was opened for use by American aircraft carriers and other ships of the US Navy. Indian Navy vessel had escorted so-called 'high value' US ships from Singapore to the Bay of Bengal in 2001 - 2002.

Partly because of Singapore's close political and military ties with the West and partly because of its relatively strong financial base, Singapore has been able to acquire a very credible mix of aircraft and warships that not only enables it to monitor the neighbourhood but also to ensure security in that zone. It operates E-2C Hawkeye AEW aircraft that are capable of monitoring South China Sea. They also have a limited ASW capability. Singapore Navy has several medium patrol vesseis that are armed with anti-ship missiles and/ or torpedos. Singapore has plans to acquire six Formidable - class (La Fayette) frigates from France that are optimised for ASW operations.

India - Singapore cooperation also reveals India's desire to extend its maritime security reach up to South China Sea if not beyond. This is reflected in the zones of their joint naval exercises and the main strategic thrust of these exercises. Joint naval exercises, that began by about 1993, gradually enlarged their scope of operation from the usual SAR, anti-piracy and pollution control to ASW operations. In 2003, in the joint naval exercise held off Kochi one of the three anti-submarine naval vessels of Singapore Navy launched a torpedo at INS Vela, a F-class submarine from India. Though it was an old Russian submarine but the ASW exercise gave the Singapore Navy a real demonstration of ASW operations. Similar ASW exercise was held off Kochi in March 2004.

While most of these joint exercises, also termed as the Lion King series, were held in the Indian waters the joint exercise of

2005, the Singapore-India Maritime Bilateral Exercise (SIMBEX -05), was held in South China Sea. Anti piracy and ASW operations were the high points of that exercise. According to Rear-Admiral Sunil K. Damle, Flag Officer Commanding, Indian Navy, Eastern Fleet, the exercise in East Asia meant that India was showing its presence there so that Indian ships, ships flying the Indian flag, have a feeling of security while on the high seas. [23] SIMBEX - 06 was held in March 2006 off the coast of Visakhapatnam. India - Singapore military related cooperation has extended beyond its maritime context. Under a new formula, land forces of Singapore will exercise on the Indian soil. Its armour will exercise in central India at Babina while its artillery will do the same at Deolali.

Indonesia: Though India's relations with other littoral state of the Malacca Straits are equally cordial yet the degree and level of interaction in terms of cooperation in areas of maritime security are on a lower key as compared to that with Singapore. Among the three states, Indonesia is closer to India, partly because of the close proximity of Sumatra to the Andaman-Nicobar Islands. The province of Aceh in North Sumatra has long been a base of radical Islamic movement challenging the central government in Jakarta. It must also be kept in mind that Indonesia is an archipelagic state spread over a large area with about 17,000 islands. Beside the question of threat of insurgency in some of these outlaying islands, Indonesia has also to look after its security concerns in South China Sea as also in the Timor Sea. Thus, India-Indonesia cooperation should be seen in the context of the wider maritime challenges faced by Jakarta as also the new threat of radical Islamic militancy at home.

Unlike Singapore, Indonesia is not a rich state and cannot afford to build a strong maritime defence capability. Most of its ships are in need of replacement. Its air-borne maritime reconnaissance capability is also limited. Despite these constraints bilateral cooperation is growing over the years. Two illustrations help to underline the mutual trust and understanding. Indian Navy was requested by Indonesia to conduct hydrographic survey of the waters off Sabang. That was conducted by survey vessel INS Jamuna in April-May 2001. [24] The other is the decision to conduct coordinated patrol in adjoining waters. The fifth coordinated patrol (CORPAT) between Indian and Indonesian naval vessels was conducted along their international maritime boundary line in the Andaman Sea during September 2005. According to Admiral Arun Prakash, "Fears of the insurgency in the troubled province of Aceh spilling over has recently prompted both countries to undertake joint naval patrols in the ANC's area of responsibility." [25] That area of responsibility of ANC, on the map at least, covers waters adjoining both sides of the northern parts of Sumatra.

Thailand and Malaysia: India's relations with Thailand and Malaysia also benefited from the 'Look East' policy initiated by Narasimha Rao in 1993 and carried forward by the successive governments. As noted in the context of Myanmar, Thailand is emerging as an important partner in India's forward policy *vis-à-vis* South - East Asia; *via* land as also *via* sea. Thailand is deeply interested in maritime security of the Malacca Straits in the context of piracy as also illegal trafficking in arms and drugs. Thai ports along the Malacca Straits are often linked to trafficking of men and material for the LTTE as also for several insurgent groups in India, Bangladesh and Myanmar. It was reported in 1997 that patrol boat of the Thai Navy had intercepted a 16-metre boat after a chase off the Thai port of Ranong. Though some arms were dumped into the sea during the chase, Thai officials succeeded in confiscating about two tons of weapons and ammunition. They included two RPG launchers, two RCL guns, 20 assault rifles, M-79 granade launchers and more than 10,000 rounds of ammunition. Four persons reportedly belonging to Manipur Revolutionary People's Front and six crew members from the Arakan region of Myanmar were apprehended. The boat was heading towards Cox's Bazar in Bangladesh. [26]

Thailand is also worried about the radical Islamic movements in its southern frontier bordering Malaysia. This area is also opposite the Indonesian Province of Aceh across the Malacca

Straits which is also facing similar problem. The increase in radical Islamic militancy in South-East Asia has also enhanced the threat of maritime terrorism.

Many of these considerations have helped to foster close maritime security linkages between India and Thailand. In that context the visit by Thai Prime Minister, Dr. Thaksin Shinawatre, to India in November 2001 was a major milestone. Discussions included cooperation on matters relating to international terrorism, drug trafficking, smuggling as also security cooperation. [27] MoU was signed in May 2005 in Bangkok between Admiral Arun Prakash and Admiral Sampop Amrapala. The focus was on joint maritime patrol to prevent piracy and arms smuggling. [28] The two countries held their inaugural CORPAT along their maritime boundary line between September 15-23, 2005.

South China Sea: India has very old friendly ties with Vietnam. When India began to implement its 'Look East' policy, it looked at Vietnam as a reliable partner. Vietnam is also apprehensive of the growing Chinese maritime influence in South China Sea. Relations between India and Vietnam in the field of maritime security were highlighted by India's Defence Minister George Fernandes. While commissioning INS Brahmaputra in April 2000, he said that Indian Navy has an interest in the ocean space extending from the north of the Arabian Sea to South China Sea. He added that Japan and Vietnam were emerging as India's key strategic partners for countering piracy from the Indian waters to the South China Sea. George Fernandes had also visited Vietnam during that period. It was reported that the two countries had decided to work together to protect the commercial highway. [29]

Vietnam's Navy comprises of old ex-Soviet vessels. It was reported that the Indian Navy donated the entire inventory of its spares of the Osa missile boats and the Petya -class frigates to the Vietnam Navy. [30] Indian Navy no longer uses the Osa or the Petya. Vessels of the Indian Coast Guard, on their visits for joint exercise with their counterpart in Japan have already initiated the move towards bilateral cooperation in maritime security with Vietnam. Indian Coast Guard also developed bilateral contacts with its counterpart in the Philippines. Ships of the Indian Coast Guard visit ports in the Philippines during their visit to Japan.

While India has succeeded in widening the area of bilateral cooperation it still has to cover some distance before it becomes a part of active multilateral regional partnership in maritime security. That is still restricted among the littoral states of the Malacca Straits proper; Singapore, Malaysia and Indonesia. Even these three states of the Malacca Straits have only 'coordinated' their patrolling in their respective territorial waters to check piracy and other illegal maritime activities. In that context the bilateral cooperation between Indonesia and Singapore to closely monitor the narrow waters of the Malacca Straits near Singapore has had fruitful results. According to Col. Kevin Santa Maria, Commander of the Coastal Command of the Singapore Navy, that had drastically reduced the number of incidents of armed robbery in that area. [31] While such a 'coordinated' patrol can prove useful in curbing crime in territorial waters of the neighbouring state it will remain inadequate in the absence of some arrangement for coordination on the right of hot pursuit. Otherwise a criminal can dodge pursuit by trespassing into territorial waters of another state. There are no reports that bilateral or multilateral agreement on overcoming this legal constraint has been reached so far.

Despite India's overtly expressed desire to participate in joint/coordinated patrol in the Malacca Straits India has not been invited to join in this multilateral venture. Foreign Minister Natwar Singh, while attending the ASEAN Plus 3 Meeting and ASEAN Regional Forum in Jakarta in July 2005 had expressed India's willingness to provide security in the Malacca Straits. Admiral Arun Prakash had also expressed similar desire if a specific request was received from South-East Asian countries. [32]

One possible reason why Indonesia and Malaysia are reluctant to collaborate in widening international participation in maritime security of the Malacca Straits is their desire to keep USA and

Japan out of it, largely due to the fear of possible adverse domestic impact and fear of jehadi backlash. USA's policy of equating regional maritime security initiative (RMSI) with proliferation security initiation (PSI) and link it with overt US involvement in this sensitive region probably proved to be counter productive. It was expected that USA's role in the relief operations after the tsunami might bring USA and Indonesia closer. It did not.

USA and Japan are also trying to enhance their cooperation with littoral states of the Malacca Straits through their efforts at enhancing their capacity to monitor the SLOC and counter threat posed by non-state actors. International Maritime Organization had held a meeting in Jakarta in September 2005 in that context. Another meeting followed in February 2006, reportedly under US initiative. These efforts aimed at a review of appropriate burden sharing interoperability, information sharing, technical assistance, training and exercises in the context of counter-terrorism. The focus was on how user states can provide help to littoral states.

Though India is acceptable to ASEAN states, they will still hesitate to involve India since many responsible officials in India are overtly justifying India's role not only in the context of curbing threats from non-state actors but also as a long-term check on China's maritime role in the Indian Ocean Region. Possibly, some of the ASEAN members may not like to see their maritime area as a potential zone of Sino-Indian rivalry with India backed by USA and Japan.

The Milan: India has succeeded in carving out a place for itself in the context of regional cooperation by initiating a biannual joint naval meet, the Milan, since 1995. The fact that India could organize such a meet was itself a proof that India had overcome the earlier 'negative' image that it was a power aiming at establishing its hegemony over the neighbours. The Milan started on a low key. In 1995, there were only five warships from India, Indonesia, Singapore, Sri Lanka and Thailand. In 1997, Bangladesh and Malaysia joined it. Number of warships participating in it rose to 17. Myanmar had agreed to participate but withdraw for the time being. [33] The fifth Milan was held in January 2006. Warships from Bangladesh, Indonesia, Malaysia, Myanmar, Singapore, Sri Lanka and Thailand participated along with those from India. Australia sent a delegation. The Milan, which has been held periodically, has broken the self imposed isolation among the maritime forces of this region. It has also proved that regional powers can coordinate their maritime activities without the 'supervision' of great powers. It has also proved that given the political will regional maritime cooperation can become a feasible proposition even without the framework of a formal alliance like the NATO.

Joint Andaman-Nicobar Command (ANC): Role of the island chain of the Andaman and the Nicobar cannot be ignored in the context of India's Look East policy. The British, in the over confidence of their naval power, had ignored that geostrategic fact which left them with no backup after the loss of Singapore to Japan in World War II. Trincomalee, to which the British Navy retreated, was never developed as a strong naval base before World War II. The same mentality prevailed in India at least during the early years of independence when India's maritime strategy was being formulated by British officers seconded from the Royal Navy to serve the interest of the British Commonwealth.

It needed the 1962 War and the possible threat of Chinese submarines operating in Indian waters to jolt decision makers in India to look beyond the traditional mindset of Andaman as the *Kalapani.* Attention at last was paid to the Andaman and the Nicobar group in the context of maritime security. President Sukarno's new found love for Pakistan as also attempt to claim some islands of the Nicobar group at that time also added to the urgency of asserting visible naval presence there.

A Resident Naval Officers' Organization was setup at Port Blair with the necessary transport and communication facilities. It was named INS Jarawa and commissioned on February 15, 1964. A naval garrison, with facilities for moving to various islands on patrol, was also stationed. [34] There were proposals for developing fuelling facilities and construction of a jetty for naval vessels at Port Blair. Lack of funds as also focus on land frontier were probably main constraints.

Andaman - Nicobar group got a new boost in the context of provisions of UNCLOS - III. Though the land area of about 573 islands, of whom only 38 are inhabited, is only 8,300 sq km., these islands have an EEZ of about 300,000 sq. km., which is almost thirty per cent of the total EEZ of India. These islands also have a large continental-shelf. Thus, fishery resources as also resources in the continental-shelf that could include oil and gas deposits have added to the economic potential of these islands. Over the years, not only the Navy but also the newly formed Coast Guard began to expand their activities in these waters. Threat of illegal fishing in these waters as also of illegal migration provided the incentive for developing facilities in this area.

Unfortunately, India's naval modernization and expansion especially the acquisition of submarines, modified Kashin - class destroyers and long-range MR/ASW aircraft from USSR and the proposal to upgrade facilities in these islands were projected as evidence of India's hegemonic intensions in the region. For political reasons, India had to retain a low posture since antagonizing regional powers of South-East Asia would have been counterproductive.

The end of the Cold War helped India to overcome some of these misapprehensions. Slowly, India came to be accepted as a cooperative regional power. That not only helped India to build bridges of understanding with regional powers but also removed the political constraints on strengthening Andaman and Nicobar group as India's major outposts in its Look East policy. The result was the setting up of the Joint Andaman and Nicobar Command.

This step has to be analysed from two complementary points of view. The one is the need to strengthen military capability in the region in the context of India's overall maritime security framework. The other is the experiment in evolving a joint command comprising of all elements involved in the process; the Navy, the Coast Guard, the Army and the Air force.

No one can dispute the geostrategic advantages of further strengthening the security around these islands. The chain of islands stretches about 450 n. miles. The 145 km wide ten degree channel separates the Andaman and the Nicobar group of islands. The important six degree channel, a major sea route, is dominated by the Nicobar group. Although these islands are about 700-750 n. miles from Chennai, Visakhapatnam or Kolkata, they are almost next door neighbours of the ASEAN states in the region. Though the mainland of Myanmar is 170 n. miles away, the nearest island of Coco is only 22 n. miles to the north. The northern tip of Sumatra is 90 n. miles from the Indira Point in Nicobar. Thai coast is 270 n. miles and Malaysian coast 420 n. miles away. Besides, these islands form the western boundary of the Andaman Sea that links the Malacca Straits with the Bay of Bengal.

As noted, ANC is an experiment in operational aspect of inter-services integration and provisions have been made to make it function smoothly. [35] There are also proposals for major military expansion in the Andaman and Nicobar islands. They include construction of three new air bases to add to the one existing at present, enhancing Coast Guard's capability and to strengthen its existing infrastructure. Vice-Admiral Arun Kumar Singh, Commander-in-Chief ANC, said that there existed a 3,000 feet World War II runway in Kamorta island which would be developed. Two other air bases will be built at Diglipur and Campbell Bay by lengthening the existing small air strips so that they can handle large transport aircraft as also fighters. [36] There is no doubt that over the years the ANC will become an effective frontline outpost of maritime security of the subcontinent, an important sentinal guarding the major SLOC of the Indian Ocean and a focal point of India's maritime cooperation with its eastern maritime neighbours.

The Arabian Sea Zone: While India's Look East policy has been promoted since the nineties the fact was never ignored that India has vital strategic interests in the Arabian Sea zone that includes the natural maritime extensions like the Persian Gulf and the Bab al- Mandeb area. These strategic interests are based upon long historical and civilizational contacts, fast growing trade, energy security and the welfare of large number of Indians working in the region, especially in the GCC countries. This is beside the role, even an obligation, as a major regional power to help secure SLOCs that traverse this zone.

India's dependence upon this zone for its energy security needs no elaboration. As India's energy demand grows India's import of oil, LNG and gas from this region will also increase. According to the statement made by Minister of State in the Ministry of Overseas Indian Affairs, Sri Jagdish Tytler, in the Parliament on August 3, 2005, there are an estimated 3.7 million Indians working in various countries of the Gulf. [37] India's trade (non-oil and gas) with this region is also increasingly rapidly.

Though India has vital strategic interests in this zone yet it has not been able to develop as close bilateral and multilateral structures of cooperation as it has succeed in the Bay of Bengal and the North Central Indian Ocean zones. One can give two main reasons for this. The first is the US argument that its relations with India be considered primarily in the context of the Seventh Fleet's zone of influence and not that of the CENTCOM and the Fifth Fleet. That effectively bars India from intruding into an area of CENTCOM preserve. That also leaves its negative imprint upon India's attempt to improve bilateral and multilateral relations with the GCC members in the context of maritime cooperation. The second reason is long-term adversarial relationship between India and Pakistan that also negatively affects India's efforts to come closer to maritime neighbours beyond Pakistan in the Persian Gulf; Iran and the GCC states.

Pakistan: There is no need to dwell upon the causes that are responsible for adversarial relations between India and Pakistan. As far as their maritime relations are concerned they get reflected in their approach to the question of maritime boundary. The focus of this controversy is the point from where the baseline should be drawn to determine the internal waters as also the territorial sea, the EEZ and the continental-shelf of both the states.

Several scholarly articles have discussed in details points of view of India and Pakistan on this subject. [38] Both states offer different legal interpretation on delimitation of their respective maritime boundary. Pakistan wants the boundary in the Sir Creek to be on the eastern bank of the creek while India insists upon applying the thalweg line principle in that area. Beyond that, into the sea, Pakistan reportedly wants to apply the principle of equity while India advocates application of equidistance formula for delimiting the EEZ and the continental-shelf.

Pakistan aims at acquiring a larger share in these adjoining waters and sub-soil thereof. Negotiations have been going on for years. It was reported that in March 2006 both sides had agreed to conduct a joint survey of the Sir Creek as a first step towards finding a solution to the problem. The disputed area is not only rich in acquatic resources but the sub-soil is also reported to be rich in oil and gas. Pakistan has been drilling in the adjoining area since long hoping to find these sub-soil energy resources. Despite drilling in several places there is as yet no report of large viable deposits of oil or gas. But hopes have not been given up.

Unresolved maritime boundary has created problems for the fishing community on both sides. Fishermen from both sides cross the disputed maritime frontier and are sometimes apprehended by the Indian Coast Guard or the Pakistan Maritime Security Agency. Their boats are impounded and fishermen are lodged in jail for long period of time till there is a drama of mutual release as a gesture of good will. One wonders why this goodwill is not shown when they are found on the 'other' side of the undemarkated maritime boundary, and immediately asked to return to their respective undisputed maritime zones. Maritime security forces from both sides that patrol these waters for stopping infiltration can be instructed to be more considerate unless the vessel is suspected of indulging in more serious crimes like promoting terrorism or well defined violations like piracy, smuggling of drugs, weapons or personnel.

This issue was taken up during the visit of Foreign Minister Natwar Singh to Pakistan in the first week of October 2005. A

MoU was signed on establishing communication links between the Indian Coast Guard and Pakistan's Maritime Security Agency so as to facilitate early exchange of information on fishermen who inadvertently stray into each other's territory as also on information on smuggling, pollution control and search and rescue operations. [39] The then Director-General of the Coast Guard, Prabhakaran Paleri, told *The Hindu* that a hot line would be setup between the Coast Guard and the Maritime Security Agency as a follow up of this MoU. [40]

Efforts are on to solve the core issue but till then steps towards greater confidence building on both sides will promote a more peaceful environment. The tense situation along that sensitive border had led to the shooting down of the Pakistan Atlantic MR aircraft near this area in August 1999. Not only did the West and other supporters of Pakistan criticise Indian action of 'shooting down' what was a sophisticated maritime reconnaissance aircraft that was snooping in its sensitive area but even some Indians also thought it fit to condemn that action. Admiral L. Ramdas, retired naval chief, writing in *The Hindu*, used this occasion not only to preach 'rules of engagement' to IAF but even vented his anger by saying, "How many more sons and daughters of both our countries are going to be sacrificed to pander to the war mongers. With the new-found Indian Nuclear Doctrine we have once again opened the Pandora's box only to frighten our entire neighbourhood. Maturity and wisdom demand that we call an immediate halt to all this hostility and jingoism, lest it is too late." [41] Admiral Ramdas not only preached peace and good will but also simultaneously condemned India for its Nuclear Doctrine, that advocated no first use and minimum deterrence, as an instrument to frighten the entire neighbourhood! Peace mongering, like war mongering, can also send distorted signals to actual or potential adversaries.

Iran: Despite the recent rhetoric of India not wanting to have one more nuclear-weapon power in its neighbourhood, India cannot ignore the long term strategic interests that underline Indo-Iranian relations. Of them four are significant. No one can underestimate the role of Iran in the context of India's energy security. Not only is India importing oil from Iran but is also negotiating for long-term commitment for the supply of natural gas and LNG from Iran. Related to that is Iran's crucial role in the free flow of oil from the Gulf *via* the Straits of Hormuz. About 15.5 mbd of oil passes through the Straits of Hormuz. Despite the massive air and naval deployment of the NATO members in that area, the security of that SLOC can never be fully guaranteed without Iranian consent. In that context, threats to launch pre-emptive strike against Iran's nuclear facilities, and many more associated/strategically defined targets, as happened in the case of Iraq in 1991 and 2003, and Iran's claims to have tested improved versions of anti-ship missiles and super fast torpedoes cannot be totally ignored because of their likely impact upon free flow of oil from the Gulf into the Arabian Sea.

Iran is also vital for India in its strategy to open the sea-land route to Russia, Central Asian republics and Afghanistan. That is the only way to bypass Pakistan's policy of denying India a role in what it claims to be its strategic depth. Associated with that is India's desire to formally associate itself with the Shanghai-Five. That cooperation is vital if India has to play a meaningful role in promoting peace and stability in its extended neighbourhood, particularly in the context of threat from sections of groups preaching violence under the banner of Islam.

A boost to Indo-Iranian cooperation was given during the visit of Prime Minister Atal Bihari Vajpayee to Tehran. Indian Prime Minister and Iranian President Mohammad Khatami signed the Tehran Declaration in April 2001. Its contents were reaffirmed in the Delhi Declaration of January 2003. The areas of cooperation included strategic convergence for strong economic relationship, energy sector as an area of strategic cooperation, exploring opportunities for defence cooperation in agreed areas and, pursuant to the trilateral agreement between the Governments of India, Iran and Afghanistan, to develop the Chahbahar route to Afghanistan and Central Asia to facilitate regional trade and transit. India's investment in the infra-structure of Chahbahar port would also contribute to enhanced regional economic prosperity.

As a follow up, in July 2004, an Indian consortium of Larsen & Toubro, IRCON and RITES led by Ashok Leyland Project Services signed a MoU with Iran's Ports and Shipping Organisation to develop the port of Chahbahar on a Built, Own, Operate and Transfer (BOOT) basis. There were provisions for construction of a rail link between Chahbahar port and Bam in Southern Iran. [42] The new routes were to supplement the earlier agreement on North-South Transport Corridor signed between India, Iran and Russia on September 12, 2000 and ratified on May 15, 2002. It is valid for ten years.

These broad agreements of cooperation were also reflected in their desire for improving their cooperation for energy and maritime security. During the meeting between Indian Foreign Secretary, Kanwal Sibal and Hassan Rowhani, Secretary of Iran's National Security Council, in October 2002, Hasan Rowhani was quoted as saying that security cooperation between Iran and Iran in the Persian Gulf and the Indian Ocean, especially for energy transit and regional energy pipelines, and reducing crisis in the region was very important". [43]

Bilateral cooperation was also reflected in the context of ensuring maritime security. *Military Balance, 2003-2004*, reported that India's Chief of the Naval Staff, Admiral Madhvendra Singh, had visited Tehran in January 2003 and had initiated a process for cooperation in defence matters. As per the *Military Balance*, India would have the right to use Iranian military bases in the event of war with Pakistan. In turn, India would provide Iran with military equipment, training and maintenance, notably warship repair facilities to be constructed at Chahbahar. India was also to maintain and upgrade Iranian MiG-29, T-72 MBT and sell anti-tank missiles to Iran. And, in the longer run, to sell missile boats and submarine simulators. [44]

As a consequence of these efforts to forge strategic links in maritime cooperation, Iranian warships visited India to conduct joint naval exercise. Fleet supply vessel Bandar Abbas and the Hengam-class logistic support ship Lavan arrived in Mumbai on

March 8, 2003 for conducting joint naval exercise with the ships of the Indian Navy off Mumbai coast. [45]

The environment of cooperation got a series of jolts after 2005. The victory of so-called 'hard liners' in Iranian election and the defeat of the group supporting Mohammed Khatami was seen as a setback to process of liberal ethos in Iran. That coincided with the IAEA accusing Iran of violating the norms of NPT and pursuing a clandestine path to nuclear proliferation. India was indirectly brought into this controversy and, reportedly, under the US pressure, took anti-Iran stand and voted on the Western sponsored proposal in the IAEA. This was seen in Iran as a demonstration of India backing the Western stand *vis-à-vis* Iran at a time when India was also negotiating a deal for US support for its civilian nuclear power programme. Indian Prime Minister sought to justify Indian stand by arguing that India would not like to have yet another nuclear-weapon power as its neighbour. One wonders how Iran, which is still years away from acquiring a credible nuclear weapon capability as also a credible long-range delivery system to target India would be more dangerous for India than Pakistan and China. USA has given an impression that it seeks total submission from India, and Iran's nuclear enrichment programme has been offered as a test case.

Unsolicited advice was also offered by USA on Iran-India-Pakistan gas pipeline as also on Indo-Iranian maritime cooperation. Some American Congressmen, raised objections to the visit of two Iranian ships, IRIS Bandar Abbas now converted as training ship and IRIS Lavan an amphibious warfare ship, to Kochi during March 3-8, 2006. Indian Navy was even accused of 'training' Iranians within a short period of fire-days; a feat in itself. Their comments could have been ignored or, if they were to have an impact on civilian nuclear power deal, quietly explained to them personally. The explanation that this was a part of maritime diplomacy almost sounded as a public apology. [46]

There are reports that Iran too has been taking a negative stance. After India had voted against Iran on a resolution in IAEA on September 24, 2005 Indian officials were bluntly told that the

CNG deal was off. As per the reports by Amit Baruah in the *Hindu* of May 14, 2006, even the project to develop Chah Bahar port and the rail-road links to Afghanistan has run into rough waters due to lack of cooperation on the part of the Iranians. It is possible that this widening gulf between India and Iran may be filled by China. China had opposed Western moves to impose strong sanctions against Iran through the Security Council. China has been keen to develop lasting links for oil and gas supply from Iran as also from Central Asia *via* Iran. It would also like Iran to be integrated within the Shanghai-Five group. These moves will further isolate India in the region. India cannot afford to chart its bilateral or multi-lateral maritime security if it is to be guided by foreign backseat drivers.

GCC States: While India has succeeded in evolving a pattern of bilateral as well as multilateral naval exercises with its neighbours in the Bay of Bengal, the Malacca Straits, the South China Sea and even with states of the Asia-Pacific, it has still to evolve that degree of maritime cooperation with countries of the Arabian Sea and its natural extensions like the Persian Gulf and the Red Sea. But Indian naval vessels do visit the states of the region during their annual naval exercise as a part of showing the flag as well as for acquiring replenishment, ration and stores. Such operation turn around (OTR) thus forms an important part of confidence building measures as also means of fostering bilateral cooperation between India and the countries of the Arabian Sea region.

India and the GCC states have yet to develop a multilateral strategy for maritime cooperation. Even the GCC states have yet to evolve such a structure among themselves. Interaction between India and some of these states is limited to occasional visit by the ships of the Indian Navy. In march 2002, Indian aircraft carrier INS Virat and INS Shakti, fleet replenishment tanker, visited Mina Zayed in Abu Dhabi, UAE. They were joined there by INS Mysore and INS Godavari. They had already visited Jubail, a commercial port of Saudi Arabia. Similar visits were made in September October 2005. As noted, such visits are almost an annual exercise aimed at showing the flag and are more a part of maritime diplomacy than of bilateral or multilateral maritime cooperation.

India is, however, developing closer bilateral relations with Oman. Though a member of the GCC, Oman is more a littoral state of the Sea of Oman and Bab al-Mandeb than a 'desert' kingdom like Saudi Arabia. It commands vital SLOCs connecting the Straits of Hormuz with the Pacific Ocean *via* Indian Ocean and the Mediterranean *via* Bab al-Mandeb.

India's close maritime security contacts with Oman grew around 1992-93 and led to the first ever exercise between the ships of their respective navies. INS Ganga and INS Khukri exercised with five Omani fast attack craft (some of whom were armed with anti-ship missiles) near Mina al-Qaboos in the middle of January 1993. It was during this period that India won a contract to carry out a hydrographic survey of the coast of Oman. This contract was won in competition with bids from other countries including UK. This US$ 5 million contract also showed Oman's trust in India in the context of a sensitive issue of national security. The survey was completed to the satisfaction of Oman. It was undertaken by one survey ship and was completed in about nine months. These contacts continued in subsequent years.

Joint exercise between naval vessels of India and Oman, Thammar al-Tayyib 2005, was held in the Gulf of Oman during February 21-22, 2005. Closer maritime cooperation between India and Oman was discussed during the visit in March 2006 to Oman by Defence Minister Pranab Mukherji. That visit was preceded by the visit of Oman's Defence Minister to India and that of India's Chief of Naval Staff, Admiral Arun Prakash, to Oman. Points that were discussed covered the possibility of establishing ship repair facilities in Oman and the possibility of tie up in ship building. [47] India and Oman could also become close maritime neighbours once the two states have finally delimited the outer limits of their continental-shelf boundary.

The Horn of Africa: India's interest in the Horn of Africa is closely related to Oman and Yemen in the southern coast of the

Arabian peninsula as also to the safety of the SLOC through the Bab al-Mandeb. Indian armed forces, including the ships of the Indian Navy, took part in UN-led peace-keeping operation in Somalia. The virtual collapse of the formal government of Somalia since late eighties has intensified the threats of piracy, armed robbery and hijacking of merchant vessels along its waters. There are also reports that the highly destabilized situation in that area has helped radical Islamic groups to develop roots thus posing additional threat to the security in those waters. In March 2006, an Indian ship Bhaktisagar with 25 crew members was 'captured' or hijacked in those waters. Since there is no organized central authority along the Somalian coast, the owner of the ship had to 'negotiate' with those who had captured the ship for the release price. Another Indian-owed ship al-Taj, registered in UAE, was also captured and was released only after the owner reportedly paid US$ 25,000 as ransom.

Those waters are being monitored by the French as also by US-led coalition from Djibouti. But their focus seems to be on 'jehadi' terrorism rather than or piracy *per se*. India and France did conduct a joint naval exercise near Djibouti. Reportedly, Djibouti has sought Indian help in managing its EEZ. But the zone is too far away for mounting effective patrol from India so as to curb threats to maritime security and freedom of navigation. Regional powers like Djibouti and Yemen do not have the resources. Thus, Oman emerges as a major partner. Even Oman will have difficulty in providing security to two SLOCs unless other maritime partners join in. It will take some time before such an arrangement can be worked out in cooperation with regional powers like Oman, Yemen, Saudi-Arabia (Red Sea), Djibouti as well as major users of the SLOC like the EU states. India can also join in such cooperative venture if it is negotiated in collaboration with all the concerned parties.

WESTERN INDIAN OCEAN ZONE

African Littoral: Though India has long established links with the African littoral of the Indian Ocean yet India has not been able to formalize any structure of maritime cooperation with them. Though ships of the Indian Navy often visit ports of these states there is as yet no evidence of regular bilateral or multilateral joint exercises. Even South Africa, that has close political and economic relations with India, has not as yet offered to extend that cooperation to strengthen maritime security. INS Gomati and INS Khukri paid a visit to South Africa in 1994. SAS Drakensberg returned the visit to Mumbai 1995. Secretary of Defence of South Africa visited India in May 1995 to discuss naval cooperation. In February 1996, India's Chief of the Naval Staff, Admiral, V.S. Shekhawat, visited South Africa. Despite this good start, cooperation in matters of maritime security seems far away.

India's willingness to go out of the way to promote such a cooperation with African littoral states is illustrated by the response to the request made by the Government of Mozambique to provide sea-ward security to Maputo while the government was hosting the Second African Union Summit between July 4-12, 2003. Indian Navy sent INS Ranjit, a missile-armed destroyer, and INS Suvarna, a large patrol vessel. They stayed in the adjoining waters from June 21- July 15, 2003. During its stay INS Suvarna also carried out some training exercises with the personnel of Mozambique Navy. [48] Similar request was made by Mozambique during the World. Economic Forum Meeting as also during the Fourth African-Caribbean-Pacific Heads of State Summit in Maputo in June 2004. [49] Operation Farishta was conducted between May 23-July 13, 2004 off Maputo.

ISLAND REPUBLICS: SEYCHELLES AND MAURITIUS

India, over the years, has developed close political and security related contacts with the island republics of the Seychelles and the Mauritius. There is the need to extend this zone of cooperation in South Western half of the Indian Ocean by including islands like Reunion, claimed by France as a part of its overseas territory, because France is also an important player in this zone.

India has increased the frequency of the visits of the ships of its Navy and the Coast Guard to Mauritius and the Seychelles. It has also helped to train their security personnel, supplied them with equipment, helped them in the survey of their EEZ as also conducted occasional EEZ patrol on their behalf. India has posted a Naval Adviser to the Government of Seychelles. India has strong social and cultural links with sections of the inhabitants of Mauritius. India is also keen to explore for oil and gas deposits in its offshore waters.

INS Nirdeshak conducted a hydrographic survey of the sea around the island of Seychelles between November 21- December 18, 2003. Seychelles had sought the help of India in monitoring its vast EEZ. India handed over INS Tarmugli, a fast attack craft, to Seychelles on February 21, 2005. India also helped to rescue ten Indian crew members whose ship was attacked by pirates and who could reach Port Victoria with difficulty. Indian crew members were brought back to India by INS Sarvekshak that was returning from Mauritius after conducting a survey of its EEZ. [50]

India's maritime security cooperation is even more intimate with Mauritius. Services of Indian pilots, navigators and ship crew from the Coast Guard, Navy and the Air Force are often provided to the Coast Guard of the Mauritius to maintain the equipment. Indians had repaired the 1,400-ton Coast Guard Vessel MCGS Vigilant. It had been acquired from Chile. But the original builders could not rectify defects and it had to be towed to India. The defects were rectified and the ship returned to Mauritius. In 2005, at the time of the visit of Prime Minister Navin Chandra Ramgolam to Kochi, there was a proposal to transfer one large offshore patrol vessel as well as the modern Dhruv ALH. Reportedly, the ship was to be a gift. [51] There is no report that the transfer has taken place.

Indian warships not only visit Mauritius to conduct joint exercise with the vessels of the Coast Guard of Mauritius but also to help patrol its vast EEZ, INS Sarvekshak, a survey vessel, visited the Mauritius to conduct a maritime survey of its EEZ and its ports so as to update the records, especially after the tsunami.

That was the first survey conducted after the nineteenth century. While the ship was there it also rendered humanitarian help to the people of the isolated island of Agalege whose landing strip had been damaged. Not only were essential goods supplied but some children were also evacuated from that island.

The change from the earlier perception of India as a hegemonic power to one of a friendly neighbour, and for some even a benign big brother, is a triumph of decades of efforts aimed at fostering the spirit of cooperation between India and its maritime neighbours in the Indian Ocean Region. Every effort must be made to see that the image is not tarnished. It was reported that India had shown interest in developing the Island of Agalega, about 1,000 km from Mauritius, for tourism. News paper reported that India was interested in that island for strategic reasons. [52] Elements that are hostile to India organized public demonstration to thwart the deal with the result that the effort to develop that island had to be put into cold storage. India needs to be sensitive that its policy of cooperation with small island republics in Indian Ocean does not backfire.

Undoubtedly, India has succeeded to some extent in its efforts to break down the earlier image of big power hegemonism. That has led to increased regional cooperation. While some success has been achieved more needs to be done to further cement these ties, especially in the Arabian Sea and its natural extensions like the Persian Gulf and Bab al-Mandeb. After the success of its Look East policy, India needs to refocus its attention towards its sensitive western flank.

Notes

1. Hiranandani, Vice-Admiral G.M., *Transition to Eminance: The Indian Navy, 1967-1990*, Lancer Publishers, New Delhi, 2005, p. 144.

2. Subramanian, T.S., "To Stay on Top", *Frontline*, February 11, 1994, quoted in Bharadwaj, Lt. Commander Atul, "Maritime Aspects of Sri Lankan Conflict", *Journal of Indian Ocean Studies*, 8(3), December 2000, p. 243.

3. Gunnaratne, Rohana, "Sea Tigers Threaten the Spread of Copycat Tactics", *Jane's Intelligence Review*, 13(3), March 2001, p. 13.

4. Hiranandani, Vice-Admiral G.M. *Transition to Eminance: The Indian Navy1967-1990*, Lancer Publishers, New Delhi, 2005, p. XVI.

5. Ministry of Defence (MoD), *Annual Report, 1990-1990*, New Delhi, 1991, p. 17.

6. *Asian Recorder,* April 2-8, 1993, p. 23033.

7. *The Hindustan Times*, February 2, 1994.

8. *The Hindu*, June 8, 2000.

9. Ibid., June 11, 2006.

10. Ibid., May 24, 205.

11. Ibid., July 20, 2006 and the *New Indian Express*, August 23, 2006.

12. *The Hindu*, October 20, 2004, quoted in *Strategic Digest*, 39(11), November 2004, p. 1578.

13. *The Hindu*, November 11, 2005, quoted in *Strategic Digest*, 35(12), December 2005, p. 1651.

14. *The Hindu*, February 25, 2006.

15. Ibid., December 15, 2005.

16. *Defence News*, quoted in *Strategic Digest*, 36(6), June 2006, pp. 739-40.

17. *The Hindu*, April 19, 2006.

18. MoD, *Annual Report, 2001-2002*, New Delhi, 2002, p. 38.

19. Ashton, William, "Chinese Bases in Burma - Fact or Fiction?", *Jane's Intelligence Review*, 7(2), February 1995, pp. 84-7.

20. MoD, *Annual Report, 1993-1994*, New Delhi, 1994, p. 5. MoD, *Annual Report, 1993-1994*, New Delhi, 1994, p. 5.

21. MoD, *Annual Report, 2001-2002*, New Delhi, 2002, pp. 6-7.

22. *Strategic Digest*, 33(12), December 2003, p. 1363.

23. *The Hindu*, March 10, 2005, quoted in *Strategic Digest,* 35(4), April 2005, p. 294.

24. MoD, *Annual Report, 2001-2002*, New Delhi, 2002, p. 38.

25. Vice-Admiral Arun Prakash, "Evolution of the Joint Andaman and Nicobar Command (ANC), and Defence of Our Island territory", Part II, *Journal of United Service Institution*, 133(551), January-March 2003, p. 28. The author has also given a map showing the area of responsibility of ANC.

26. "Thailand Seizes Illegal Arms Bound for Manipur", *Jane's Intelligence Weekly*, March 26, 1997, p. 11.

27. MoD, *Annual Report, 2001-2002*, New Delhi, 2002, p. 10.

28. *The Hindu*, May 21, 2005.

29. Ibid., April 15, 2000, quoted in *Strategic Digest*, 30(6), June

2000, pp. 870-71.

30. "India's Friendship Diplomacy", *India Today*, February 13, 2006, p. 54.

31. *Jane's Naval Intelligence*, 107(2), May 2004, p. 32.

32. Sakhuja, Vijay, "Management of Straits of Malacca and Singapore: Considerations for India", *Journal of Indian Ocean Studies*, 12 (3), August 2004, p. 219.

33. Roy-Chaudhury, Rahul, "Maritime and Naval Cooperation in the Indian Ocean", *Asian Strategic Review, 1997-98*. IDSA, New Delhi, 1998, pp. 271-73.

34. MoD, *Annual Report, 1963-1964*, New Delhi, 1964, p. 45.

35. For details, Vice-Admiral Arun Prakash, "Evolution of the Joint Andaman and Nicobar Command (ANC) and Defence of Our Island Territories, Part I and II, *Journal of United Service Institution of India*, 132 (550), October- December 2002 and 133 (551), January-March 2003.

36. *The New Indian Express*, March 17, 2006.

37. *Strategic Digest*, 35(9), September 2005, p. 1168.

38. Menon, Rear Admiral K.R. (Retd.), "Maritime Conflict Resolution and Confidence Building in South Asia", *Indian Defence Review*, 10(4), October-December 1995, pp. 33-5, Roy-Chaudhury, Rahul, "The Indo-Pakistani Dispute Over Sir Creck", *Journal of Indian Ocean Studies*, 6(3), July 1999, pp. 246-56 and Vohra, Ravi, "The Sir Creek Affair: Can We Accelerate the Resolution?" *Maritime Affairs*, 2(1), Summer 2006, pp. 1-15.

39. *Strategic Digest*, 35(11), November 2005, p. 1565.

40. *The Hindu*, April 29, 2006.

41. Ramdas, L. "Sir Creek and the Pakistan Atlantique", *The Hindu*, August 31, 1999.

42. Hiranandani, Vice-Admiral G.M., "Developments Along the Makaran Coast." *Defence Watch*, April 2005, p. 22. Hiranandani, Vice-Admiral G.M., "Developments Along the Makaran Coast." *Defence Watch*, April 2005, p. 22.

43. *Strategic Digest*, 32(11), November 2002, p. 1403.

44. *The Military Balance, 2003-2004*, I.I.S.S., London, 2004, p. 286.

45. *Jane's Defence Weekly*, We, 39, March 19, 2003, p. 140.

46. *The New Indian Express*, April 2, 2006.

47. *The Hindu*, March 12, 2006.

48. MoD, *Annual Report, 2003-2004*, New Delhi, 2004, p. 40.

49. Sakhuja, Vijay, "Management of Straits of Malacca and Singapore", *Journal of Indian Ocean Studies*, 12(3), August 2004, p. 222.

50. *The Hindu*, April 12, 2006.

51. Ibid., October 25 and 28, 2006.

52. *Times of India*, November 25, 2006.

7

LOOKING AHEAD

CHANGE IN THE MINDSET

Over the past few decades there has been a change in the mindset concerning maritime affairs. It is no longer confined to the role of the Navy and merchant shipping. Its scope has been widening under the impact of new advantages conferred upon coastal states under the terms of UNCLOS-III as well as the growing realization that India's economic development in future is increasingly related to its ability to utilize its advantage as a major maritime nation. One can even say that this marks a shift from the traditional 'continental' mindset to a 'maritime' mindset.

India's growing maritime interest was best summed up by Admiral Arun Prakash in his address delivered on October 16, 2004, while inaugurating the Chair for Maritime Studies and Research, University of Calicut. He said, "India's national objectives lie in ensuring a secure and stable environment which will permit the economic development and social uplift of its masses, so that the country can ultimately take its rightful place in the international comity of nations. Within this overall objective our primary maritime interest is to ensure national security and provide insulation from external interference, so that the vital tasks of fostering economic growth and undertaking developmental activities can take place in a secure environment." [1]

Thus, maritime security would be directly related to promoting and protecting national maritime assets like ports and harbours, major strategic installations like oil and gas storage tanks and refineries, nuclear installations near the coast, off-shore oil and gas installations and pipeline network, fishery resources, SLOCs both overseas and coastal etc. from threats posed by state as well as non-state actors as also by natural hazards and man-made pollution. The expanding areas of maritime interests as also of the multiple sources of threats have thus not only widened the scope of maritime security but have also widened the network of agencies that benefit from it and hence ought to contribute in their own ways towards strengthening maritime security.

There has been a change in the nature of threats to maritime security as also in actors that pose such threats. Earlier, threats came primarily from conflicts among state actors. Even during the Cold War era, the global threat came from the clash of two major power blocs as illustrated by the Korean war and the long-drawn Vietnam war, as also from conflicts among middle powers. Arab-Israeli wars, long-drawn Iraq-Iran conflict, India-Pakistan armed conflicts are some of the illustrations.

Things began to alter since 1990. The Kuwaiti crisis of 1990-91 was no longer a bilateral regional conflict. It had taken a global role. Unanimously passed Security Council resolutions applied economic and political sanctions. They were also used to legitimise multilateral military operation, conducted primarily by USA, UK and France, against a regional power in 1991. UN continued to impose economic and political sanctions against Iraq even after the signing of the ceasefire agreement in 1991.

Soon, even this fig leaf of legitimacy through UN Security Council resolution was dispensed with and unilateralism was invoked to selectively 'punish' so-called rogue regimes through military action. though 'successful' as conventional military operations, they taught the bitter lesson that such victories can not only be illusory but can also drag the victor into long-drawn low intensity campaign for years without a credible exit policy. These lessons are reflected now in the public hard line stance but refusal to do an Afghanistan or Iraq to Iran on the issue of nuclear proliferation. This does not mean that the great powers have abandoned their policy or reduced their capability for force projection or for conducting littoral warfare in faraway places. Threat of great power intervention in the Indian Ocean Region under some pretext or the other will remain a matter of concern for all regional powers and will influence their approach to maritime security *vis-à-vis* state actors.

While the threat of conventional warfare between state actors remains, a new threat has been added since the past three decades if not more. Non-state actors are now being projected as a major source of threat to maritime security. The new types of threat need different strategies to counter them. While enough literature is available on how to improve conventional war fighting capability by the application of principles like revolution in military affairs (RMA) and network-centric warfare (NCW), not enough breakthrough has been achieved in combating threats posed by non-state actors.

MARITIME SECURITY AND STATE ACTORS

Since the Navy is the prime enforcement agency in the context of maritime security, it is natural that its views would have to be given prime consideration. This is specially true when neutralizing threat from state actors; both great powers as also middle powers. In such cases it is essential to anticipate the maritime environment in the years to come, assess the threat and seek counter-measures both in terms of weapons acquisition and related strategy as well as diplomacy.

The focus on neutralizing maritime threat from state actors has influenced maritime strategy since ages. Even after the end of the Cold War, the main strategic thrust has not changed much except that two factors are getting greater prominence; force projection across the oceans, and fighting a conventional was against middle powers under the new concept of littoral warfare. This new orientation, in fact, poses greater threat to small and medium powers in the post-Cold War period as compared to the Cold War period when the primary focus of one great power was the other adversary great power. Even conventional operations involving the Navy, as in Korea and Vietnam, were conducted in the context of the Cold War rivalry.

Strategy of regional powers has not undergone major changes even after the end of the Cold War. India-Pakistan naval thrust is still based upon the premises of post-1971 war; Pakistan's major thrust being on sea denial while India's is on strengthening of its sea control role with ASW warfare as a part of that overall thrust.

Indian Ocean Region boasts of only a few maritime powers capable of playing a major role even in the areas of their immediate responsibility. Thailand, Malaysia and Singapore in South-East Asia have credible maritime capabilities. They are seeking to enhance their capability for ASW operations as also sea control in their immediate neighbourhood in the context of growing naval capability of China, and its likely power projection not only in South China Sea but also beyond it into the Indian Ocean Region. In that context, their strategic needs dove-tail with those of India. Bilateral naval exercises between India and these states, especially Singapore, points in that direction.

Navies of the GCC states are yet to emerge as a viable maritime force in their own waters. They will remain over-shadowed by the presence of the Vth Fleet in that area. Sometimes their warships do exercise with those of the US-led coalition but most of them would prefer not to be associated overtly with USA because of possible domestic backlash. They, however, need to strengthen their homeland security. That, among other things, would mean enhancing their very limited mine-counter measure capability in the shallow waters of the Gulf and the Straits of Hormuz. They also need to develop greater regional maritime cooperation on a sustained basis.

Iran, a strong maritime power in the Gulf during the days of the Shah, gradually eroded its naval power during long-drawn Iraq-Iran war and in continued confrontation with USA in the subsequent years. Its major surface combatant forces are old and getting obsolete. Iran, despite its three Kilo-class submarines and undisclosed number of midget submarines as well as large number of patrol craft, some of them armed with SSMs, has been reduced to the status of a land power. Even its sea denial capability in the coastal waters is largely based upon land-based anti-ship missiles. That role is not likely to change for some time to come because it is a part of Iran's overall security framework that aims at land-based deterrence rather than confronting major power on the high sea. One likely season for such a policy is the dominant role played by the Revolutionary Guards (Pasdaran) even in maritime security. However, Iran's role in the security of SLOC through the Straits of Hormuz as also in the narrow and shallow Persian Gulf cannot be under-estimated. In that context, Iran's maritime capability as well as related political role is of vital concern for India.

NON-STATE ACTORS

While the strategy of using maritime power *vis-à-vis* state actors will remain a valid proposition as long as there are state actors, the focus of maritime strategy has gradually shifted towards neutralizing the challenges that are being posed by non-state actors. These threats can be analysed under three main heads; level or type of threat, source of threat and provocation or reason for the same.

Threats posed by non-state actors range from petty theft and armed robbery near the coast, piracy and hijacking, smuggling of arms, drugs and personnel, terrorist targets upon shipping on the high sea, in the anchorages near the port or in the port, major strategic targets near the coast like refineries, oil and LNG terminals and storage tanks and nuclear facilities near the coast. Sources of threat can be foreign power as well as non-state actors on their own or acting as proxy for state actors and foreigners in collaboration with section of local population. Provocations for such acts can range from greed, social, ethnic and religious propaganda, as also a state pursuing its own agenda behind the cover of non-state actors.

An attempt is being made to give a 'form' to this new threat. Earlier, it was sought to be covered under the broad label of piracy. In the post-9/11 period there is the tendency to label it as a part of jehadi terrorism, thus giving it a religious overtone. Such an exercise not only seeks to over simply a complex ethno-religious and political protest movement by seeking to demonise it but it also ignores other equally serious non-state actors like the LTTE, the war-lords of a disintegrated state like Somalia, as also the well-established nexus between smugglers and various terrorist groups on land. This is specially true of India's large maritime zone extending from the Bay of Bengal to the Arabian Sea.

Role of smugglers in landing explosives as also trained terrorists along India's Arabian Sea coast is also an important source of threat. These non-state actors are not necessarily part of organized global network though there are reports of al-Qauda and LTTE having a global network. Most of these non-state actors are small groups that would like to act as independent actors rather than be subjected to an organized centralized command. Hence, unlike state actors, these groups can be neither easily identified non effectively targeted.

This also means that 'war or terror', especially in its maritime dimension, cannot be a unified global effort. War on terror cannot be a war between state actors *versus* non-state actors *per se* at the global level. Hence, cooperation can be only among interest partners as also in selected areas of concerns. The Proliferation Security Initiative (PSI), Maritime Regional Security Initiative MRSI), Container Security Initiative, International Ship and Port Facility Security Code are some of the illustrations of such bilateral or multilateral sets of cooperation designed to reinforce maritime security of such concerned states in the context of threat from non-state actors.

Two factors act as major constraints in evolving regional or global mechanism in war on terrorism. They are inadequate legal provisions under customary international law as also under UNCLOS-III, and the strong commitment to the concept of state sovereignty among small and middle powers. Attempts are being made to overcome these constraints, like the signing of SUA Protocol of 2005 that seeks to modify the provisions of the SUA Convention of 1988. Yet, that Protocol also respects the concept of state sovereignty. [2] That is one season for retarding the progress in creating RMSI in the Malacca Straits. Even India, that has close understanding with regional powers, is allowed only coordinated patrol and not joint patrol in each others territorial waters. Thus, a state has no option but to strengthen its own homeland security against maritime threats posed by non-state actors.

HOMELAND SECURITY

The Indian Navy has not fought a conventional war since December 1971 but India's maritime security has been threatened since the seventies, if not earlier, by non-state actors. Activities of the smugglers was considered in the fifties and the sixties as an economic offence but not a maritime threat. Similarly, the illegal fishing in India's EEZ was seen as an encroachment upon India's exclusive economic rights under UNCLOS-III rather than a threat to the nation's security. Activities of the non-state actors began to be seen or equated as a form of threat to maritime security following the activities of Sri Lanka's Tamil militants since the early eighties. That has kept the Navy and the Coast Guard busy along the southern coast of Tamil Nadu since then.

Unlike the level of threat that probably had been deliberately kept at a low level by Sri Lankan Tamils and their local supporters, Bombay blasts of March 1993 revealed the real nature of threat to security, peace and stability of the country. That threat could be traced directly to erstwhile smugglers, acting as proxies for foreign agents, using their contacts to land large quantity of explosives in Vasai, Thane creek and Mumbra near Mumbai.

The *Annual Report* of the Ministry of Defence, *1994-95*, commenting upon the new threat said, "Instead of peace and tranquillity and a new world order, we are witnessing today new form of conflict and continuing disorder. It is not so much interstate violence but international terrorism and proxy war by external power that characterises the global security environment at present." [3] Thus, India was aware of this threat long before the West discovered it.

These threats prompted India to launch several operations like Operation Tasha since June 1990, and Operation Nakebandi since August 1996 along the Tamil Nadu coast and Operation Swan since 1993 along the Arabian Sea Coast. The Indian Navy and the

Coast Guard as also the BSF in the Cutch region are now engaged almost on a daily basis in trying to sanitize the coastal waters of elements that can harbour hostile intentions.

Since the eighties, India has undertaken *ad hoc* as also mission-specific operations to confront the new challenge. There is need to formulate a national policy for strengthening homeland security *vis-à-vis* threats posed by non-state actors.

While the Navy has the primary responsibility of maritime security *vis-à-vis* state actors, burden of maritime security in the context of threat from non-state actors need to be shared not only by the Navy and the Coast Guard but also by agencies that stand to gain from exploitation of maritime resources and whose operations can be targeted by hostile non-state actors. Thus, agencies like the port authorities, those dealing with oil, gas, and petroleum products, customs and immigration as well as fishery also need to contribute towards strengthening maritime security.

Equally important is the need to define the role of coastal states in this context. Till now an impression was being created that maritime security was the exclusive responsibility of the Central Government. Increasingly, it is being realized that the coastal states also need to contribute towards that, especially in the crucial zone that covers inland sea, the territorial sea and if need be even beyond. Not only is the state responsible for intermediate and minor ports but also for the management of fishery up to the limits of the territorial sea. The coastal state is also responsible for maintaining law and order in the adjacent water, up to the limit of the territorial sea. Thus, responsibility of maritime security in these adjoining waters needs to be seen as an extension of land-based 'thana' jurisdiction over the immediate coastal waters of these states in India.

Such a policy needs a common understanding about the shared responsibility between the States and the Central Government as well as among the adjoining states. There are reports of proposal to strengthen maritime security with active involvement between the Central Government and respective State Governments.

Decision has been taken to strengthen coastal security through an arrangement under which the Central Government will provide assistance to the coastal states for setting up coastal police stations and for acquisition of vehicles and vessels for mobility along the coast and in the coastal waters. These proposals also provide for the formation of marine police in coastal states. Under this scheme Ministry of Home Affairs would meet the non-recurring expenditure that is estimated to be about Rs. 400 crore, as also recurring expenditure of about Rs. 151 crore on fuel, repairs and maintenance of vessels for a period of five years. The State Government is required to provide the necessary personnel. The scheme has been approved for implementation in the coming five years beginning 2005-2006.

The High Level Empowered Committee under the Home Secretary has approved an outlay of Rs. 329.52 crore for setting up of 68 coastal police stations under the scheme in nine coastal states and in the Union Territory of Pondicherry. These police stations will be equipped with 184 vessels, 124 jeeps and 279 motor cycles for coastal patrolling and surveillance. A lump sum assistance of Rs. 10 lakh per police station has been approved for acquisition of equipment, computer and furniture.

Other steps are also being suggested beside the formation of marine police and coastal police stations to strengthen homeland security. There is scheme for joint coastal patrolling off the coast of Gujarat and Maharashtra. These are designated as vulnerable coasts for cross border activities. Patrolling of area between international boundary with Pakistan off Gujarat up to north of Goa is being conducted jointly by the Navy, the Coast Guard, the Customs and the state police. The Navy and the Coast Guard are to patrol the high seas while a joint contingent of the Navy, the Customs and the state police would patrol waters close to the coast by deploying trawlers. They would eventually be replaced by interceptor boats. It was also proposed to set up three Coast Guard stations in 2005-2006 at Veraval, Dhanu and Murad Janjira and to equip them with interceptor boats. The scheme is to be implemented jointly by the Ministry of Home Affairs and the

Ministry of Defence. Non-recurring expenditure of about Rs. 342.56 crore would be met by the Ministry of Home Affairs, while the recurring expenditure of about Rs. 25.15 crore per year is to be met by the Ministry of Defence. [4]

While these steps are to be welcomed they would be inadequate without the active cooperation of other agencies that are intimately related to maritime affairs and whose security will be enhanced if they too contribute to the overall scheme of homeland security. These agencies are the authorities of both major and intermediate ports, fishery department including those responsible for fishing harbour and landing sites, environment protection agencies, those that are related to exploitation of off-shore oil and gas resources besides the customs and the immigration authorities. Those who benefit have a duty to contribute towards the maintenance of the security of their assets. Hence some mechanism needs to be evolved so that these agencies can also share the overall burden of homeland security against threats emanating from the sea.

Equally important is the need to evolve a framework of interaction among these various agencies so as to avoid duplication of efforts as also to ensure more effective coordination of available resources. In this context one will need to take into account the capability of these agencies as also the legal framework (or constraint) under which they will be operating under the provisions of UNCLOS-III. Jurisdiction of state police will extend only up to 12 n.miles limit of the territorial sea, that of the customs and immigration up to 24 n.miles limit of the contiguous zone and that of the Coast Guard up to 200 n.mile limit of EEZ for fishery violations. There are several grey areas in the field of international law and India will need to evolve state practice to buttress the clauses of UNCLOS-III so as to enhance the legal basis for its actions.

It is also necessary to evolve a framework for interaction at horizontal level among the various agencies operating along the coast, as also at the vertical level from the coast up to the EEZ or continental-shelf limit; an area of operation of the Navy and the

Coast Guard. While state police, port authorities, state fishery department etc. can interact along the coast horizontally up to the limit of the territorial sea, they can interact vertically with the customs, immigration and pollution control authorities up to at least 24 n.m.miles, and with the Coast Guard and the Navy beyond that. Such a synergy may even require a coordinating body like Coastal Maritime Security Agency which can be entrusted with the task of coordinating these activities.

What is needed is the realization of the changing nature of maritime threats among various agencies, that are so threatened, to work out modalities of their responses and the need for synergy between their responses and those of other enforcement agencies like the Navy, the Coast Guard and the state police. Such an arrangement will throw a multi-tiered cordon of security in which the affected parties have a role as also responsibility and their actions are coordinated at different levels or zones for more effective synergy among various maritime enforcement agencies.

This also calls for a review of the outmoded national laws and regulations dealing with the subject. Some of them, like the laws on piracy, were enacted in the nineteenth century. It is time that an expert committee is constituted to look into domestic laws pertaining to these subjects and to recommend appropriate legislation to update them and to fill the gaps where necessary. Such a unified and codified law of maritime security will not only delimit responsibilities of various agencies but also help the enforcement agencies in framing appropriate charges and for the judiciary to swiftly pass the judgement.

The concept of homeland security can also be an effective instrument of diplomacy for encouraging cooperation at bilateral, regional or even global level. It has two main advantages. First, it helps to enhance maritime security of each independent state which, in turn, contributes to enhancing the security of other states as well. Non-state actors also need a base for their operations in some state or the other. Hence, helping a state in sanitizing its coast will help restrict the operational capability of such non-state actors. This cannot be done by outsiders.

Respective state authorities are best suited to carry out that task. Regional and global cooperation can help strengthen, to the extent possible, the role of each littoral state.

Secondly, showing respect for state sovereignty of these states in their respective waters will provide the right environment for ensuring their willing cooperation in bilateral or multilateral security initiatives. Main objection to MRSI in the Malacca Straits by some regional powers rests on the ground that it violates the spirit of national sovereignty. One can draw the lesson from the quiet diplomacy of Japan and the brusque offer of MRSI by USA. Obviously, Japan scored points.

In this context a word of caution needs to be added. Care has to be taken that states/regimes that welcome such cooperation are not utilizing that political, economic and military support for their own regime security rather than for regional maritime security. India has succeeded in developing bilateral maritime security cooperation with Sri Lanka as well as with smaller island republics of Seychelles, Mauritius and the Maldives.. India needs to be extra careful lest it be is accused of offering covert support to a regime that is not popular. The Maldives is going through a process of domestic turmoil. Demand for greater democracy is gaining momentum especially among the younger generation. Indian maritime cooperation should not be seen as taking sides in the internal politics of that island republic lest it becomes counter productive.

NEED FOR SYNERGY

Synergy of resources and activities of different enforcement agencies is seen as the best way to optimise national resources in the field of maritime security as well. In the case of maritime threat posed by state actors, the strategy needs to be based upon the synergy of related national enforcement agencies like the Navy, the Coast Guard and the Air Force that can together project maximum coordinated power over the water/space of national concern.

In this context one can even evaluate comparative advantages of the concept of joint command *vis-à-vis* of synergy of action and shared responsibility of different agencies involved. Andaman-Nicobar Command (ANC) represents the concept of joint command. It is still at an experimental stage and confined to a group of islands isolated from the mainland by about 700 miles. The concept of joint command not only seeks to integrate various services under one command but also requires the psychological preparedness to 'subordinate' ones own service to some one else under a joint command. What happens when that person goes back to his own service after serving under the joint command? How does he readjust, may be with a sigh of relief of being on 'familiar' grounds.

By contrast, the concept of synergy of action and shared responsibility maintains the existing command structure, distributes responsibility to each component unit or service according to its capability, while at the same time evolves modes of participatory cooperation for a more cost-effective performance by avoiding duplication of men and resources.

Thus, there is an emphasis upon 'networking' rather than subordination that is obligatory under joint command. India's maritime sea and air space is vast and demands vary from sectors to sector. Hence, networking or synergy rather than joint command concept will be more effective in the context of a vast sub-continent and its immediate water/space environment.

This concept of networking is already operational. Jaguars armed with Sea Eagle ASMs, manned and operated by the Indian Air Force, are an intrinsic part of maritime strike capability. In future, when IAF is able to arm Su-30 with air-launched version of BrahMos missile and extend the range of the aircraft with mid-air refuelling, or when the IAF acquires AWACS aircraft, the reach and sophistication of naval-air strike and surveillance capability will be further enhanced.

India is entering into the space age in military-related affairs. Unfortunately, race has begun to 'own' space under the aero-space concept. Air Marshal S.R. Savur, Chief of the Southern Air Command, speaking to media persons at Thiruvananthapuram, said that the city stood a good chance of hosting the headquarters of the proposed Aero-Space Command of the Indian Air Force. He said that a committee of the Chiefs of Staff was considering the matter. Proximity to various sea routes and various facilities of the Indian Space Department gives the city an edge over other cities. He added that the chance of establishing a tri-service command in the Capital as a pre-cursor to a full-fledged aero-space command was also high. [5] As and when the Aero-Space Command is established, networking or synergy will be acquiring a higher level of technological sophistication. It is, therefore, essential that *ad-hoc* arrangements for synergy among various agencies that exist at present be given an organizational framework for smooth operation not only in peace time but also in times of emergency.

This is equally true of the role of the Navy and the Coast Guard. Increasingly, the Coast Guard is being entrusted with greater responsibilities like SAR operations, combating piracy and terrorism and even in the field of maritime diplomacy and training of foreign coast guard personnel. Indian Coast Guard, though operating at a lower threshold of maritime power projection, can become a useful instrument of regional cooperation and maritime diplomacy.

The Coast Guard, because of the nature of its operational role, can never acquire the fire power capability or the responsibility of the Navy. It is also true that under certain conditions the Navy may have to intervene for maritime security even in peace time in the coastal waters. But, these areas of their overlapping responsibility can be converted into an asset if the Coast Guard, especially its larger (200-300 ton) offshore patrol craft and offshore patrol vessels (about 1500-2,000 tons) can be modified, if need be, for ASW operations in the coastal waters. Helicopter-equipped large patrol vessels and smaller offshore patrol craft equipped with active sonar, ASW mortars and depth changes can help sanitize at least parts of offshore waters and thus deter activities of hostile submarines. That will enable the Navy to deploy its more sophisticated ships to contain the threat from hostile submarines on the high seas or in high risk zones. Maritime reconnaissance aircraft of the Coast Guard already play a useful role in keeping a large part of coastal waters under surveillance. Thus, the Navy and the Coast Guard can work out their respective zones of responsibility and capability as also modes of cooperation under given circumstances. This will not only ensure streamlining of their respective functions but also prevent avoidable duplication of equipment on both sides.

This cooperation can be further enhanced if some mechanism can be worked out under which officers of the Navy and the Coast Guard can be rotated. When officers of the Navy operate along with those of the Coast Guard in Coast Guard vessels they would not only gain valuable experience of operating in the coastal waters but also have a better appreciation of the role of the Coast Guard. Similarly, officers of the Coast Guard can be deputed to serve for a certain period in comparable ships of the Indian Navy. Thus, not only the Navy and the Coast Guard would benefit by shared experience but young officers of both the services will develop a healthy respect for each other; an essential factor in fostering the spirit of cooperation and, therefore, of synergy.

CONCLUSION

To conclude, one can say that of late the range of maritime security in India has widened in its scope. It has evolved in response to changing regional and international environment, increasing areas of adjacent waters and sub-soil there of coming under coastal state's control for exploitation, changing perception of maritime interests like trade, exploitation of maritime resources and the need to protect them, as also the new threat from non-state actors.

India's responses to these multiple variables had been largely *ad hoc*. The burden of maritime security has been laid exclusively upon the Navy and the Coast Guard. Other agencies that ought to share this burden of security have virtually abandoned their responsibility. It is time that all those who benefit must also share the responsibility.

It is necessary that Indian decision makers, instead of responding piece-meal to the challenges, decide to take stock of the entire spectrum of maritime security and take concrete steps not only to strengthen each concerned section to the extent necessary but also to formulate structures of coordination among them to ensure effective synergy so that instead of obstructing each other they cooperate with each other to further strengthen nation's maritime security. It seems too ambitious a project. But, ambitions need to be translated into concrete action so that they can be finally achieved over a given period.

Notes

1. Admiral Arun Prakash, "Indian Maritime Doctrine", in Nambiar, E.K.G., and Suryanarayan V., eds., *Lectures on Maritime Studies*, Publications Division, University of Calicut, 2005, p. 24.

2. Beckman, Robert, "The 1988 SUA Convention and the 2005 SUA Protocol: Tools to Combat Piracy, Armed Robbery and Maritime Terrorism", *Maritime Affairs* 2(2), Winter 2006, pp. 29-52.

3. Ministry of Defence, *Annual Report, 1994-1995*, New Delhi, p. 1.

4. Ministry of Home Affairs, *Annual Report 2005-2006*, New Delhi, 2006, p. 40.

5. *The Hindu*, August 31, 2006.

Index

Index